Outside Money

Outside Money

Soft Money and Issue Advocacy
in the 1998 Congressional Elections

edited by
David B. Magleby

ROWMAN & LITTLEFIELD PUBLISHERS, INC.
Lanham • Boulder • New York • Oxford

ROWMAN & LITTLEFIELD PUBLISHERS, INC.

Published in the United States of America
by Rowman & Littlefield Publishers, Inc.
4720 Boston Way, Lanham, Maryland 20706
http://www.rowmanlittlefield.com

12 Hid's Copse Road
Cumnor Hill, Oxford OX2 9JJ, England

British Library Cataloguing in Publication Information Available

Library of Congress Cataloging-in-Publication Data

Outside money : soft money and issue advocacy in the 1998 congressional elections
edited by David B. Magleby.
    p.   cm.
    Includes bibliographical references and index.
    ISBN 0-7425-0042-X (cloth : alk. paper)—ISBN 0-7425-0043-8 (paper : alk. paper)
    1. Campaign funds—United States.   2. Pressure groups—United States.
  3. United States. Congress—Elections, 1998.   I. Magleby, David B.
JK1991.O695   2000
324.7'8'09739049—dc21   99-049349

Printed in the United States of America

♾ ™ The paper used in this publication meets the minimum requirements of American
National Standard for Information Sciences—Permanence of Paper for Printed Library
Materials, ANSI Z39.48-1992.

To Linda and our children

Contents

Acknowledgments

This book grows out of an experiment. With the proliferation of interest-group campaign advertisements and party soft-money expenditures, students of elections have less reliable information on campaign spending and communication. The 1994 and 1996 elections were early harbingers of this phenomenon, as were the special elections of 1997 and early 1998. Given this potential for extraordinary party and interest-group activity, I applied for a grant to the Pew Charitable Trusts to recruit teams of academics to closely monitor all forms of election communication and the undisclosed campaign spending in the U.S. House District or state they resided in. We were breaking new ground in monitoring nonbroadcast communication by parties and interest groups, and we were also the first academics to systematically track broadcast communications using local stations as a primary source of data.

All of the political scientists who agreed to be investigators on this project had a willingness to build networks with political reporters, campaign staff, party staff, consultants, former students, friends, and neighbors. Most investigators had not previously published on campaign finance issues. When discussing the project with one Washington practitioner, I was told that academics lack the tenacity of news reporters—that academics are too used to getting their data the easy way. The data we summarize in this book demonstrate just the opposite. Academics can and did learn a great deal about party and interest-group electioneering and the tone and content of these communications, and they are well positioned to put this development into context.

I wish to thank all of my colleagues who participated in this project. They are Sandra Anglund, Lonna Atkeson, Thad Beyle, Michael Bowers, DeLysa Burnier, Michael Burton, Allan Cigler, Anthony Coveny, Russ Dondero, Dennis Dresang, Tim Fackler, Nathalie Frensley, Jay Goodliffe, Donald Gross, Ferrel Guillory, John Haskell, Eric Herzik, Ted Jelen, Robin Kolodny, Todd Kunioka, Clyde McKee, Penny Miller, William Moore, Doug Nilson, Michael Rodrigues, John Shockley, Sandra Suarez, and Danielle Vinson. Space limitations preclude including all of their case studies in this volume. But throughout the volume, we refer to the work of other participants in the study, and I want to thank them for their fine work.

This project would not have been possible without the strong support of the Pew Charitable Trusts. Rebecca Rimel, president of the Trusts, has provided leadership in the effort to restore trust and build confidence in our democratic processes. Paul Light, former director of Public Policy at Pew, was willing to take a risk on a new approach to learning about campaign finance. His remarkable leadership at Pew has made a difference in democratic processes and governance as well as public policy more generally. Sean Treglia, program officer in Public Policy, helped navigate the grant through the submission and approval process and provided constant encouragement.

I was fortunate to have an extraordinary research assistant to help me with this project. Marianne Holt, who wrote chapter 2 of this volume, helped coordinate the efforts of the investigators in the sixteen case studies, assisted with the preparation of the monograph for the event at the National Press Club, and oversaw logistics for that event and other parts of the project. Her hard work and superb interpersonal skills greatly assisted with this project. Marianne became an expert on campaign finance, preparing the script for a local PBS television program on outside money. She was also interviewed by Brooks Jackson at CNN in its coverage of our study.

Marianne has been succeeded by two outstanding research assistants, Anna Nibley and Michelle Reed, who have been extensively involved in the revision and publication of this book and who will provide the staff support necessary for a similar study of the 2000 election cycle. Both Anna and Michelle have strong research and writing skills and have helped juggle the completion of this book, while launching a new large research effort. Ralf Gruenke was our Washington, D.C.–based research assistant; Jason Beal helped with the project generally and particularly with the documentary; Eric Smith assisted with computing; and Eric Jarvi helped maintain a secure home page for investigators in our sixteen races. The Annenberg Public Policy Center's D.C. office provided space from which to do our Washington, D.C., research. I would also like to thank a supportive department secretary, Irene Fuja, as well as Kelly Patterson and Clayne Pope, chair and dean, respectively, for their encouragement. Gary Reynolds of the Brigham Young University Office of Research and Creative Activity was helpful in logistics at BYU, and Kevin Walker assisted with budgeting and financial management. Lillian Miller was most helpful in my travel arrangements as well as those for the investigators.

The research reported in this book meant I needed the assistance of numerous practitioners and experts. I benefited from the input of Charlie Cook, Stu Rothenberg, Bernedette Budde, party committee staff at all six major party committees in Washington, D.C., and reporters at *Congressional Quarterly*. Lloyd Leonard and Jee Hang Lee of the League of Women Voters helped facilitate our collaboration with League members in our states and districts. Jane Mentzinger at Common Cause provided similar assistance with members of Common Cause. In the postelection phase, I was fortunate to be able to interview key participants in the historic 1998 congressional elections. They are widely quoted throughout this book, and I appreciate their willingness to take time to talk with me.

Jennifer Knerr, executive editor, lived up to her reputation for careful attention to manuscripts and knowledge of the discipline. I wish to also thank Janice Braunstein, production editor, for excellent and timely production and Bonnie Dorsey for copyediting.

Throughout my intense year of research and travel, my wife, Linda, and children have been patient and supportive.

1

The Expanded Role of Interest Groups and Political Parties in Competitive U.S. Congressional Elections

David B. Magleby

Voters in competitive U.S. House and U.S. Senate elections encountered a different kind of campaign in 1998 than has been the norm in American politics. In addition to the competing candidate campaigns, interest groups and political parties aggressively tried to influence the vote. This noncandidate campaign activity, what we call outside money, differs from candidate campaigns in that groups and parties have no contribution limits: the sky is the limit for interest groups and party spending. Notably, these limitless expenditures can largely avoid the disclosure laws that apply to other money in our federal election system. Independent expenditures, important in the early 1980s and to a lesser extent today, are unlimited but disclosed.

Outside money was important in several competitive 1998 congressional races. We often found estimated campaign expenditures by interest groups and political parties exceeding the amounts spent by the candidates; and in contests where the candidates spent more, the parties and groups together spent an average of $500,000 or more in House races and $2 million or more in Senate races. This expanded role for parties and interest groups marks an important departure from the candidate-centered campaigns so common in American politics.

American politics has long been characterized by weak political parties and interest-group pluralism. Parties in the United States are generally only observers in the nomination process, and although parties play a greater role in general elections, they are still not as important as the candidates' own organizations. Indeed, Martin Wattenberg's work on the rise of candidate-centered politics has been widely accepted as describing presidential elections in the last two decades.[1] Herbert Weisberg also argued that politics has evolved into a more candidate-centered environment, asserting that the 1960s literature on voting behavior stressed partisanship, while the later revisionist perspective emphasized the issues. But most modern political analysts emphasize candidates.[2] The candidate-centered campaign thesis applies just as well to congressional elections, where the work of Mayhew and Fiorina demonstrates the importance of the reelection motive and the desire on the part of representatives and senators to provide constituency service as a way of broadening their electoral base.[3] Congressional candidates build their own support base among voters and campaign donors and work to broaden and solidify their appeal in their state or district as well as with those who contribute to congressional candidates.

Diana Dwyre's research demonstrates that political parties play a larger role in congressional campaign finance than previously reported.[4] Part of the reason for this enlarged role is soft money, or what is called in the law nonfederal money, which can be raised in unlimited amounts. This exception to the more general contribution limits in the Federal Election Campaign Act (as amended by Congress in 1979 and interpreted by the Federal Election Commission and the courts) was used first in presidential campaigns but has now been discovered by party congressional campaign committees. Will the ability of parties to raise and spend this soft money make them major players in American electoral politics as we move into the next century? Or will candidates find ways to harness soft money to their purposes? Dwyre's work suggests that soft money enhances the party roll by "providing funds with which the national party committees can maintain and improve the organization and therefore offer more and better services."[5] A counterhypothesis would be that parties have become financial institutions raising money candidates cannot and then spending it on candidates. If this is true, parties as institutions act only as brokers of funds and are not appreciably strengthened as institutions. One of our primary research questions is whether the use of outside money strengthens parties.

Both political parties developed a large-scale soft-money strategy in 1998. The disclosed and limited hard-money contributions to candidates by parties actually declined in 1998, while soft-money spending roughly doubled. But unlike hard-money party spending, soft money by law cannot involve coordination or collusion with the candidates.

Campaign spending by interest groups in the guise of "issue advocacy" has also grown dramatically in recent election cycles and has given the political parties a new argument to use when raising soft money. The argument is that parties need millions of dollars to respond to well-financed attacks against their partys' candidates by interest groups. The fear of interest groups targeting candidates has also meant candidates have cooperated with their parties in the surge in soft-money fund-raising and spending we observed in 1998.

Interest-group involvement in congressional elections also changed in 1998. Competition among interest groups occurs at all levels of American government and in a variety of settings. Campaign finance has been no exception. One important set of interests in congressional campaign finance is organized labor. The unions pressed for legislation permitting political action committees (PACs) in the early 1970s, in part because of the fear of pending litigation. The Federal Election Campaign Act (1971, 1974) permits unions to have PACs, but for the first time it also authorizes corporations to form them as well. The greatest growth in PAC activity in the last two decades has been in the business sector. Labor and business each fund their favored candidates, who are generally incumbents, with labor money going mostly to Democrats and corporate money more evenly divided but going primarily to Republicans.[6]

Labor unions were ahead of other interest groups in a second mode of participation in congressional campaigns as well: in 1996, in addition to the campaign contributions given to the candidates and the Democratic Party, organized labor engaged in interest-group election advocacy in forty-four congressional races. The Christian Coalition and the NRA spent money trying to influence voters in 1994, but this effort was dwarfed by what the unions did in 1996. Not surprisingly business interests responded with election advocacy campaigns of their own in 1996. The campaign spending by outside groups in 1994 and 1996 was limited to a relatively small number of contests, generally competitive races. This is not to say that interest groups spending $1 million or more in a U.S. House race is insignificant. But in most contests, interest groups played their familiar game of giving to incumbents and occasionally investing in an open-seat race.[7]

But as we will see, in 1998 interest groups and political parties altered their strategy (see fig. 1.1). Political parties and interest groups now view competitive congressional elections as important terrain on which they will battle. The close party balance in both houses makes winning competitive elections essential, and because interpretations of campaign finance rules permit unlimited and undisclosed activity, such outside campaigns are changing the nature of the electoral system. The phenomenon of interest-group election advertising and large-scale party soft money in congressional elections is new and not well understood.

THE HISTORIC 1998 MIDTERM ELECTION

The 1998 midterm election for the House of Representatives was historic. The President's party picked up five seats in the House of Representatives, surprising most pundits and ending the long-term trend.[8] Not since 1934 has a president's party won seats in a midterm election. At one point before the election, Speaker Gingrich speculated that Republicans might pick up as many as forty seats in the House.[9] Democrats also denied the Republicans any net gain in the U.S. Senate, despite Republican preelection hopes of electing a "filibuster proof" Senate. As we will demonstrate, campaign finance was an important part of the story of the 1998 elections.

STRATEGIC ENVIRONMENT OF THE 1998 ELECTIONS

Political science research has pointed to two macro-level indicators of the degree to which the president's party loses seats in midterm elections, the state of the economy and the level of presidential popularity.[10] The economy clearly benefited Clinton and the Democrats, especially among a group whom public opinion analyst Bill Schneider calls the "new rich"—individuals whose financial situation has become more stable since Clinton took office—who credit Clinton for better jobs and more reliable health care. Schneider contends that when Republicans turned the election into a referendum on the President and on impeachment, the Democrats benefited because this group did not want to see him impeached, and they voted that way.[11]

Before the election, strategists from both parties had reason to be concerned. Would the scandal discourage Democratic voters from going to the polls in 1998? Or would it generate a "rally around the President effect?" Christian conservatives who have been important to Republican coalitions in the past were offended by the scandal, but it was unknown whether they would channel their anger towards greater levels of participation or whether they would shun the entire process.

As we will describe in this book, one of the most important elements of the 1998 elections was voter mobilization and turnout. Which candidates, groups, and parties would be most able to mobilize their constituency? Would turnout continue to decline or would the scandal activate voters? The 1996 presidential election saw the lowest voter turnout since 1924.[12] The 1998 election followed suit with the lowest turnout in the primaries in over forty years, with only 36 percent of the voting-age population voting in the general election, compared to 45 percent four years earlier.[13] Despite overall lower voter turnout, some candidates, parties, and groups did a better job than others in mobilizing turnout. Turnout was especially low among self-declared conservatives. In 1994, 37 percent of all voters considered themselves conservatives, in 1996 conservatives' share of the vote fell to 34 percent, and in 1998 it fell still further to 31 percent.[14] Conservatives did not come out to vote in 1998, but moderates did—this time in greater numbers, and they voted Democratic 54 percent of the time.[15] The liberal proportion of the vote has been constant since 1994.[16] African Americans were one segment of the population that voted in larger proportions in some states with competitive races than in past midterm elections. Among this subpopulation the tendency to vote Democratic remained near 90 percent in 1998.[17] The role that parties and interest groups played in mobilizing voters or failing to do so is an important part of the story of this election.

The strategic environment of the 1998 elections was unusual because of the specter of impeachment and the widespread attention given to the Clinton/Lewinsky scandal. Democrats feared that the scandal could keep Democrats away from the polls.[18] Democrats largely avoided the impeachment issue, instead fo-

Figure 1.1   Number of Issue Ad Campaigns by Week in 1998: Interest Groups and Political Parties

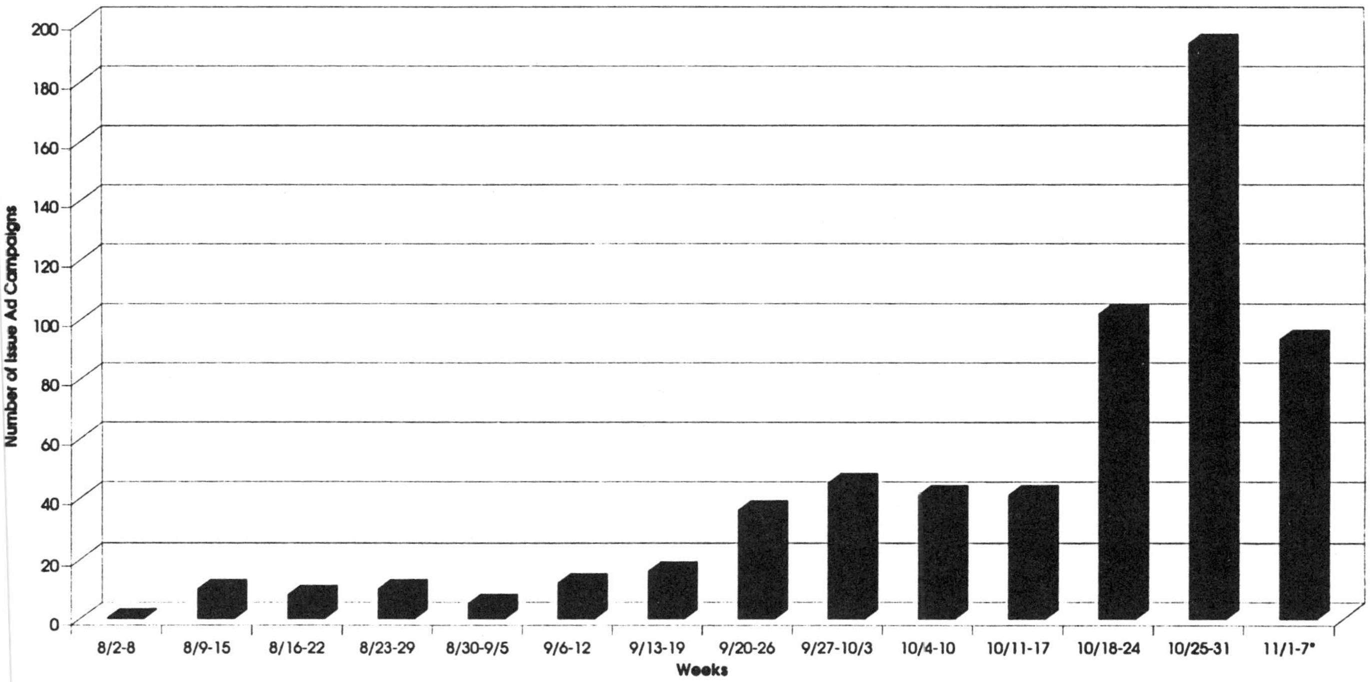

Source: Data from the *Outside Money* Data Set.
*Estimated for the whole week from November 1–3 data.

cusing on three broad themes: Social Security, education, and health care.[19] Republicans took another approach to the scandal and impeachment issue. They said very little about the issue until the end of the campaign, when the National Republican Congressional Committee (NRCC) spent $10 million on three television advertisements and direct mail raising the issue of honesty and integrity in government and within the presidency. The blitz was aimed at selected midwestern and southern states. The media, already preoccupied with the scandal, gave widespread coverage to the ads and the Republican decision to make impeachment an issue. Speaker Gingrich's election postmortem recognized the strategic mistake that sidetracked the media and the public's attention from other campaign issues. "We underestimated the degree to which people would get sick of the scandal through repetition . . . we did what we thought would be effective, but our expectations did not fit with what happened on Election Day."[20]

Gingrich set himself up for a fall when he continued throughout the election, including on election day, to predict double-digit victories for the Republicans in Congress. Some argued that he relied on too few confidants and did not lay any groundwork for seat losses in the House.[21] The NRCC mistake cost Speaker Gingrich his job and resulted in wholesale staff and leadership changes at the NRCC.

In terms of impacting the actual vote, most voters responding to national exit polls indicated that the scandal was not a factor in their decision.[22] The Republicans, at least on the House side, invested heavily in trying to make impeachment and Clinton's character an issue. But as Gary Jacobson has pointed out, this strategy overlooked "the public's distinction between Clinton the president and Clinton the person." This distinction "freed Democrats to campaign on Clinton's policy agenda without defending his character or behavior."[23] The view that the scandal did not matter was also shared by consultants like Republican pollster Glen Bolger of Public Opinion Strategies who said, "Monicagate was much ado about nothing."[24] Not long after the election, however, others interpreted the election as a referendum on the scandal, with more than two-thirds of voters surveyed after the election saying the Clinton/Lewinsky scandal was a major reason "why the Republicans did not do as well as anticipated."[25] While it may not have helped either party at the ballot box, the scandal appeared to help with party fund-raising. DNC Chairman Steve Grossman attributed the increase in donations to people wanting to help.[26]

One impact of the scandal was a "placid period" of limited campaign advertising between August 17, when the President admitted that he had misled the American people, and October 21, when Congress finally adjourned for the election campaign.[27] Candidates, parties, and groups did not know how to adjust their strategy to these new circumstances; therefore, the intense media campaign was delayed. We also found in our data a delay in the advertising campaigns in several races until mid-October.

Both parties saw 1998 as strategically important, long before the Clinton/Lewinsky scandal and the threat of impeachment raised the stakes of the 1998 elections. The slim majority of only eleven seats in the House was the closest in forty-six years, and Democrats believed that several Republican incumbents were vulnerable. Republicans had been the minority in the House for forty years and knew the historic trends might help expand their majority. In the Senate, as noted, Republicans knew that the mix of open seats and competitive races gave them an opportunity to expand their majority. Both parties worked hard at recruiting quality candidates for competitive races.[28] To attract a candidate in a competitive contest, one Democratic candidate was promised a seat on the House Appropriations Committee if the candidate ran and won.[29]

While both parties saw the election as important and both aggressively courted possible candidates, all agreed that relatively few 1998 contests would be competitive. A combination of safe seats resulting from partisan gerrymandering, incumbency advantages, early fund-raising, and fewer open seats contributed to this phenomenon. Gary Jacobson asserts that the "Clinton-Lewinsky scandal probably scared off high quality challengers in potentially winnable districts."[30] If so, this may have reduced the number of competitive races as well. Table 1.1 presents the number of competitive U.S. House elections in July of each election year for the 1990s. Because only fifty-eight U.S. House contests in 1998 were competitive (a substantial decrease from recent years), the focus on these competitive races was intensified.

In the spring of 1998, Democrats optimistically believed that they would pick up seats. Claiming credit for good times and the first balanced budget in twenty-nine years, Democrats expected that voters would "find it easier to vote for Democratic candidates on the basis of tobacco, campaign finance, or HMO reform."[31] Republicans also claimed credit for the good economic times and the balanced budget but, lacking the unified voice of the presidency and distracted by the Lewinsky scandal, had a harder time focusing the public on their accomplishments.

Campaign finance was also an important part of the 1998 elections story. Party committees, building on their record-setting soft-money fund-raising in 1996, set new fund-raising and expenditure records for a midterm election in 1998. Soft money, which had previously been used primarily by the national party committees in presidential races rather than the congressional campaign committees, became a central part of both parties' congressional committee strategies, especially the Republicans. Overall, party soft-money spending in 1998 was more than double party soft-money spending in the 1994 midterm election.

Table 1.1   Competitive U.S. House Races over Time

Year	1992	1994	1996	1998
Races	138	108	123	58

Source: Data from Charlie Cook, "How Big Will Republican Gains Be?" *National Journal* 30, no. 39, 2252.

Party soft-money fund-raisers reported that certain campaign finance practices helped them motivate contributors to give generously in 1997–98. Contributors were told that the parties needed large amounts of soft money to respond to the issue ads run by groups such as organized labor, the Business Roundtable, or Americans for Limited Terms. Debts from the 1996 presidential races, the costly tobacco legislation fight of spring 1998, and interest-group advertising during the special elections of March and June 1998 gave this fund-raising argument credibility.

Interest-group involvement was important for reasons beyond being a fundraising foil. Not only can interest groups spend money on radio and television airwaves to attack some candidates and support others, they can also mount ground offenses of targeted telephone and mail campaigns. This form of campaigning usually falls under the radar screen of television or radio advertising. Phone banks and direct mailers were major parts of interest-group and political party strategies in the 1998 campaign. The outside-money study was designed to systematically retrieve information on these types of campaign activity.

Party committees' growing use of soft money for voter identification and activation, combined with interest-group spending, significantly alters the campaign finance landscape of American federal elections. Voters can no longer assume that the candidates are the only ones seeking to influence their vote. The Federal Election Commission provides only partial disclosure on interest-group and soft-money expenditures; and in the most competitive races, in which the stakes are highest, unlimited and undisclosed campaign activities are likely to play a major role and see larger expenditures. This research project was designed to learn the extent of outside money in competitive races, how the money was spent, and what effect it is having on our electoral democracy.

Limited Media Coverage

When congressional races have the kinds of soft-money expenditures and interest-group activities that our study saw in competitive 1998 contests, it is much harder for voters to distinguish and assimilate all the information and competing messages. Because soft-money spending and interest-group electioneering are not disclosed, voters must rely on the news media to help them understand the campaign. This new environment of elections is challenging for news media to report, in part because the groups and parties often do not disclose what they are doing. One of the study's research questions is the extent to which the news media understood and reported on the role of outside money in our sample of competitive races.

Generally, media coverage of the 1998 elections was sparser than in previous years. In a study of 1998 gubernatorial elections, the Annenberg Center found that local television news devoted less time to elections than in previous years.[32] Speaking more generally, political pundit Stuart Rothenberg correctly predicted in August that "much of the political story of 1998 is going unreported and even unrecognized." Rothenberg also predicted that "TV advertising in politically and financially competitive races probably won't decide as many races as will alternate voter contact methods, including absentee ballot programs and get-out-the-vote efforts."[33]

In the absence of informative news coverage about which groups and parties are attempting to influence the election, voters are at a loss to know who to hold accountable for exaggerated claims or negative messages they do not like. Voters can hold candidates accountable at the ballot box, but they cannot hold interest groups or parties accountable. In this new world of large-scale party and interest-group electioneering the media have an added responsibility to inform the public of the full range of campaign activities, including those by noncandidate campaign entities.

STUDY DESIGN AND METHODOLOGY

Given the importance of soft-money and issue-group election advocacy, the Pew Charitable Trusts generously funded a grant to place academic researchers in sixteen competitive districts or states to gather data on the unregulated and undisclosed campaign activity by parties and interest groups in the 1998 general election. The sample of contests selected was based on the competitiveness of the race and the probability of outside money flowing to the district.

This project studied the impact of outside money on the contests where it was most likely to be spent; that is, in the most competitive races, districts, or states with media markets providing good value for the investment. The sample of contests was drawn from published lists of competitive races by the *Cook Political Report,* the *Rothenberg Political Report,* and Congressional Quarterly's *On Politics* newsletter.[34] The list of competitive races was then circulated to a small sample of party and PAC professionals who identified places where outside money was most likely to impact the elections. The sample for U.S. House elections had equal numbers of Democratic incumbents, Republican incumbents, and open seats. In the U.S. Senate, the sample had two Democratic incumbents, one Republican incumbent, and one open seat. Overall there were more Senate Democratic than Republican incumbents in 1998 Senate elections. Table 1.2 presents the sample of contests selected.

Outside money in Senate races is especially likely to be allocated to states where parties or groups can get more "bang for the buck." In earlier research I established that less populated states have generally seen much higher spending in terms of dollars per voter.[35] This greater efficiency of spending in sparsely populated states not only reflects the less expensive media markets but the reality that a senator from Nevada has the same power as a senator from New York. In 1998, Nevada U.S. senatorial candidates spent $20.01 per voter, whereas in New

Table 1.2   Sample U.S. House and Senate Races

Race	Democrat	Republican	Incumbency
Connecticut 5**	Jim Maloney	Mark Nielsen	Democrat
Idaho 2**	Richard Stallings	Mike Simpson	Open
Illinois 17**	Lane Evans	Mark Baker	Democrat
Iowa 3**	Leonard Boswell	Larry McKibben	Democrat
Kansas 3**	Dennis Moore	Vince Snowbarger	Republican
Kentucky 6**	Ernesto Scorsone	Ernie Fletcher	Open
New Mexico 3**	Tom Udall	Bill Redmond	Republican
Ohio 6**	Ted Strickland	Nancy Hollister	Democrat
Oregon 1**	David Wu	Molly Bordonaro	Open
Pennsylvania 13**	Joseph Hoeffel	Jon Fox	Republican
Utah 2*	Lily Eskelsen	Merrill Cook	Republican
Wisconsin 1**	Lydia Spottswood	Paul Ryan	Open
Kentucky Senate**	Henry Baesler	Jim Bunning	Open
Nevada Senate**	Harry Reid	John Ensign	Democrat
North Carolina Senate**	John Edwards	Launch Faircloth	Republican
South Carolina Senate**	Ernest Hollings	Bob Inglis	Democrat

*Races considered tilting to one party or worthy of watching.
**Races considered toss-ups or highly vulnerable.

York, senatorial candidates spent $9.32 per voter. I did not assume that parties and interest groups would ignore populous states, but rather that resources would be more concentrated and have a greater payoff in less populated states.

After determining the sample of sixteen races, I selected the academics. In some instances, scholars who had already published on money and politics issues taught at institutions in the district or state. In other cases, I contacted respected academics to inquire about scholars in the district or state who would have an interest in the topic, who were well connected with political elites in the district or state, and who had a reputation for solid scholarship.

All participating academics were provided with detailed training documents, including information on the intent of the study, a brief review of the soft-money and issue-advocacy literature, and a detailed description of the proposed methodology. The scholars participating in the study were urged to come to the training sessions with suggestions on how to improve the methodology and with any adaptations necessary for their state or district.[36] The study design called for the academic observers to create a network of contacts with political parties, campaigns, other political science departments, former students, reporters, consultants, and citizen-activist groups. The academics in each district or state employed graduate or undergraduate students to assist with the monitoring. Effort was made to expand the networks as broadly as possible. In some cases, professors even incorporated this project into class curricula, where students helped with monitoring efforts. This reconnaissance offered daily monitoring of campaign activities such as telephone banks and direct mail. The scholars and their networks periodically tracked print advertising and stories by local reporters covering outside money, and traveled to broadcast, cable, and radio stations to access public political files which contain records of issue and candidate advertisements.[37]

I also contracted Strategic Media Services, a media marketing and tracking firm in Alexandria, Virginia, to monitor political advertisements on television. Once a new advertisement has been coded by Strategic Media, they track and record each following appearance of that advertisement in the top seventy-five markets nationwide. Table 1.3 lists the twenty media markets in the study's sample that were monitored by Strategic Media. Our study permits us to verify the accuracy of this new method of tracking television advertising because in several markets we obtained actual media-buy contracts from television stations.

Volunteers from the League of Women Voters, Common Cause, and alumni of Brigham Young University assisted in gathering mail and reporting on telephone contacts during and shortly after the campaign.[38] We designed a form for these individuals to fill out, which included questions about the content and tone of the message. Academic investigators contacted the groups making phone calls or sending mail to learn the extent and cost of their activity. Our collection of telephone reports and mail permits us to assess the timing, tone, and message used in the mail strategy.

Table 1.3   Media Markets Monitored by Strategic Media Services

Connecticut Fifth	Hartford, CT, and New York, NY, markets
Idaho Second	No markets monitored
Illinois Seventeenth	No markets monitored
Iowa Third	Des Moines, IA, market
Kentucky Sixth and Senate	Lexington, KY, Louisville, KY, and Huntington/Charleston, VA, markets
Kansas Third	Kansas City, MO, market
Nevada Senate	Las Vegas, NV, Salt Lake City, UT, markets
New Mexico Third	Albuquerque, NM, market
North Carolina Senate	Charlotte, NC, Raleigh/Durham, NC, and Greensboro/Winston/Salem/High Point, NC, markets
Ohio Sixth	Charleston/Huntington, VA, Columbus, OH, and Cincinnati, OH, markets
Oregon First	Portland, OR, market
Pennsylvania Thirteenth	Philadelphia, PA, market
South Carolina Senate	Greenville/Spartanburg/Asheville, SC, market
Utah Second	Salt Lake City, UT, market
Wisconsin First	Milwaukee, WI, market

Academic observers in the sample contests were encouraged to regularly interview political reporters, campaign staff, and party professionals to learn about the campaign activities of individuals, groups, and parties that are otherwise not disclosed. Good working relations were sought with the campaign staff of all major party candidates. We assumed the campaign staff would be among the first to know about noncandidate campaign activity. We expected that they would share information about efforts aimed at hurting their candidate or helping their opponent. Often, they share this information with the press or supporters of a candidate in a weekly fax or e-mail press release. We sought to be included on such mailings with both candidates. In several of our study's contests, academic investigators generally achieved good working relations with both campaigns.

We identified and interviewed consultants involved in all party, candidate, and interest-group election efforts in our sample contests, and we also interviewed state party directors. Consultants and party staff often know much about the workings of campaigns. Postelection interviews with many campaign consultants revealed their frustration with outside campaigns and the general inability to maintain a candidate's agenda and to balance negative and positive media with interest groups and political parties waging wars that the consultant could neither manage nor anticipate. There was greater satisfaction with national party committees' ground-war and voter-mobilization efforts, as these activities help increase overall voter turnout.

The material results of this methodology include not just anecdotes, information on campaign finance, and stories of campaign tactics and strategies, but also hard figures on actual spending on television or radio by parties and groups. The broadcasting, radio, direct mail, phone bank, and newspaper data from the sample races were transmitted weekly to a secure home page at Brigham Young University that permitted regular monitoring of the data and feedback to the investigators. Internet reporting forms were designed to minimize multiple data entry. With over 1,600 entries, this database contains information on message tone, cost, and distribution circulation. The database allows us a comprehensive view of interest-group and party activities across a range of states as well as a detailed look at specific strategies in each race. The growth in party soft-money–funded communications with voters was a major development in 1998, one well documented in our data set.

We realized that because our study broke new ground, we would encounter some research difficulties. For example, the level of cooperation from radio and television stations was uneven and many stations were unaware of the FCC rules and were unprepared for the onslaught of advertising requests. With some notable exceptions, political reporters in the states and districts were not informed about this new world of unregulated and undisclosed money. As a result, voters often lacked information to help them understand who was truly funding the advertisements. In addition, the coverage by the network of volunteers and contacts helping monitor mail and phones was uneven across districts but appeared to work well in several districts or states. We knew gathering these data would be difficult but, as the events of 1998 demonstrated, they were essential to understanding the outcome.

OVERVIEW OF BOOK

We begin the book by examining the major development of the 1998 election cycle, the surge in soft-money spending, and the extent to which it was targeted to competitive races. Chapter 2 examines this soft-money surge and its implications for congressional campaign committees, congressional leadership, campaign committee leadership, and candidates in competitive races. Marianne Holt demonstrates that both parties made soft money an important part of their 1998 effort, both in broadcast advertising and in the ground war. The chapter also examines the strategic role parties now play because of soft money and the implications of a growing reliance on soft-money donors for our political system generally.

Chapter 3 examines the three types of communication that interest groups engage in: pure issue advocacy on an issue for purely educational or informational purposes; legislative issue advocacy on a policy issue that is being considered by government; and interest-group electioneering, which is spending by an interest group to influence the outcome of an election focusing on one or both of the candidates. All three types of advocacy are sometimes labeled issue advocacy, but in fact they have quite different aims. For our purposes, we will emphasize interest-group electioneering, which continued to grow in 1998 and which was important in several competitive congressional elections. It is important to note that advertisements run by the political parties near election time are also sometimes called issue ads. In every important respect these party ads are electioneering.

One of the important developments of 1998 was the ground war of voter registration, identification, and mobilization. Past studies of issue advocacy have been limited to broadcast advertising, and little research has been done on how party soft money is spent on ground-war activities. Chapter 4 summarizes what we learned about the ground war in 1998 and the implications of outside money spent on these activities for other low-turnout elections like primaries and the 2002 midterm election.

Chapters 5 through 7 present case studies of outside money in U.S. Senate and U.S. House elections in 1998, where party activity was important. We begin in chapter 5 with the Kansas Third Congressional race, detailing its heavy party and interest-group involvement consisting of extensive ground-war activity and creating a highly negative tone for the candidates to balance. We then turn in chapter 6 to the South Carolina Senate election where outside party money allowed the Democratic candidate to compete in the newly Republican-leaning state. Chapter 7 examines the Nevada Senate elections, which saw extraordinary party soft-money and candidate spending, bolstered by the get-out-the-vote (GOTV) efforts of organized labor and environmental groups.

Chapters 8 through 11 emphasize the successes and failures of interest-group spending and influence. Chapter 8 discusses the New Mexico Third Congressional race and the efforts made by environmental groups to wage war against Bill Redmond as well as Republican efforts in his defense. The Connecticut Fifth District race, chapter 9, reveals the power of interest-group pledges: the successful Democratic candidate signed three separate interest-group pledges, eliminating conservative interest-group threats, leaving the Republican candidate alone to battle labor and environmental groups. Chapter 10 addresses the Utah Second District race and the intense involvement of Americans for Limited Terms through television and ground-war techniques against the successful Republican incumbent Merrill Cook. The concluding case study, chapter 11, details both the Kentucky Senate and the Sixth Congressional District elections. Providing an interesting interplay between contests, the Kentucky sample reveals the successful party efforts in the Senate race and the heavily influential interest-group efforts in the Sixth Congressional District.

Chapter 12 presents the overall findings and implications of our research. It evaluates the effectiveness of various campaign strategies in primary, midterm, and presidential elections; examines the efficacy of soft money; and provides implications for the major players in our electoral democracy: candidates, parties, voters, interest groups, and the media.

NOTES

1. Martin P. Wattenberg, *The Rise of Candidate-Centered Politics: Presidential Elections of the 1980s* (Cambridge: Harvard University Press, 1991).

2. Herbert F. Weisberg and David C. Kimball, "Attitudinal Correlates of the 1992 Presidential Vote: Party Identification and Beyond," in *Democracy's Feast: Elections in America,* ed. Herbert F. Weisberg (Chatham, N.J.: Chatham House Publishers, Inc., 1995), 72–111. See also Paul Herrnson, *Congressional Elections: Campaigning at Home and in Washington* (Washington, D.C.: Congressional Quarterly, 1998).

3. See David R. Mayhew, *Congress: The Electoral Connection* (New Haven: Yale University Press, 1986).

4. Diana Dwyre, "Spinning Straw into Gold: Soft Money and U.S. House Elections," *Legislative Studies Quarterly* 21, no. 3 (August 1996).

5. Ibid., 420.

6. For an overview on PACs see Frank J. Sorauf, "Political Action Committees," in *Campaign Finance Reform: A Sourcebook,* ed. Anthony Corrado, Thomas E. Mann, Daniel R. Ortiz, Trevor Potter, and Frank J. Sorauf (Washington, D.C.: Brookings Institution Press, 1997), 121–64.

7. For an overview of interest-group activity in campaigns through 1996 see Mark J. Rozell and Clyde Wilcox, *Interest Groups in American Campaigns: The New Face of Electioneering* (Washington, D.C.: Congressional Quarterly, 1999).

8. Long before the Clinton/Lewinsky scandal, Stuart Rothenberg and Charlie Cook commented on the possibility of the Democrats picking up House seats in 1998, but concluded this was unlikely, given the long-term trend of the President's party losing seats. *Cook Political Report,* 2 July 1998, 2; *Rothenberg Political Report,* 21 May 1998, 1.

9. Jim VandeHei, "Speaker Predicts Republicans Could Gain Up to 40 Seats in Fall," *Roll Call,* 16 July 1998.

10. Edward Tufte, "Determinants of Outcomes of Congressional Midterm Elections," *American Political Science Review* 69, no. 3 (September 1975), 812–26.

11. William Schneider, "To the 'New Rich,' Bill's OK," *National Journal,* 14 November 1998, 2746.

12. Rhodes Cook, "Big Picture," *CQ On Politics,* 12 August 1998, 1; U.S. Department of Commerce, Bureau of the Census, *Statistical Abstract of United States, 1997* (Washington, D.C.: GPO, 1997), 289; and Leslie Wayne, "The Nation: The Price of a Vote," *New York Times,* 8 November 1998, D4.

13. Cook, "Big Picture."

14. James A. Barnes, "The 1998 Vote: Gauging Mid-Term Political Performances," *The Public Perspective: A Roper Center Review of Public Opinion and Polling* (December/January 1999): 5.

15. Richard Benedetto, "Pay Attention—It Was About Something," *The Public Perspective: A Roper Center Review of Public Opinion and Polling* (December/January 1999): 34.

16. "The Expectations Come When Groups Are Actually Changing Their Relative Population Size," *The Public Perspective: A Roper Center Review of Public Opinion and Polling* (December/January 1999): 106.

17. "How Key Demographic Groups Voted For the US House of Representatives, 1984–1998," *The Public Perspective: A Roper Center Review of Public Opinion and Polling* (December/January 1999): 70.

18. David S. Broder and Thomas B. Edsall, "Amid Election Apathy, Parties Bet on Core Voters," *Washington Post,* 7 September 1998, A1.

19. Marc Sandalow, "Dwindling Hopes for GOP Landslide; Lewinsky Influence Proves Hard to Predict," *San Francisco Chronicle,* 21 October 1998, A1.

20. Marc Birtel, "Democrats' Victories Buck History of Midterm Elections," *Congressional Quarterly* 5 (November 1998): 7.

21. Richard E. Cohen, "The Rise and Fall of Newt," *National Journal,* 6 March 1999, 598–606.

22. Decision98 National Exit Poll conducted by MSNBC on election day revealed that the scandal was not on the minds of the voters when they were in the booth. When asked "Was one reason for your vote for Congress today to express support for Bill Clinton, to express opposition to Bill Clinton, or neither," 60 percent of voters said neither. When asked what one issue was most important in voting for a representative, the scandal was the lowest ranked of seven items including education, Social Security, health care, taxes, moral and ethical standards, and the economy. Overall, the Clinton/Lewinsky matter only received 5 percent of the voters' main concern when voting.

23. Gary C. Jacobson, "Impeachment Politics in the 1998 Congressional Elections," *Political Science Quarterly* 114, no. 1 (spring 1999), 31–51.

24. Glen Bolger, "Lessons of Victory and Defeat '98," *Campaigns and Election* (December/January 1998): 66–70.

25. *Public Opinion OnLine,* Question 15, Roper Center, 5 November 1998.

26. "Democratic Donors Hear 'Call to Arms,' " *Des Moines Register,* 29 January 1998, A7.

27. Remarks of Kathleen Hall Jamieson to the Congressional Quarterly postelection conference, Washington, D.C., 5 November 1998.

28. Staff of congressional campaign committees, interview by author, August 1998.

29. Richard Stallings of Idaho was promised the Appropriation Committee assignment. Stallings lost the election to Mark Simpson.

30. Gary Jacobson, "Impeachment Politics in the 1998 Congressional Elections," 13.

31. Stuart Rothenberg, "House Outlook '98: Democrats Still Poised to Gain Seats," *Rothenberg Political Report,* 21 May 1998, 2.

32. Kathleen Hall Jamieson, "Tracking Gubernatorial Elections in Ten States" (report of a grant funded by the Pew Charitable Trusts, Washington, D.C., 1 December 1998).

33. Stuart Rothenberg, "Is '98 Election Coverage Missing the Boat?" *Roll Call,* 13 August 1998.

34. The *Cook Political Report* rates candidates in one of seven different categories: "Solid Democrat/Solid Republican," "Likely Democrat/Likely Republican," "Leaning Democrat/Leaning Republican," and "Toss-Up." For our methodological purposes, we considered only those candidates in the "Toss-Up" or "Leaning" categories. The *Rothenberg Political Report* rates races on a system of "Toss-Up," "Tilt Republican/Tilt Democrat" or "Democrat/Republican Favored." We studies the races with either "Toss-Up" or "Tilting" candidates. *CQ On Politics* ranked all races in categories of "Highly Vulnerable," "Potentially Vulnerable," and "Probably Secure." Within their ranking system, we targeted the "Highly Vulnerable" and "Vulnerable" races.

35. David B. Magleby, *More Bank for the Buck: Campaign Spending in Small State U.S. Senate Elections* (paper presented at the annual meeting of the Western Political Science Association, Salt Lake City, Utah, March 1989).

36. Most academics were trained in person at the American Political Science Association annual meeting in Boston over Labor Day weekend 1998, while others were trained in calls generally involving several researchers as well.

37. We acknowledge the useful advice provided by Andy Schwartman at the Center for Media Access and Bobby Baker at the Federal Communications Commission on the difference between public files, candidate files, and political files under the law.

38. We acknowledge Jane Metzinger at Common Cause and Lloyd Leonard and JeeHang Lee at League of Women Voters for their help at the national level of organizing and for inviting their members to participate in this research project.

2

The Surge in Party Money in Competitive 1998 Congressional Elections

Marianne Holt

In recent years both parties have used soft money to fund a wide range of activities, from voter registration drives and get-out-the-vote efforts to television ads. Intended as a means to enhance the role of parties in elections, soft money has clearly accomplished that goal. But as Tony Corrado, the leading authority on soft money, has said, "Soft money is the most controversial and complicated form of funding in the political finance system."[1] Why is it so controversial? First, because it allows unlimited contributions. Second, because it allows parties to raise money "in violation of the spirit of the FECA and it violates the letter of many state laws."[2] Third, because it largely avoids disclosure, at least as to its expenditure.

Concern regarding soft money grew in 1996 following revelations of record levels of soft-money spending by both parties and by soft-money fund-raising practices by the Clinton/Gore campaign. These campaign activities included hosting White House "coffees" for large soft-money donors, inviting large soft-money donors to spend a night in the Lincoln Bedroom, and possibly contributing of Chinese money through intermediaries.

Learning from the presidential campaign of 1996, both parties raised and spent soft money on the 1998 congressional elections, doubling amounts spent in the 1994 midterm election cycle. In this chapter we explore party involvement in federal campaigns—how soft money is expanding the campaign agenda-setting role of political parties through attack advertisements and election advocacy.

PARTY MONEY

Party Hard Money: Limited and Disclosed Contributions

Under the Federal Election Campaign Act (FECA), parties are allowed to contribute directly to candidates. Once a contribution is made, the party relinquishes

control of the money and the candidate controls spending. U.S. House candidates can receive a $5,000 contribution from each of their national party com-
mittees, in each election stage (primary, runoff, and general), for a total of
$15,000; Senate candidates can receive a slightly higher total contribution of
$17,500 in a campaign cycle. State parties can also contribute $5,000 to senatorial
candidates each election cycle.[3]

A second way parties can help finance campaigns is through coordinated expenditures, in which the parties and candidates share spending control.[4] Candidates in the most competitive congressional races have come to expect the party's
financial support through both direct contributions and coordinated campaigns.
Coordinated campaigns include polling, direct mail, and get-out-the-vote
(GOTV) drives. Coordinated expenditures for U.S. Senate candidates vary with
the population of the state, from a low of $65,100 to a high of $1.5 million. In
1998, U.S. House candidates were allowed to spend a maximum of $32,550 in
coordinated expenditures from national parties and the same amount from state
parties.[5] State parties can also transfer their spending limits to the national parties through "agency agreements." These agreements, most commonly seen in
hotly contested races, essentially double national party limits for coordinated expenditures.

Coordinated expenditures and direct contributions are fully disclosed and limited by law. Table 2.1 presents the combined party committee hard-dollar contributions and coordinated expenditure totals for 1978 through 1998 in 1998 dollars. Since 1992, political party hard-money expenditures given directly to
candidates through contributions and coordinated expenditures have fluctuated,
but the general trend has been downward. In 1998, both parties in the aggregate
gave at least 43 percent less real hard-money contributions to candidates than
they did in 1994, the previous midterm election. Real coordinated expenditures
also fell by at least 59 percent in both parties. Although overall hard-money contributions to political parties are increasing, political parties are generally giving
less of this money to candidates and spending more of it on their own campaign
efforts, including election advocacy. The executive director of the National Republican Senatorial Committee (NRSC) explained the change in 1998. He said,
"In the past, incumbents have kind of looked at the coordinated money as a kind
of God-given right, and they expected to get it no matter what kind of race they
were in. Quite frankly, that did not happen this time."[6]

Party Soft Money: Unlimited Contributions and Expenditures

Political parties have bolstered their soft-money fund-raising. Soft-money
contributions are unlimited and may come from individuals, political action
committees (PACs), unions, corporations, and other party committees. Political
party, nonfederal, or "soft money" accounts, though established prior to the
1979 FECA amendments, were expanded through the 1979 legislation, explicitly

permitting soft money to pay for a portion of party-building activities, including voter identification and registration and slate mailers.[7] National party soft money and hard money spent on such party building and overhead administrative expenses are divided into a ratio of 40 percent soft and 60 percent hard money in nonpresidential election years and 35 percent soft and 65 percent hard money in presidential election years.[8] State and local soft-money formulas take into account the number of federal and state offices on the election ballot, the ballot composition method; the amount of hard versus soft dollars received at a fund-raising event, the funds-received method; and the amount of time or space given to a candidate, i.e., a phone bank ratio compares the number of questions dedicated to federal candidates to the total number of questions, the time/space ratio method. These various ratio formulae often result in a more favorable soft-to-hard-dollar ratio than the national fixed percentage.[9]

Following the 1970s reforms, political party fund-raising took a back seat to candidate fund-raising. Pressure mounted within the system because some large donors wanted to contribute to the political process beyond the hard-dollar limits. Soft money was the pressure valve that allowed for greater contributions. In the late 1970s and early 1980s soft-money contributions were new and not widely engaged in, but political parties soon discovered loopholes in the soft-money regulations and benefited from court rulings on campaign finance that enabled them to spend dollars on a wider range of campaign activities, avoiding the constraints of hard money.[10] Parties have emphasized the unlimited soft-dollar–funded campaign activity (see figure 2.1). The soft-money graph does not document pre-1992 soft money because political parties were not required to disclose soft-money contributions prior to the 1992 election cycle; however, the data available are sufficient to show the recent surge in party soft-money expenditures.

There is no indication that this growth in soft-money expenditures will diminish. Political parties have consistently spent over $50 million in soft money since 1992, more than double what they spent before 1992. By the 1996 presidential election, Democrats had tripled their soft-money spending from 1992 to over $120 million. Republicans spent slightly more soft money in the 1998 midterm election than they did in the 1996 presidential election year. Looking to the 2000 elections, all four party congressional campaign committees created special programs to court donors willing to give $200,000 or more for the 1999–2000 election cycle.[11]

Scholars have noted the expansion of soft-dollar expenditures. Political scientist Gary Jacobson observes that national party committee involvement in campaigns represents an abrupt departure from previous campaign practices.[12] Paul Herrnson also notes that national political parties have become more involved in funding federal campaigns than ever before, while state and local parties have diminished their role in funding these campaigns.[13] With the growth of soft-money expenditures, national party committees have devoted more of their efforts to running national uniform campaigns with consistent themes. The na-

Table 2.1 National Party Committee Candidate Contributions and Coordinated Expenditures, 1978–1998 (in 1998 dollars)

	1978	1980	1982	1984	1986	1988
DNC						
Candidate Contribution	$150,000.00	$78,137.14	$210,420.33	$1,452,209.20	$30,488.14	$190,140.95
Coordinated Expenditure	$150,000.00	$7,798,928.86	$244,486.49	$4,181,958.75	$510,636.17	$11,170,314.22
DSCC						
Candidate Contribution	$1,000,000.00	$952,481.80	$895,233.16	$659,193.02	$867,506.52	$592,038.60
Coordinated Expenditure	—	$1,183,561.99	$3,170,890.52	$6,194,705.97	$9,022,067.85	$8,552,935.17
DCCC						
Candidate Contribution	$1,250,000.00	$1,214,779.26	$951,151.45	$1,196,641.20	$908,457.30	$922,822.50
Coordinated Expenditure	—	$68,614.30	$334,337.49	$1,763,423.11	$2,298,323.80	$3,342,124.17
Total Democratic	*$2,550,000.00*	*$11,296,503.35*	*$5,806,519.44*	*$15,448,131.25*	*$13,637,479.78*	*$24,770,375.61*
	1978	1980	1982	1984	1986	1988
RNC						
Candidate Contribution	$2,250,000.00	$1,663,678.09	$2,871,634.34	$1,331,601.75	$521,164.24	$448,408.45
Coordinated Expenditure	$750,000.00	$10,587,619.50	$393,503.96	$10,695,890.57	$3,123.18	$11,421,261.19
NRSC						
Candidate Contribution	$1,250,000.00	$820,722.80	$943,080.84	$883,323.51	$936,167.30	$1,043,846.21
Coordinated Expenditure	$6,500,000.00	$9,941,817.06	$14,708,067.68	$10,561,507.34	$14,811,777.28	$14,123,733.68
NRCC						
Candidate Contribution	$4,500,000.00	$3,967,512.97	$4,315,571.11	$4,050,022.88	$2,461,731.30	$2,164,754.36
Coordinated Expenditure	$2,000,000.00	$2,431,370.51	$8,349,736.65	$9,827,161.75	$6,095,231.82	$5,662,082.64
Total Republican	*$17,250,000.00*	*$29,412,720.93*	*$31,581,594.58*	*$37,349,507.80*	*$62,178,702.92*	*$34,864,086.53*

	1990	1992	1994	1996	1998
DNC					
Candidate Contribution	$57,555.09	$3,602.73	$94,838.06	$30,425.63	$6,894.00
Coordinated Expenditure	$146,446.83	$13,092,812.93	$383,029.10	$6,955,625.55	$6,029,492.00
DSCC					
Candidate Contribution	$538,627.08	$689,526.02	$588,427.30	$560,994.26	$300,500.00
Coordinated Expenditure	$5,643,169.75	$13,053,606.96	$13,523,832.83	$8,723,594.82	$8,424.00
DCCC					
Candidate Contribution	$558,380.38	$973,385.35	$1,089,954.16	$1,076,021.28	$425,281.00
Coordinated Expenditure	$3,588,348.35	$4,805,027.39	$8,062,907.79	$5,910,847.50	$2,954,058.00
Total Democratic	*$10,532,527.48*	*$32,617,961.38*	*$23,742,989.14*	*$23,257,509.04*	*$9,724,649.00*
	1990	1992	1994	1996	1998
RNC					
Candidate Contribution	$318,739.20	$912,013.46	$598,494.87	$505,314.54	$442,494.00
Coordinated Expenditure	$57,797.03	$13,070,337.98	$5,179,736.35	$23,668,784.32	$3,891,039.00
NRSC					
Candidate Contribution	$868,014.28	$804,189.49	$683,323.06	$723,578.71	$276,359.00
Coordinated Expenditure	$9,583,145.39	$19,143,364.80	$11,994,578.27	$320,553.16	$36,775.00
NRCC					
Candidate Contribution	$1,180,617.61	$846,303.44	$866,628.77	$1,308,804.81	$782,742.00
Coordinated Expenditure	$3,529,985.12	$6,029,419.96	$4,322,814.99	$7,614,853.03	$5,069,215.00
Total Republican	*$15,538,298.63*	*$40,805,629.13*	*$23,645,576.31*	*$34,141,888.57*	*$10,498,624.00*

Source: Data from FEC press releases, 1980–98.

Figure 2.1 Soft-Money Expenditures, 1992–1998 (in 1998 dollars)

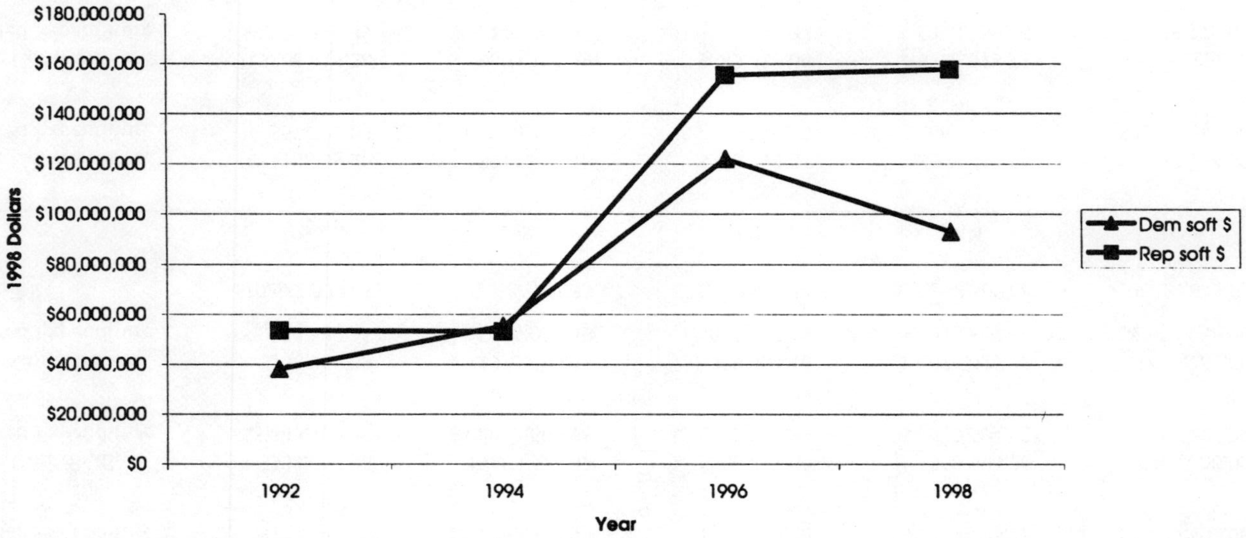

Source: Data from press releases, 1992–1998.

tional Republican Party used this tactic in 1994 with their "Contract with America" platform, which united many federal candidates and their campaigns throughout the United States.

The growth of party soft-money activity has also changed the agenda of campaign finance reformers. The campaign finance reform bills, including Shays-Meehan, which passed in the House in 1998, was filibustered to death in the Senate that same year.[14] Campaign finance reformers have essentially stopped advocating spending caps in federal elections financed with public funds and instead aim at restraining spiraling party soft-money campaign expenditures in federal elections.[15]

Another way to bypass the contribution limits of the Federal Election Campaign Act is to create a leadership political action committee (PAC). Candidates can solicit funds not only for their own campaigns but for their leadership PAC as well. Leadership PACs in their early incarnation were used by aspiring members who wanted to win friends in the party for leadership votes down the road. But more and more members have seen it as a way to raise more money and indirectly benefit their own campaigns by distributing funds to their friends' campaigns and pay for incidental, non-campaign-related activities. One newly elected member even formed a leadership PAC before being sworn into office. The use of leadership PACs has also grown because of soft-money contributions that are unlimited and that can be used by candidates to make contributions to state and local campaigns to pay for their political travel and to hire pollsters and other consultants. For instance, in the 1998 cycle Senator Ashcroft (R-MO) received a $400,000 soft-money contribution from The House of Lloyd.[16] Many leadership PACs are registered in Virginia, which has minimal disclosure and allows unlimited contributions from corporations and individuals.

Loopholes Exploited: State Parties and Soft-Money Campaigns

Federal law requires disclosure of soft-money contributors, but unlike party hard-money contributions, soft-money expenditures are not line-item reported at the federal level. Many states have weaker soft-money disclosure requirements and some states do not require disclosure of soft money.[17] In some states, limited or no disclosure effectively means that state parties may hide from the public the amount of contributions, contributors' names, how soft money is spent, and conduct a state-run campaign with limited accountability. John Bibby argues that state parties have been losing autonomy and that to survive, have integrated themselves into strengthened national party committees.[18] State parties have developed the infrastructure and means to conduct election advertising and large-scale ground-war tactics, including direct mail, person-to-person contacts, and GOTV efforts that are in larger part funded by federal soft dollars. In the early 1990s national parties learned to route soft money to state and local parties for GOTV drives because of lower disclosure requirements and more favorable state hard-to-soft-dollar ratios.[19] This has increased the state and local party role as they spend more and more soft money.

State parties have also become laundering stations for national party soft dollars. State parties receive soft-money transfers from national party committees and then pass them back to the national party as hard-money contributions. State parties even keep a bit "off the top" for this service. An example of this type of transfer service occurred in 1997 when the Democratic National Committee (DNC) approached its state committees proposing to trade soft dollars, offering a soft-money commission between 10 and 15 percent for conducting the transfer. Between January 1997 and April 1998, the DNC sent soft money in amounts ranging from $11,000 to $172,500 to selected states and often, within days, received back a hard-dollar transfer in the exact sum minus the state's commission.[20]

Such campaign activity has not only strengthened the national party committees but has infused the state parties with a vitality and power not seen in the past two decades. So long as national party committees continue to exploit the soft-money option for raising and laundering money and large contributors are constrained by contribution limits in federal campaigns, state parties will continue to see a good deal of the campaign action.

Loopholes Exploited: The Court's Impact on Party Involvement

Political parties have also benefited from court rulings on campaign finance reform. In the landmark 1976 court case *Buckley v. Valeo*, the Supreme Court established that noncandidate-run communications that did not explicitly say " 'vote for,' 'elect,' 'support,' 'cast your ballot for,' 'Smith for Congress,' 'vote against,' 'defeat,' or 'reject' " could not be limited to a set dollar amount.[21] Interest groups interpreted the ruling to mean that as long as they did not mention these "magic words" in campaign advertisements they would not have to report these expenditures to the FEC because these ads would not be considered electioneering.

In 1996 the courts enlarged the role of political parties in elections. The case of *FEC v. Colorado Republican Federal Campaign Committee* sought to more broadly define the limits of political party election involvement.[22] In a 5–4 split decision, the Supreme Court ruled that political parties could participate in independent expenditures advocating candidates as long as their expenditures were disclosed and paid for by hard-dollar contributions and as long as no coordination took place between candidate and political party.

In *FEC v. Massachusetts Citizens for Life* and other similar cases, federal courts held that interest groups and political parties could run issue-advocacy campaigns that did not expressly advocate a candidate by steering clear of the language mentioned in *Buckley*.[23] This ruling allowed parties to pay for indirect attack or support campaigns through the federally prescribed ratio of hard and soft money. It is still undecided whether such campaigns may be coordinated with the candidates or not, but evidence in 1996 and 1998 suggests such coordination has taken place.[24] Indeed, U.S. District Judge Joyce Hens Green opened the door in 1999 for increased coordination by nearly absolving the Christian Coalition of any wrongdoing, arguing that illegal coordination only occurs when a group engages in "substantial discussion or negotiation" on content, timing, location, or other factors. GOP election lawyer Jan Baran explained the impact of this ruling, saying, "There's kind of a sense of, boy, if they didn't find coordination in this case, they're not going to find it with the AFL-CIO or environmental groups or the business groups that engage in issue advertising. So I think it has some potentially major consequences for the 2000 election."[25]

These so-called "issue ads," more accurately called "election advertisements" or "party election advocacy," are becoming the mainstay of political party activity in campaigns and were the primary expenditure of soft and hard money at the national and state levels in 1996 and 1998.[26] These ads do two things. First, they reinforce the candidate's message or theme by mirroring the candidate's own advertising. State parties are heavily involved in this type of election advertisements to best address the relevant issues within a given district or state. Political parties are also able to conduct more ground-war campaigns through direct mail and phone banks to individualize the more general broadcast message on television and radio run by political parties. For more information on the ground-war efforts of political parties, see chapter 4.

Second, political parties are able to conduct attack campaigns on their candidates' opponents so that their candidate can spend money on more positive campaign messages. Dr. Kathleen Hall Jamieson and the Annenberg Public Policy Center conducted the most thorough evaluation of the tone of political party campaign ads since the influx of issue ads in an election context. Annenberg found that in 1996, 41 percent of all party-funded election advertisements were pure attack on one of the two federal candidates.[27] The 1998 campaign cycle did not see any fewer negative attack campaigns, with parties running attack advertisements 41 percent of the time and increasing the attack campaigns to nearly 60 percent of all party-run ads in the last two months of the campaign.[28]

Election advocacy and attack ads increase political party visibility and importance because of the amount of money parties are able to spend on such tactics. Political parties prefer these election advocacy campaign tactics because they enable complete messages and strategy control.

1996 SOFT-MONEY CAMPAIGN EXPENDITURES

Soft money was critical to the strategy of both parties in the 1996 election cycle. The parties had learned from the example of labor unions and health care organizations in previous elections how to conduct election advocacy, and the parties aggressively raised soft money. The Democrats in 1996, on the urging of Dick

Morris, spent $85 million on party election advocacy that focused on issues like the national budget and education, as well as re-election ads for President Clinton.[29]

The fixation of the Clinton/Gore campaign and the Democratic National Committee (DNC) with soft-money fund-raising came to light only after the campaign. Large soft-money donors were sometimes guests in the White House Lincoln Bedroom, while other donors were hosted at White House policy discussions over coffee. Controversy later surrounded the possible foreign sources of large soft-money donations. While not as visible or controversial, the national Republican Party hosted large contributors to policy discussions with Speaker Gingrich and Senate Republican Leader Lott. The Republican Party went into debt raising even larger amounts of soft money in 1995–96, trying to compete with labor's very aggressive campaign against Republican freshmen House members. Both parties offered perks to large soft-money contributors in the 1999–2000 election cycle, including exclusive issue briefings with congressional leaders and a weekend stay at the Kennedy family compound in Hyannisport, Massachusetts.[30]

The shift to soft money in 1996 meant that Fat Cats were more important for both parties. More soft-money donations to multiple national party committees were made in 1996 than ever before, the greatest amount going to the two House and Senate congressional committees.[31] This signifies, especially in a presidential election year, the growing importance of party committees and the surge in soft money for the purpose of supporting federal candidates through election advocacy campaigns. Table 2.2 breaks down all $100,000-plus contributors to the national party committees in 1996.

Not all of this money used in election advocacy campaigns was spent on television. Paul Herrnson reports that in 1996 parties increased soft-money receipts and spent record amounts on grassroot mail campaigns, phone banks, voter-to-voter contacts, and registration efforts.[32] Democrats spent almost $40 million (soft and hard money) to fund state party-building activities, buy voter lists, run direct mail campaigns, and establish phone banks. The DNC alone spent nearly $20 million to contact 14.3 million voters through direct mail and 11 million through phone banks. The Republicans spent $48.3 million on similar campaigns, sending out 84.8 million mailers and 14.5 million voter identification phone calls.[33]

Congressional party committees were also more active than ever before in raising and transferring money to state parties for federal and presidential campaign assistance.[34] In 1996 the Democratic Congressional Campaign Committee (DCCC) and the Democratic Senatorial Campaign Committee (DSCC) each transferred over $8 million to state parties to run ads in sixty House races against freshmen Republicans and in the fourteen states with the most competitive Senate races. The National Republican Congressional Committee (NRCC) ran large ad campaigns in thirty competitive races while the NRSC spent $2 million in five states with close Senate races.

Table 2.2   Contributors of $100,000 or More to a Political Party

Year	Total Number
1996	303
1998	204

Contributor Bedfellows

Contributors giving to more than one Republican Party committee

1996	9
1998	16

Contributors giving to more than one Democratic Party committee

1996	5
1998	10

Bedfellow Breakdown*

Number of contributors giving to the following combinations of party committees

REPUBLICAN PARTY COMMITTEES

	NRSC & NRCC	NRSC & RNC	RNC & NRCC	ALL THREE
1996	6	4	3	2
1998	9	8	3	2

DEMOCRATIC PARTY COMMITTEES

	DSCC & DCCC	DSCC & DNC	DNC & DCCC	ALL THREE
1996	3	2	2	1
1998	5	2	5	1

Source: Data from FEC reports, 1995–98.
*Those contributors that gave to all three party committees are included in the number of contributors that gave to any of the two-committee combinations.

Political party involvement in 1996 expanded the issue-advocacy loophole and took advantage of recent court decisions allowing for party-independent expenditures. Paul Herrnson and Diana Dwyre evaluated the 1996 party election advocacy campaigns and found that political parties played a greater role than before in setting the agenda and that national party committees increased their power and nationalized congressional politics. They also noted that in the future, election advocacy campaigns will drive campaign costs even higher. Our study has substantiated these claims and given further evidence as to the changing nature of congressional campaigns.[35]

SOFT MONEY IN THE 1998 MIDTERM ELECTIONS

Both parties approached the 1998 election cycle assuming that they needed to raise as much soft money as possible to counter campaign activity by the opposing party, to effectively check the unlimited spending that interest groups could launch against candidates from their party, and to force issues onto the national agenda. If 1996 was any indicator, many millions of dollars would be spent on election advocacy and the parties would rely heavily on soft money to support their efforts.

Because of the limited number of competitive races, political parties specifically targeted tight House and Senate races and poured their soft money and campaign efforts into winning those key races, sometimes outspending the candidates themselves. For example, the Republican and Democratic parties and interest groups spent over $4.3 million on campaign advertising in the Kentucky Senate race between Scotty Baesler (D) and Jim Bunning (R), while the candidates only spent $4 million on advertising. The NRCC targeted fifty-seven competitive races, including eleven of the twelve House races we monitored. Both party senatorial committees targeted all four of our targeted senatorial races. Large-scale party involvement affected all of the close Senate races we monitored, and some House races also saw some extraordinary independent spending. All sixteen of the sample races were targeted by one or the other party or both.

The 1998 Party Ground War

The ground war fought by parties, interest groups, and candidates to register and mobilize voters was a major part of the 1998 drama. We discuss this topic at length in chapter 4. Party soft money and cooperation between committees and candidates were central to the ground-war efforts. Matt Angle, former executive director of the DCCC, noted after the election that "the election emphasized the use of soft and hard money for party building and voter turnout efforts to protect the party base from cynicism caused by interest-group advocacy."[36]

The Democratic Party's ground war proved to be the backbone of their successful campaign. Republicans focused on television and direct mail while the Democrats ran a more diversified campaign with a strong emphasis on the ground war. The Democratic Party strategies were more effective because of their ability to mobilize their base, especially African Americans and women. The House Republicans' "Operation Breakout" television campaign and their last-minute attack on Clinton attracted much negative media attention and put the Democrats further ahead. Figure 2.2 reflects the amount and type of each campaign activity run by political parties in the sixteen contests we studied.

African Americans, when they vote, are predictably Democratic, a fact not lost on the leadership of the DCCC. Charles Rangel (D-NY), cochair of the DCCC, and DCCC Matt Angle worked tirelessly with former chair Martin Frost (D-TX) and the Black Caucus on joint campaign efforts to mobilize the African American vote. Young blacks were targeted on hip-hop radio with themes like "Vote—It's a Power Thing" and in radio segments voiced by celebrities and well-liked black congressmen. This power message resonated well with young African

Figure 2.2 Political Party Activity by Campaign Type

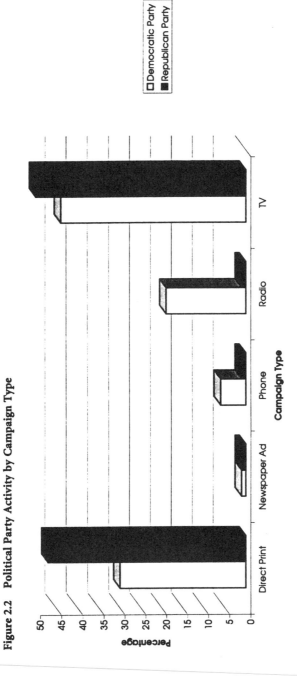

Source: Data from the *Outside Money* data set.

American voters who not only planned on voting but also became very active in Democratic voter mobilization efforts in their communities. Democratic mobilization efforts cost approximately $2 million and were targeted at states like Georgia, North and South Carolina, and Illinois.

But the Democratic breakthroughs in 1998 were not limited to mobilizing African American voters. In several of the districts where Democrats picked up previously Republican seats there were very few African Americans, like the New Mexico Third Congressional District race between Tom Udall (D) and Bill Redmond (R). In this context, Democrats courted the environmental vote. In other districts or states, Democrats benefited from greater activation of union households. In short, the party adopted its strategy to the state or district.

Although each party committee ran election advocacy campaigns, no party committee received as much widespread attention as the NRCC's Operation Breakout. The advertising blitz focused on fifty to sixty competitive races in thirty states and sixty-two media markets bought at "saturation levels."[37] Operation Breakout advertisements were most often "cookie-cutter" ads that touted the success of the 105th Congress or focused on generic issues like health care or Social Security, but ended with the name and face of the local candidate. Such ads did not address candidate agendas or local issues and generally fared poorly with voters.

As will be discussed extensively in chapter 4, the parties feel that the type of medium used for campaign ads is critical. Matt Angle, former executive director of the DCCC, believed that had Operation Breakout run its last-minute campaign in direct mail or phone messages rather than on television, the campaign would have been more successful at influencing the targeted voters.[38] Broadcasting the messages to all voters ran the risk of activating some Democrats, and alienating others who had tired of the Clinton scandal.

The NRCC decided late in the campaign to make Bill Clinton an issue. They tried to target this message, but the media made it a national issue. The House Republicans ran a series of three advertisements in the midwest and south during the last week of the campaign that focused on Clinton, honesty, lying, and integrity in government. Republican pollsters had been polling consistently throughout the election asking about the two greatest concerns in the country. The two most common answers were the President's character and the general moral decline in America. According to an editorial in the *New York Times* written by Republican pollsters William Dalbec and Michael Dabadie, this $10 million advertisement blitz targeted:

> Republican and independent women—more specifically, married, suburban baby boomers who may think Mr. Clinton is doing a decent job but are embarrassed by his personal life. These women don't know what to tell their children when they ask about the President's dalliance with Ms. Lewinsky, and the ads play on their concerns.[39]

The pollsters argued that these ads were needed to push independents and swing voters to the polls. They recognized that there was some risk of backlash, but if the ads gained "three voters for every one who is pushed to the Democrats or who decides not to vote" then the ads would have been worth it.[40] Unfortunately for the Republicans, they did not predict the great backlash the advertisements had with the national media. Instead of gaining more votes, these ads lost votes because they left Republicans open to charges of being obsessed with scandals and impeachment rather than policy.

Republican Congressional Committee leaders insist that they also had an extensive voter identification and GOTV effort.[41] The day after the election, Representative Livingston (R-LA) expressed a contrary view when he stated that they had been "beat on the ground" and that "relying on TV was a major tactical mistake."[42] One effect of relying on national media campaigns, as Representative Livingston alluded to, is that there is a greater chance that a generic or more national message will not resonate with local voters, backfiring on the candidate and the party advertising campaign altogether.

In addition to directing their advertisements too broadly to the wrong medium, Republican committees hurt candidates in at least three of this study's sample races by not attacking the Democratic candidate and by not reinforcing the Republican candidates' issue agenda. In the Iowa Third District race between Leonard Boswell (D-incumbent) and Larry McKibben (R), the NRCC ads emphasized the accomplishments of the Republican Congress and other national themes, while McKibben spent his resources responding to Democratic Party attacks. A Republican consultant close to this race told academic investigator John Haskell that McKibben's campaign was severely damaged because the national GOP ads constrained his strategic options and ability to set the agenda, thus diverting his limited resources and time to campaign tactics that the party could have conducted.[43]

It is also clear from our research that there was some congruence in message between party and candidate campaigns. Collusion between parties and candidates is not necessary given the openness of our political system; the Democrats, for instance, made no secret of their plans to emphasize education, Social Security, or health care in their party ads. The party then ran ads on one or more of these issues that matched the politics of the district. The lack of a consistent, focused message that centered on Republican candidates and their issues hurt the GOP.[44]

1998 Party Soft-Money Contributions and Expenditures

In 1998 the party congressional committees raised, spent, or transferred more than double the amounts spent in the 1994 midterm election. Democrats raised over 92.8 million soft dollars in the 1998 election cycle: an 89 percent nominal fund-raising increase over the 1993–94 midterm election. Republicans increased their soft-money funds 151 percent nominally over the 1993–94 midterm, rais-ing $131.6 million in 1997–98.[45] In 1998, soft money accounted for nearly two-thirds of Democratic committees' receipts and nearly one-half of Republican committees' revenues, with most of the soft-money increase in the senatorial and congressional campaign committees (see table 2.3).

All party committees took advantage of state party soft-money transfers in 1998. Tables 2.4a and 2.4b show the amount of soft money transferred to our fifteen sample states by each party committee in the 1998 election cycle. These totals reveal some soft-money trends. First, the Republicans transferred more soft money to the sample state parties than the Democrats did. Second, the na-

Table 2.3   National Party Soft-Money Activity, 1992–98 (in 1998 dollars)

		1992	1994	1996	1998
DNC	Receipts	$36,429,368.41	$48,309,940.00	$103,290,841.48	$56,966,353.00
	Disbursements	$32,982,078.74	$49,600,721.82	$99,126,081.36	$57,411,879.00
	Cash on Hand	$3,836,286.91	$642,079.22	$4,864,190.11	$1,364,084.00
DSCC	Receipts	$657,705.58	$409,642.54	$14,617,447.30	$25,880,538.00
	Disbursements	$588,289.42	$458,361.06	$14,437,260.10	$25,858,673.00
	Cash on Hand	$94,327.39	$81,934.45	$236,493.37	$191,126.00
DCCC	Receipts	$510,005.27	$5,623,987.24	$11,337,544.47	$16,865,410.00
	Disbursements	$4,667,607.82	$5,648,414.14	$10,694,656.48	$16,617,533.00
	Cash on Hand	$526,417.97	$460,477.20	$1,031,349.52	$1,044,695.00
Total	Receipts	$42,122,856.17	$54,051,173.95	$127,103,762.89	$92,811,927.00
Democratic*	Disbursements	$38,197,894.01	$55,415,101.20	$122,115,937.95	$92,987,711.00
	Cash on Hand	$4,457,032.27	$1,184,490.86	$6,131,919.75	$2,599,905.00
		1992	1994	1996	1998
RNC	Receipts	$41,751,404.38	$49,351,778.37	$114,625,536.31	$74,805,286.00
	Disbursements	$39,038,013.21	$46,647,658.96	$114,990,845.39	$74,325,722.00
	Cash on Hand	$3,214,038.18	$3,814,795.03	$2,760,721.34	$2,213,597.00
NRSC	Receipts	$10,530,714.33	$6,139,460.99	$27,738,960.81	$37,866,845.00
	Disbursements	$8,881,514.49	$7,179,374.60	$26,644,295.82	$37,283,103.00
	Cash on Hand	$1,636,705.89	$204,404.42	$1,371,943.68	$908,311.00
NRCC	Receipts	$7,059,446.35	$8,107,211.95	$18,974,040.45	$26,914,059.00
	Disbursements	$7,214,061.67	$5,221,636.81	$28,468,816.42	$24,092,993.00
	Cash on Hand	n/a	n/a	n/a	n/a
Total	Receipts	$57,842,848.09	$57,767,951.21	$146,654,669.59	$131,615,116.00
Republican*	Disbursements	$53,647,652.09	$53,219,270.13	$155,420,089.64	$157,730,744.00
	Cash on Hand	$4,850,744.07	$4,019,199.45	$4,132,665.02	$3,121,908.00

Source: Data from FEC press release, *FEC Reports on Political Party Activity for 1997–98,* 9 April 1999.
*Totals do not include intercommittee transfers.

Table 2.4a National GOP Transfers to State Parties' Hard and Soft Money in the 1997–98 Election Cycle

State	RNC		NRSC		NRCC	
	Federal	Nonfederal	Federal	Nonfederal	Federal	Nonfederal
Connecticut	$92,500.00	$406,500.00	—	—	$100,000.00	—
Idaho	$130,408.00	$619,361.00	—	$146,250.00	$126,000.00	$102,000.00
Illinois	$7,187.00	$366,716.00	$192,000.00	$473,000.00	—	$90,000.00
Iowa	$45,528.00	$396,372.00	—	$250,000.00	$170,000.00	—
Kansas	$2,000.00	$25,000.00	—	$25,000.00	$80,000.00	—
Kentucky	$8,222.00	$346,500.00	$578,052.00	$890,750.00	$125,000.00	—
Nevada	$255,502.00	$1,288,211.00	$379,960.00	$1,347,625.00	$75,000.00	$20,000.00
New Mexico	$164,413.00	$708,583.00	—	$205,000.00	$133,234.00	$996,000.00
North Carolina	$22,275.00	$287,530.00	—	—	$90,000.00	—
Ohio	$2,200.00	$1,309,800.00	—	—	$25,000.00	—
Oregon	$15,000.00	$75,000.00	—	—	$115,000.00	—
Pennsylvania	$36,250.00	$225,750.00	—	—	$160,000.00	—
South Carolina	$258,357.00	$946,134.00	$282,800.00	$719,473.00	—	—
Utah	$107,030.00	$267,253.00	—	$70,000.00	$25,000.00	—
Wisconsin	$104,500.00	$617,000.00	$964,925.00	$1,029,785.00	$40,000.00	—
Total	$1,251,372.00	$7,885,710.00	$2,397,737.00	$5,156,880.00	$1,264,234.00	$1,208,000.00

Source: Data from FEC press release, FEC Reports on Political Party Activity for 1997–98, 9 April 1999.

Table 2.4b   National Democratic Party Committee Transfers to State Parties' Hard and Soft Money in the 1997–98 Election Cycle

State	DNC		DSCC		DCCC	
	Federal	Nonfederal	Federal	Nonfederal	Federal	Nonfederal
Connecticut	$90,538.00	$562,529.00	—	$225,850.00	$22,200.00	—
Idaho	$97,792.00	$247,038.00	$4,000.00	—	$89,640.00	$242,726.00
Illinois	$54,734.00	$200,526.00	$325,900.00	$2,616,100.00	$64,935.00	$227,565.00
Iowa	$86,868.00	$650,200.00	—	$46,000.00	$42,940.00	$25,560.00
Kansas	$36,450.00	$45,000.00	—	—	$38,000.00	$5,000.00
Kentucky	$113,603.00	$526,939.00	$1,086,217.00	$1,357,317.00	$88,357.00	—
Nevada	$13,610.00	$51,000.00	$561,000.00	$885,000.00	$55,480.00	$194,556.00
New Mexico	$42,820.00	$53,271.00	—	—	$179,681.00	$770,205.00
North Carolina	$176,232.00	$524,980.00	$1,173,770.00	$998,966.00	$71,098.00	—
Ohio	$65,521.00	$1,368,701.00	$195,509.00	$579,301.00	$19,018.00	$48,280.00
Oregon	$79,068.00	$37,000.00	—	—	$120,850.00	$323,550.00
Pennsylvania	$74,003.00	$310,351.00	—	—	$138,112.00	$254,884.00
South Carolina	$37,906.00	$17,500.00	$919,075.00	$312,500.00	$2,895.00	$8,682.00
Utah	$26,953.00	$10,000.00	—	—	$39,965.00	$128,051.00
Wisconsin	$185,139.00	$993,634.00	$275,000.00	—	$113,830.00	$44,560.00
Total	**$1,181,237.00**	**$5,598,669.00**	**$4,540,471.00**	**$7,021,034.00**	**$1,087,001.00**	**$2,273,619.00**

Source: Data from FEC press release, *FEC Reports on Political Party Activity for 1997–98,* 9 April 1999.

tional parties utilized state parties for soft-money laundering and soft-money spending on election advertisements.

To fund soft-money transfers to state parties, election advertisement campaigns, and ground-war tactics, all six party committees were very active at recruiting contributions and expanding their fund-raising base. In 1998, 204 contributions exceeded $100,000 each. Twenty-two percent of these contributors gave more than once in the two-year campaign cycle. This number is up slightly from 1996 contributors, perhaps because in a midterm election there are fewer contributors and they are relied upon more heavily by the party committees. Table 2.2 shows soft-money contributions received in the 1998 election cycle. Because 1998 was a midterm election, the number of contributions that went to two or more party committees from donors giving over $100,000 doubled for the Democrats. Contributors gave most often to both congressional committees. The soft-money data (see table 2.3) also show that over the past three election cycles, from 1994 to 1998, soft-money contributions to the Senate and House campaign committees have steadily increased in both presidential and midterm elections.

Both political parties conducted major fund-raising in 1998 to stockpile their soft money war chests for election advocacy. They targeted large organizations, businesses, and their own members of Congress, and leadership PACs. In 1998, Republicans far outspent Democrats. The DCCC spent $7 million on election ads, while the NRCC spent $25 million on a national election advertising campaign dubbed Operation Breakout.[46] Each committee had a fund-raising campaign goal to raise between $7 million and $37 million, specifically for election advocacy campaigns in the most competitive races. Specific DSCC targets included $2 million in Kentucky and $1.5 million in North Carolina. The NRSC raised $9 million, spending $6 million on election-related advertisements in Wisconsin, North and South Carolina, Kentucky, and Nevada.[47]

Although candidates still expected more coordinated expenditures and direct contributions, the political parties departed from the norm by pursuing more election advocacy campaigns and aimed these campaigns at fewer targets. As Dave Hansen, political director for the NRSC, stated, "In the words of Senator McConnell, we were not going to be chasing windmills and we were not going to be buying landslides. We were going to target the money and target it as well as we possibly could."[48]

Nevada provides a useful illustration of soft-money transfers in 1998. The NRSC transferred $1.3 million in soft money to Nevada's state Republican Party, and the RNC transferred another $1.3 million. This was an extraordinary allocation for a sparsely populated state with inexpensive media markets.

In New Mexico, the state party spent $288,465 on 1,991 election advertisements that indirectly supported the Republican incumbent, Bill Redmond. The RNC transferred $708,583 soft dollars to New Mexico and purchased $45,170 worth of advertising time; the NRCC also transferred $996,000 soft dollars to the state Republican Party. The DNC and the DCCC transferred $53,271 and $770,205, respectively, to the state party and ran only one ad 197 times in the last two weeks of the campaign. Even though the Democrats were outspent, they received 6,000 more absentee ballots than usual because they targeted direct mail and phone banks extensively in precincts where Democratic performance was over 65 percent. They also targeted individuals likely to vote Democratic with recorded messages from Hillary Clinton and popular former Congressman Bill Richardson. Another interesting variable in New Mexico's race was a strong third-party candidate Carol Miller (Green Party). The Republicans used some of their direct mail to portray both the Green Party candidate and the Republican candidates in a positive light, trying to sway the Democrats and Independents against voting Democratic. Chapter 8 further details the soft-money impact in the New Mexico Third District House race.

SOFT MONEY AND THE FUTURE OF POLITICAL PARTIES

As discussed earlier in this chapter, political party committees are increasing their power and influence in election cycles by dramatically increasing their soft-money fund-raising and expenditures on campaign-related advertising and effective voter mobilization efforts. Critics of political parties have long thought the parties weak and undisciplined, but there are indications of change. With the rise of the political party committees and soft-money contributions, parties may now become filters between candidates and large contributors that may lessen the claim these donors have on candidates and increase the visibility of the party. Alternatively, large donors may expand their influence by giving soft money to the party with the expectation that this money will benefit a specific candidate, thereby reducing the party to the role of middleman.

Political parties have taken advantage of the soft-money loophole to increase their activity and influence in federal campaigns. In some contested races their campaign spending approached the spending by candidates and, according to our study, parties now surpass interest groups.[49] Parties have extended the boundaries of party-building activities through court decisions and FEC rulings. Political party activity has come to include advertising blitzes or mail and phone calls attacking or defending specific candidates. Promoting or opposing individual candidates in advertisements extends the party role beyond voter mobilization and registration. With the recent increase in party involvement, candidates focus more on issues because they expect political parties to come in with advertisements lambasting the opponents. One such example of this was in the Nevada Senate race, where both state parties spent more than a combined total of $4.3 million on negative ads attacking the opposing party and candidate so that their candidates would not have to claim the negative advertisements as their own. Political parties will continue to utilize election advertising in the veiled language of issue advocacy, mirroring candidate advertisements and themes.

Because they benefit the entire party line, parties will increase traditional party-building efforts like voter identification, mobilization, and slate party mailers funded by soft money. These activities encourage participation, inform voters on party slate candidates, including state, local, and federal candidates, and strengthen the relationships between national and state parties. A party now has more campaign options than ever before because of the increased power of soft money and legitimacy of election advocacy.

Because of the fund-raising expansion undertaken to buttress elaborate political party candidate campaigns, one must wonder what the implications are for more large donors willing to contribute unlimited amounts to political parties. It seems that the Fat Cats have returned, and with them, more opportunities to influence the individuals who are asking for the checks—party committee leaders, majority or minority leaders and their PACs, and the candidates who indirectly benefit from outside campaigns. Where does the potential influence stop? How many party leaders become indebted to large soft-money donors because of their contributions? What are the paybacks for such large soft-dollar contributions? These are questions that deserve consideration, given the dramatic growth of interested money in American elections.

NOTES

1. Comments by Tony Corrado, Round 4 of Discussion, "Topic: Soft Money," Brookings Working Group on Campaign Finance Reform, at <http://brook.edu/gs/campaign/workgrp/round4.htm>, 4.

2. Comments by Frank Sorauf, "Topic: Soft Money," 10.

3. Federal Election Commission, "FEC Announces 1998 Party Spending Limits—Amounts Range From $130,000 to $3 Million," press release, 6 March 1998.

4. See U.S. Code 2 § 441a.

5. Coordinated expenditures are adjusted for inflation annually, and in states where there is only one congressional district, the coordinated expenditure limit of $32,550 is doubled. See *FEC Record* 24, no. 3 (March 1998), 4–5.

6. Dave Hansen, lunchtime discussion panel at the Pew Press Conference, "Outside Money: Soft Money & Issue Ads in Competitive 1998 Congressional Elections," National Press Club, Washington, D.C., 1 February 1999.

7. Congress's decision in the 1979 FECA codified previous FEC Advisory Opinions discussing use of nonfederal funds for general party activity used in soft- and hard-dollar ratios prescribed by the FEC. See FEC Advisory Opinion 1978–10, "Allocation of Costs for Voter Registration," in *Campaign Finance Reform: A Sourcebook,* ed. Anthony Corrado, Thomas E. Mann, Daniel R. Ortiz, Trevor Potter, and Frank Sorauf (Washington, D.C.: Brookings Institution Press), 190–93.

8. The ratios of hard and soft dollars emerged after the 1988 presidential election,

when both parties raised in excess of $22 million and the FEC decided to create new soft-money disclosure rules and expenditure options. (See the 1991 FEC regulations, 11 C.F.R. § 102, 104, 106.)

9. FEC, "Campaign Guide for Political Party Committees," press release, August 1996, 49. In 1996, ratios ranged from a low of 25 percent hard dollars in Rhode Island to a high of 75 percent hard dollars in Maryland.

10. For a summary of the most important administrative and court rulings on soft money see Anthony Corrado, "Party Soft Money," in *Campaign Finance Reform: A Sourcebook,* ed. Anthony Corrado et al. (Washington, D.C.: Brookings Institution Press, 1997), 165–224. See also <www.book.edu/campaignfinance>.

11. Alison Mitchell, "Congress Chasing Campaign Donors Early and Often," *New York Times,* 14 June 1999, A1 and A18.

12. Gary C. Jacobson, *The Politics of Congressional Elections* (New York: Longman, 1997), 63.

13. Paul S. Herrnson, *Party Campaigning in the 1980s* (Harvard University Press, 1988), chapters 3 and 4; and *Congressional Elections: Campaigning at Home and in Washington* (Congressional Quarterly, 1998), chapter 4.

14. The Senate version of Shays-Meehan is McCain-Feingold.

15. Diana Dwyre, "Who Controls the Dialogue of Democracy? Campaign Communications in 1998" (paper presented at the 1999 Western Political Science Association Conference, Seattle, Washington, 25–27 March 1999), 5.

16. Susan B. Glasser and Juliet Eilperin, "A New Conduit for 'Soft Money': Critics Decry Big, Largely Untraceable Donations to Lawmakers' 'Leadership PACs,' " *Washington Post,* 16 May 1999, A1.

17. Michael Malbin and Thomas Gais said that even with partial disclosure laws in states, the "disclosure chain" still does not reach the voters because state legislatures fail to give state agencies the power and resources they need to disclose the most basic campaign finance information. They also state that "efforts to limit political parties in most states have been even more fruitless than efforts to limit large, powerful interest groups." Michael Malbin and Thomas L. Gais, *The Day After Reform: Sobering Campaign Finance Lessons from the American States* (Rockefeller Institute Press: New York, 1998), 168–69.

18. John Bibby, "State Party Organizations: Coping and Adapting to Candidate-Centered Politics and Nationalization," in *The Parties Respond: Changes in American Parties and Campaigns,* 3rd ed., ed. Sandy Maisel (Boulder, Co.: Westview Press, 1998), 24.

19. James A. Barnes, "Guess Who's OK'd Another Loophole," *National Journal,* 2 May 1998, 1000. The Republican Party is currently litigating a case seeking to end hard- and soft-money ratios for issue advocacy in congressional elections.

20. Scott Wilson, "DNC Swaps Funds with Its State Affiliates; Exchange Increases Latitude in Spending by Avoiding Limits," *Washington Post,* 24 April 1999, A1.

21. *Buckley v. Valeo,* 424 U.S. 44 n.52 (1976).

22. *Colorado Republican Federal Campaign Committee v. Federal Election Commission,* 116 Sup. Ct. 2309 (1996).

23. *Federal Election Commission v. Massachusetts Citizens for Life, Inc.,* 479 U.S. 238 (1986).

24. For coordination evidence in 1996, see Paul Herrnson and Diana Dwyre, "Party Issue Advocacy," in *The State of the Parties,* 3rd ed., ed. John C. Green and Daniel M.

Shea (Lanham, Md.: Rowman & Littlefield, 1999), 90. For coordination evidence in 1998, see *Outside Money: Soft Money & Issue Ads in Competitive 1998 Congressional Elections,* ed. David Magleby and Marianne Holt (report of a grant funded by the Pew Charitable Trusts, 1999).

25. Bill Miller and Susan B. Glasser, "A Victory for the Christian Coalition," *Washington Post,* 3 August 1999, A1.

26. For a discussion of the 1996 party ads, see Darrell M. West, *Air Wars: Television Advertising in Election Campaigns, 1952–1996,* 2nd ed. (Washington, D.C.: Congressional Quarterly, 1997), 191–93.

27. "Issue Advocacy Advertising During the 1996 Campaign: A Catalog," a report by the Annenberg Public Policy Center, 16 September 1997, 9.

28. Jeffrey D. Stanger and Douglas G. Rivlin, "Issue Advocacy Advertising During the 1997–1998 Election Cycle," a press report by the Annenberg Public Policy Center, 1, 7.

29. Dick Morris, *Winning the Presidency in the 90s: Behind the Oval Office* (New York: Random House, 1997), 139.

30. Alison Mitchell, "Congress Chasing Campaign Donors Early and Often," *New York Times,* 14 June 1999, A1.

31. This number does not include a joint Senate and House Republican nonfederal dinner account that was established annually to benefit candidates in both houses.

32. Paul Herrnson, "Parties and Interest Groups in Post-reform Congressional Elections," *Interest Group Politics,* 5th ed., ed. Allan Cigler and Burdett A. Loomis (Washington, D.C.: Congressional Quarterly, 1998), 161.

33. Ibid., 159–62.

34. See Elizabeth Drew, *Whatever it Takes: The Real Struggle for Political Power in America* (New York: Penguin Books, 1997).

35. Herrnson, "Parties and Interest Groups in Post-reform Congressional Elections," 102–03.

36. Matt Angle, lunchtime discussion panel at the Pew Press Conference, "Outside Money: Soft Money & Issue Ads in Competitive 1998 Congressional Elections," National Press Club, Washington, D.C., 1 February 1999.

37. NRCC press release, " 'Operation Breakout' Goes Nationwide," 6 October 1998.

38. Angle, Pew Press Conference.

39. William Dalbec and Michael Dabadie, "You Don't Need Every Vote," *New York Times,* 30 October 1998, A35.

40. Ibid.

41. Vic Gresham, "Why Didn't Conservatives Turnout?" *Campaigns & Elections,* February 1999, 56.

42. Ruth Marcus, "Outside Money Wasn't Everything," *Washington Post,* 5 November 1998, A39.

43. John Haskell, "A Profile of Iowa Third Congressional District," in *Outside Money: Soft Money & Issue Ads in Competitive 1998 Congressional Elections,* ed. David Magleby and Marianne Holt, (report of a grant funded by the Pew Charitable Trusts, 1999), 93–102.

44. Vic Gresham, a Republican consultant, stated that the "participation of conservative voters is directly proportional to the quality of an issue-driven campaign message combined with the discipline and consistency with which that message is delivered" and

that Republicans never focused attention on the campaign message and lost millions of voters because of it (Gresham, "Why Didn't Conservatives Turnout?").

45. Money raised by the parties also went to pay off debts from the 1996 presidential campaign: the DNC still has $3 million in debt left from $15 million incurred in 1996 for Clinton's legal defenses, and the RNC paid off its $9.6 million in debt in the summer of 1998. See FEC, "Reports on Political Party Activity for 1997–98," press release, 9 April 1999, 8.

46. "Outlook '98; Politics is a Billion Dollar Industry," *National Journal Cloakroom,* at <http://www.nationaljournal.com/hotline/>, 26 October 1998.

47. Tim Curran, "McConnell Asks GOP Senators for $9 Million, *Roll Call,* 24 September 1998, 1–2; and Jill Abramson, "Political Parties Channel Millions to 'Issue' Attacks," *New York Times,* 26 October 1998, A1.

48. Ibid.

49. Jeffrey Stanger and Douglas Rivlin at the Annenberg Public Policy Center in Washington, D.C., reported in their "Issue Advocacy Advertisements During the 1997–1998 Election Cycle," that political parties represented 70 percent of all issue advocacy after 1 September 1998.

3

Interest-Group Election Ads

David B. Magleby

Interested groups and individuals have a variety of ways to invest money in campaigns and elections and, more generally, to influence legislation or the political process. They can make contributions as individuals or as political action committees to candidates, parties, and other PACs. At the federal level there are generally contribution limits on money given to candidates, other PACs, and to parties (with the exception of soft money). Contributions given for these purposes, including soft-money contributions, require disclosure of the contributor for contributions above minimally specified amounts. Individuals and political action committees can also spend money independently of parties and candidates in what are called independent expenditures. Independent expenditures must also be disclosed.

Individuals and interest groups may spend money advocating their point of view about issues. Such expenditures, known as issue advocacy, are not regulated or limited. The Supreme Court has argued that as long as an advertisement or communication does not expressly call for the election or defeat of a candidate the advertisements are presumed to be issue and not candidate related.[1] Often interest groups run ads whose content is, in all-important respects, indistinguishable from a candidate-paid commercial, phone message, or mailer. These "issue advertisements" often include photos of one or both candidates, use the names of the candidates, and emphasize voter action. Issue ads urge voters to express concern, call, or write the candidate, rather than mention voting. Yet, candidate-centered interest-group ads are very rarely played in a nonelection year—they always correlate with elections, whereas legislative issue ads and pure issue-related advertisements run at any time throughout the year. Steve Rosenthal, the political director of the AFL-CIO, stated that "the only way issue ads will work is if they are done in an electoral context. In other words, running an issue ad in a district where a member of Congress gets reelected with 75 percent of the vote does not really do much; but running an issue ad in a district where

41

you are trying to pass a minimum-wage bill, for example, in a district where a member of Congress was reelected with 53 percent of the vote is a very, very valuable tool in our legislative program."[2]

Over the past three election cycles, interest groups have discovered and exploited what our study calls *interest-group election ads*, which are often indistinguishable from independent expenditures or candidate-run election ads. These ads often show the likeness or image of one or both candidates, mention the candidates by name, praise or condemn the candidates all in the context of an election campaign and are in effect, election ads. Interest groups exploit the fiction of their ads being about issues by urging voters to call Congresswoman X and tell her you oppose her views on a particular subject. Others use the same tactic with a positive spin. This chapter briefly reviews the history of independent expenditures and issue advocacy and then summarizes the outside money study's findings on the use of these new forms of electioneering in 1998.

LEGISLATIVE ISSUE ADVOCACY

Interest groups have long used advertising to advocate their position on public policy issues. Notable examples include the ads run by the sugar lobby during tariff deliberations in Congress over eighty years ago,[3] and the American Medical Association's (AMA) campaign in the early 1950s against President Truman's health care plan through newspaper, magazine, and radio ads.[4]

More recently the Health Insurance Association of America (HIAA) ran advertisements against President Clinton's health care reform efforts. These ads showed a middle-aged couple talking about the complexities of the original Clinton proposal. The ads came to be known as "Harry and Louise," referring to the two characters in the commercial. The ads generated national publicity even though they were mainly run in New York and Washington, D.C., and in select congressional districts represented by key committee members with jurisdiction over health care legislation. Total cost of the advertising campaign has been estimated to be $12 million, and despite the limited ad buys, the commercials received national attention and were even mentioned on occasion by President Clinton. The commercials positioned HIAA as the lead opposition to the White House health care plan. Representative Dan Rostenkowski (D-IL), then-chairman of the Ways and Means Committee, argued that more advertisements by outside groups would be seen because they had become effective but that issue ads would lose their effectiveness as they became more pervasive.[5] Rostenkowski was correct in the first instance and incorrect in the second.

Tobacco companies essentially copied the HIAA approach in the spring and summer of 1998. Kathleen Hall Jamieson of the Annenberg Public Policy Center estimates that $40 million was spent by the five largest tobacco companies on an issue ad campaign between April and July of 1998.[6] The tobacco industry's media-buy campaign was much shorter than the health care campaign, lasting only three and a half months, but had much greater reach with ads running in more than fifty markets and with greater frequency than the Harry and Louise ads. The tobacco companies specifically avoided high-profile media markets like Washington, D.C., and New York in an effort to keep media attention down and opted for cable and local station buys. The tobacco companies faced little opposition on the airwaves; the American Cancer Society ran only one week of advertisements in May 1998.[7] This near monopoly permitted tobacco interests to redefine the issue from tobacco-free kids to an attack on the working class through increased taxes. The campaign shifted the political ground, and, in the end, the Senate lacked the votes needed to stop a filibuster and the bill was sent back to committee.

Tobacco companies were not the only groups running legislation-related issue ads during 1998. Business groups including the U.S. Chamber of Commerce and the Business Roundtable came together to form the Health Benefits Coalition (HBC). This group aired ads opposing HMO reform. The Health Benefits Coalition ran ads in over thirty-seven locations, warning against further regulation and increased government bureaucracy in the managed care industry.[8] The Business Roundtable also financed its own separate $27 million campaign against managed care reform legislation. One advertisement said the following: "Had enough? Say no to the Kennedy Bill. No to increased health care costs."[9]

Media campaigns like the tobacco tax, Harry and Louise, and HMO reform are issue advocacy to influence legislation on a particular issue. They may include a reference to contact your representative, but the immediate purpose is not to influence the outcome of an election. Interest groups can also run ad campaigns that are more "educational" in nature. Campaigns like this are rare and are generally run in anticipation of a future political battle to shore up public opinion in support of the group's position. In 1998 true issue ads, urging people to vote, were run by the People for the American Way and the Annenberg Public Policy Center.

Legislative issue ad campaigns are often expensive. The estimated $40 million spent by the tobacco companies on the 1998 tobacco tax fight is an example of a high-cost effort. But when the $40 million is measured against the $310 billion more the tobacco companies would have had to pay had the McCain tobacco tax legislation passed, it is a wise investment. Other interest groups in the future will make the same cost/benefit calculations, and for this reason, issue advocacy is a potential growth field for political consultants.

INDEPENDENT EXPENDITURES IN CONGRESSIONAL ELECTIONS

Independent expenditures are expenditures made by individuals, interest groups, or party committees relating to federal elections that are not in any way coordinated with candidate campaigns. The 1976 Supreme Court decision in *Buckley v. Valeo* exempted such independent spending from any limits because of protected First Amendment rights.[10] The Court permitted requiring disclosure of who is making independent expenditures and the expenditure costs. Since the *Buckley* ruling, the Court has consistently affirmed that independent expenditures may not be limited.[11] The first test of *Buckley* came ten years later in 1986 with *Federal Election Commission v. Massachusetts Citizens for Life, Inc.*[12] This case dealt with an actual voter guide that did not expressly advocate a candidate using the detailed *Buckley* language but did expressly say "Vote Pro-Life" and listed the names of the pro-life candidates. The Court found such wording, although "marginally less direct," was expressly advocating the election of a candidate more than addressing the issues. This case has been cited by the FEC in court cases asking for clarification of what constitutes express advocacy.[13] As mentioned in chapter 2, the courts have ruled that political parties may engage in independent expenditures as long as they used hard dollars to pay for the ad and the expenditure is disclosed.[14]

Much of the independent expenditure activity in the late 1970s and early 1980s came from conservative groups. One such group was the National Conservative Political Action Committee (NCPAC), which targeted vulnerable Democrats in the 1980 congressional elections, especially U.S. senators who had voted for the 1978 Panama Canal Treaty. NCPAC spent over $1 million in negative advertising against these incumbents on defense spending, government spending, and abortion issues.[15] Holding onto Ronald Reagan's coattails, Republicans picked up twelve U.S. Senate seats in 1980 and regained the majority in the U.S. Senate for the first time in twenty-six years. Four of the Republican upsets occurred in races where NCPAC had run independent expenditure campaigns: Senator Frank Church in Idaho, Senator George McGovern in South Dakota, Senator Birch Bayh of Indiana, and Senator Gaylord Nelson of Wisconsin. Following the election, NCPAC claimed credit for pushing the Republican challengers over the top against these Democratic incumbents.[16] In rejoicing over the Republicans' success, the late John "Terry" Dolan, NCPAC's founder, once claimed that NCPAC "could elect Mickey Mouse to the House and Senate."[17]

NCPAC was active again in 1982, but Republicans fell below their expectations of winning a House majority, and Democrats appeared to have learned how to run against such independent expenditures. Democratic Senator Paul Sarbanes of Maryland was the number one NCPAC target in 1982, in part because NCPAC expected that defeating another incumbent within the Washington, D.C., media market would enlarge NCPAC's reputation among members of Congress and the media elite. Implicit in the NCPAC strategy was the veiled threat that other incumbents with voting records not sufficiently in line with NCPAC's leanings would be targeted with similar negative campaigns in the future.[18]

Another Democrat in the 1982 NCPAC crosshairs was Montana Senator John Melcher. NCPAC ran one thousand television ads against Melcher, claiming his vote against Reagan's tax and budget plans was "out of step with Montana." Sarbanes and Melcher were more prepared for the NCPAC assault than their colleagues in 1980. Melcher responded to the NCPAC attack with an ad that showed two cows telling viewers that outsiders had come into the state trying to influence the vote, but that they had been "stepping in what they had been trying to sell."[19] Sarbanes responded by using NCPAC as a fund-raising tool throughout the nation, portraying himself as a target of NCPAC. Coached by other Democrats targeted in 1980, Sarbanes also tied NCPAC to his opponent Lawrence Hogan (R), forcing Hogan to defend NCPAC.[20] Sarbanes, Melcher, and nine of the dozen candidates opposed by NCPAC were reelected.

NCPAC spending constituted 52 percent and 58 percent of all 1980 and 1982 independent expenditures.[21] But its defeats in 1982 hurt fund-raising for 1984, and in that year the PAC nearly declared bankruptcy. NCPAC toppled from $10 million in contributions in 1982 to $2.2 million in 1988 and to a meager $366,600 in 1990.[22] Although NCPAC was only a factor in two election cycles, its existence was not without long-term effects on the electoral system. NCPAC demonstrated that noncandidate campaign activity could be important. NCPAC founder Dolan once bragged that NCPAC could make false statements in advertising without its affecting the candidate. He said, "A group like ours could lie through its teeth and the candidate it helps stays clean."[23]

The tendency of the noncandidate campaign to be more negative persists in the campaign efforts of interest groups in the 1990s. Prior to the NCPAC attacks in 1980 and 1982, independent campaign consultants only used personal attacks on opponents out of desperation, and even then the strategy was thought to be apt to backfire on the groups.[24] NCPAC effectively used personal attacks that quickly became the industry standard. "One Democratic consultant put it this way: 'People say they hate negative campaigning. But it works. They hate it and remember it at the same time.' "[25]

Over time candidates and campaigns have adjusted to negative advertising, largely by using the tactic themselves, and as the 1982 election demonstrated, candidates learned how to respond to NCPAC and independent expenditures in the election cycle following its large-scale introduction. Will candidates be able to show the same adaptability to the unlimited and undisclosed election advocacy mounted by interest groups?

PRE-1998 INTEREST-GROUP ELECTION ADVOCACY

Beginning in 1994, interest groups like the Christian Coalition and the NRA began using loopholes in federal campaign finance rules to spend greater amounts of undisclosed funds on federal elections. It is estimated that the Christian Coalition spent $25 million on its 1994 grassroots effort through voter guides. These voter guides were distributed widely at churches, shopping malls,

convenience stores, and even gas stations. The most successful place for the religious right to distribute its message is at churches because, as one observer said,
it "anoints" the voter guide.[26] Several million dollars more was raised for the
same purpose at the local level.[27] In most states where the Christian Coalition
saw success, like Oklahoma and South Carolina, it was because it operated within
a strong and united Republican structure. The Christian Coalition's efforts backfired, however, in Virginia (and other similar states) because its issues and efforts
divided the party and contributed to defeat for the Republicans on election day.[28]
The Christian Coalition continued its efforts into 1996 and 1998, building its
voter guides and grassroots campaign. Ever since its organization in 1989, the
Christian Coalition sought tax-exempt status as a 501(c)(4) social welfare organization, but in 1999 the Internal Revenue Service denied its bid, forcing a reorga-
nization for the 2000 election cycle.[29] Though this failure will marginally affect
its tax burden and will not likely affect its donation rate—donations to 501(c)(4)
organizations were never tax deductible—the greatest impact will be on
churches: leaders may be reluctant to allow coalition members to speak and distribute material to their congregations for fear of losing their own tax-exempt
status.

The 1996 elections saw a surge in interest-group election advocacy, as organized labor spent over $35 million, much of it on television, aimed at defeating
105 members of Congress, including thirty-two heavily targeted Republican
freshmen.[30] Labor broadcast television commercials in forty districts, distributed
over 11.5 million voter guides in twenty-four districts, and ran radio ads in many
others.[31] While falling short of labor's stated goal of a Democratic majority, the
1996 election results reflected the impact of labor's efforts: twelve of the forty-
four targeted freshmen members were defeated, and voter turnout among union
members rose by 2.32 million over 1992.[32] The scope of labor's 1996 election
advocacy and the negative tone of the message generated widespread coverage,
despite the fact that labor did not officially disclose any of this activity.

To avoid charges of collusion and coordination with the party committees, a
necessary condition to avoid contribution limits and disclosure, labor unions instead talked about when it would send PAC money, with party and union leaders
understanding that the targets would be the same.[33] But labor was not alone.
Religious conservatives, gun owners, environmentalists, business, and abortion
groups all actively campaigned for their agendas and for candidates who supported such agendas. Many groups who engage in election advocacy are tax-
exempt groups like the Sierra Club, Americans for Tax Reform, or the Citizens
for the Republic Education Fund. This last example was created to respond to
advertisements run by the AFL-CIO.[34]

No one interest group countered labor's campaign efforts as much as the National Federation of Independent Business (NFIB) and a coalition of five pro-
business groups: U.S. Chamber of Commerce, the National Association of
Wholesaler-Distributors, the National Restaurant Association, and National As-

sociation of Manufacturers, and the NFIB, called the Coalition: Americans Working for Real Change. The coalition was active in thirty-seven House races, spent $5 million on over 13,000 television and radio commercials, and mailed over two million letters, mainly in support of Republicans, to owners of small businesses.[35] The coalition may have helped Republicans beat back the labor push but did not claim to beat labor at its own game.

Labor's 1996 initiative had some important consequences. First, labor showed other interest groups the potential power and influence that can come through successful election advocacy. Second, labor's campaign motivated political parties to raise and spend soft money, in part to counter million-dollar election-advocacy campaigns aimed at their more vulnerable incumbents and at competitive open seat races.

INTEREST-GROUP ELECTION ADVOCACY IN 1998

The 1997–98 election cycle began with interest groups running election ads in special elections in New Mexico and California. In the Santa Barbara, California, special election, Americans for Limited Terms spent more than $300,000 attacking defeated State Assemblyman Tom Bordonaro because of his refusal to sign its term-limits pledge.[36] Campaign for Working Families, a conservative PAC headed by Gary Bauer, spent nearly $200,000 in the campaign against Democrat Lois Capps for not supporting a ban on late-term abortions.[37]

There was substantial interest-group election advertising in the 1998 elections. More groups ran issue ads in 1997–98 than in 1995–96, and the overall amount of money spent on issue ads also rose.[38] Several of the races in our sample had as much campaign activity by interest groups as by candidates. Interest groups focused their efforts on the relatively small number of competitive House and Senate elections. In the twelve House and four Senate races we monitored, 111 interest groups were active in 1998. These groups ran 218 ads on TV or radio and mounted 258 phone banks or direct mail efforts. Most records show that groups used direct mail from preprimary to the day of the election, whereas they used phone banks more in the final month. Television ads aired throughout, but most heavily in the final month and a half of campaigning. Our data also show that interest groups produced more direct print, radio, and phone banks than the political parties, but that the parties focused more on television advertisements (see fig. 3.1). One race, not in our sample, was an excellent example of heavy interest-group and party involvement. In the Washington First Congressional District open race between Brian Baird (D) and Don Benton (R), an estimated $800,000 was spent in the last week by noncandidate campaigns.[39]

Interest groups adapted their strategies to the size and nature of the district. For some House districts in metropolitan areas, television ads were inefficient.

Figure 3.1 Campaign Activity

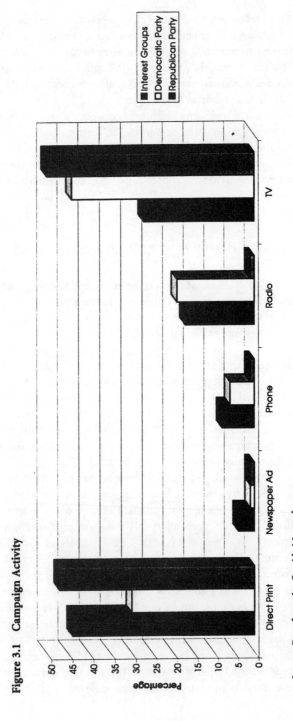

Source: Data from the *Outside Money* data set.

In these contests, resources went to telephone contacts and direct mail. In districts where television markets more closely matched district boundaries, we found more television advertising. But much of the interest-group activity of 1998 was not broadcast advertising. Rather, interest groups adapted to a low-turnout midterm election and spent resources on voter identification and activation. For a more complete description of these ground-war tactics, see chapter 4.

Interest-Group Campaign Strategies in 1998

Interest groups sometimes enter the campaign very early, and in some instances before the primaries, in part to set the agenda of the campaign. In New Mexico, the Sierra Club began running advertisements on four radio stations in Santa Fe and Albuquerque at the end of June, continuing the blitz through the middle of July. Sierra Club political director Dan Weiss explained, "We want to make the environment a part of the dialogue as the campaigns heat up."[40] The Sierra Club felt that its message would be "drowned out" with the millions of candidate campaign dollars after Labor Day. The Sierra Club was right about the extraordinary advertising blitz in these and other races. The AFL-CIO ran its ads 437 times in September in the New Mexico Third Congressional District.

Another election advocacy strategy by interest groups was to discuss candidate value to state or district. Sometimes the content of the ad focuses on the concerns of the interest group, but other times these ads may be more focused on issues unrelated to the interest group. In an attempt to unseat incumbent Harry Reid, the trucking industry funded Nevada's Foundation for Responsible Government, whose ads talked about taxes rather than trucking issues.

Interest-group election advocacy is often negative in tone. In fact, in the last two months before election day, 51 percent of issue ads run by parties and interest groups were pure attack ads.[41] Such ads portray the individual's voting history or character in a negative light, although both character advertisements and issue-related candidate ads may also be used in a positive way.

In several of our races we found an implicit division of labor, with outside money used to attack one candidate or the other in hope of helping the favored candidates. As Kathleen Hall Jamieson has observed, "Candidates don't have to attack because others will do it for them."[42] Mark Mellman, experienced pollster, concurs that money spent by outside groups "increases the negative tone of races," and in his view, "the public blames the candidates."[43] Research has found that voters who watch negative ads become more cynical about the responsiveness of public officials and the electoral process, which in turn fosters lower turnout.[44]

Interest Groups and the Ground War

Interest-group election involvement in 1998 was more multifaceted than in 1996, with some of the most important activities aimed at mobilizing voters in a low-turnout election (see table 3.1). To do this, groups used targeted mail, phone banks, and person-to-person contacts. In the sixteen races we studied, many interest groups used their local affiliates to assist them in their campaign efforts. For example, six state labor unions actively worked on Labor '98's campaign activities. Labor spent approximately $18 million on the ground war in what has been called the "best kept secret" of the 1998 election. Labor coordinated a state/national get-out-the-vote (GOTV), including over 13 million targeted union members. Efforts included extensive phone calls, GOTV efforts, and rides to the voting booth on election day. Labor doubled the number of coordinators in 1998, compared to the 1996 presidential year, and aimed these organizers at half as many targeted races. Former executive director of the National Republican

Table 3.1   Top Interest Groups and Their Communication Strategies

Interest Group	Direct Print	Newspaper	Phone	Radio	TV	Total*
AFL-CIO, Victory '98 (national)	X		X	X	X	53
Sierra Club	X	X	X	X	X	50
National Rifle Association (NRA)	X			X		27
National Education Association	X			X	X	20
Campaign for America					X	17
League of Conservation Voters	X		X		X	16
Service Employees International Union	X					16
American Medical Association	X			X	X	13
National Right to Life Committee	X		X		X	13
People for the American Way	X				X	13
Americans for Limited Terms	X		X		X	12
Christian Coalition	X		X			10
Kentucky Educational Association	X		X			8
Philadelphia Federation of Teachers			X		X	8
Planned Parenthood	X		X			8
We the Parents					X	8
Wisconsin Citizen Action	X					8
National Right to Work Committee	X					7
Right to Life				X		7
Voices Heard Coalition				X		7
AARP	X	X				6
AFL-CIO (Wisconsin)	X					6
U.S. Term Limits	X				X	6
Citizens for a Clean America		X			X	5
Totals	**18**	**3**	**9**	**7**	**13**	**344**

Source: Data from the *Outside Money* data set.
Note: An "X" indicates that the group ran at least one ad campaign in that medium.
*The "Total" column indicates total number of ad campaigns run by the groups in our sample.

Congressional Committee, Ed Brookover, lists the defeat of Mark Baker (R) in the Illinois Seventeenth Congressional District as the result of "union campaigning."[45]

Labor was not alone in mounting a large ground war in 1998. Americans for Limited Terms used phone banks, and at least seventy groups sent mail. Groups like the Sierra Club worked first at activating its membership. We discuss the full scope of the ground war in greater detail in chapter 4.

Voter Guides

Another ground-war tactic is voter guides. Interest groups like the Sierra Club and the Christian Coalition have consistently created voter education direct mailers based on surveys given to candidates or based on a representative's legislative history. These guides portray numerous issues on which the candidates have either voted or voiced their platform; the interest groups judge these responses with a thumbs up or down or a numerated scale. Although these guides claim to be objective, the voter guides clearly portray which candidates are supported by the interest groups and which are not. For example, the Sierra Club "voter education" pamphlet shows two columns and the issues upon which each candidate differs with a check where the Sierra Club's position was the same and a thumbs down where the Sierra Club's position differed. In the Kentucky Senate race, the Christian Coalition distributed more than 500,000 voter guides. This ground-war effort to mobilize voters occurred at the same time interest groups and parties were spending money on negative ads, which foster lower turnout. The reason for this seeming contradiction in strategy is that get-out-the-vote efforts are aimed at segments of likely voters while broadcast ads are aimed at much broader audiences, sometimes with the intent to suppress turnout.

Interest-Group Pledges

One interest-group strategy in recent cycles has been to ask candidates to make pledges on policy questions, and if one candidate refuses to make the pledge in support of the interest group's position, the group then mounts a substantial campaign against the candidate who refused the pledge. The group most identified with this tactic is Americans for Limited Terms; other groups, however, have been active on issues like flag protection and tax reduction. Representative Maloney in the Connecticut Fifth Congressional District signed three pledges in 1998—tax reform, flag protection, and term limit support—to avert interest-group retaliation.[46] Candidates' acquiescence to signing pledges, when confronted with the prospect of a group spending nearly $400,000 against them, is understandable. This tactic has the effect of making candidate elections into referendums on one or more issues that otherwise might not be central to the contest. Pledges are powerful agenda-setting tools for interest groups. The use of pledges in several competitive races in 1998 reinforces the broader finding that candidates are losing control of their campaigns. Other groups concerned with gun control, abortion, or Social Security will likely consider the candidate-pledge tactic in future elections.

There are several unanswered questions for elections in general: Will candidates really stick to the pledges they sign, or are there ways to benefit from the attack on their opponent and avoid action in the future? Will the threat of substantial money coming into a race, if one candidate does not sign, mean both candidates sign the pledges? Can a pledge be used as an effective campaign tool by the candidate who refuses to sign? With the use of this form of interest-group coercion on the rise, these questions deserve further exploration. The 2000 election may provide a test, as at least three candidates have recanted their pledges to limit themselves to three terms and one has begun to waver on her pledge.[47] Republican George R. Nethercutt Jr., the representative who unseated House Speaker Thomas Foley in 1994, claims that his term-limits pledge could have been a mistake, "I know what I said and I wish I hadn't said it. I have lived and learned."[48]

Interest-Group Collusion

One strategic tactic for interest groups in 1998 was to collude with each other on a common agenda. Americans for Limited Terms and U.S. Term Limits are two interest groups that work toward one common goal: getting federal candidates to sign their term-limits pledge. These groups are nonpartisan, although more Republicans sign their three-term-limits pledge than Democrats. This group was active in four of our races and in more than one race told the candidates that if they did not sign the pledge, the groups would use over $100,000 against them in issue ad campaigns.[49] Such was the case in the Utah Second Congressional District, where Lily Eskelsen voluntarily signed the pledge, but where Representative Merrill Cook would not. U.S. Term Limits President Howard Rich called Representative Cook and asked him to sign the pledge. Cook said that when he declined, Rich threatened to run $100,000 against him.[50] Although Cook deemed this action as "political blackmail," Howard commented that "pressure is a good thing."[51] This "pressure" resulted in not just $100,000 but rather $380,000 targeted to direct mail, phone calls, and television and radio advertisements against Cook. Similar "pressure" was put on both candidates in Connecticut Fifth Congressional District and Wisconsin First Congressional District races as well as in twenty-one other House races nationally. Other examples of interest groups working together include the Christian Coalition, Right to Life, and Campaign for Working Families, who joined together to oppose Scotty Baesler (D) in the Kentucky Senate race,[52] and the National Council of Senior Citizens working with labor unions in mass mailings in the Kansas Third Congressional District race.[53]

As Elizabeth Drew notes, "On each side, the various participants swim in the same pond of pollsters, ad-makers, and consultants. They all had access to the same information . . . the [issue advocacy] ad buyers could simply check time availabilities . . . to find out who's doing what."[54] In some of the 1998 campaigns we monitored, interest groups shared lists of voters, adopted the same theme and messages as the candidates, and became part of the voter mobilization strategy at the end of the campaign.

Interest-Group Pluralism

Interest-group conflict is a part of the issue-advocacy story; sometimes the candidates become mere bystanders. The Christian Right has always heavily encouraged voters to vote conservative; they pass out millions of voter guides the Sunday before the election at places of worship. In 1996, one scholar reports, the Christian Coalition distributed 46 million voter guides in 125,000 churches.[55] In 1998, an interest group called the Interfaith Alliance, a more moderate counter to the Christian Coalition, challenged the Christian Right's campaign tactics. The alliance's spokesperson, Walter Cronkite, wrote a letter to hundreds of thousands of pastors asking them to keep Christian Coalition voter guides out of their places of worship. This effort was completely ground run and did not include any air time. On other issues like abortion, the environment, and health care, our study saw groups competing with each other in the context of congressional races. Right to Life competed with NARAL; HMOs competed with the American Medical Association and insurance groups.

Some groups ran ads on television and radio in anticipation of another group's involvement in a race. In the Kansas Third Congressional District race in 1996, a business group called Triad spent $287,000 for the Republican candidate, Snowbarger. Triad is accused of being a front for heavy individual and business contributions in races to support Republicans in 1996. Acting on Triad's possible future involvement in Snowbarger's 1998 campaign, a quickly created interest group, Citizens for a Clean America, ran television, radio, and newspaper ads in the Kansas district to lessen Triad's impact, should it have entered the contest. Although Triad did not enter the race, the campaign agenda shifted to make way for its potential influence.

Disguised Identity

Voters often have only limited information about which interest groups are attempting to influence their vote. Sometimes the group includes its name and identity in the mailing or in a "tag line" at the end of the commercial. But some interest groups avoid even this very limited disclosure and use front groups to hide their identity and avoid raising suspicions about the groups' motives. These fronts also help "private interests evade public disclosure rules governing lobby-

ing and campaigning."[56] Groups that are formed solely for issue-advocacy purposes mask their intent with obscure and generic names and are thus able to skirt
attention while making significant effects on the races they enter. A prime example of this was Triad in 1996. Triad was a funnel for campaign money from conservative business groups like Koch Industries. Triad weighed in heavily in selected races in 1996, significantly affecting the outcome of the Kansas Third
Congressional District race between Snowbarger and Judy Hancock (D). Examples of disguised identity occurred again in 1998. The Coalition to Make Our
Voices Heard was the AFL-CIO in the Connecticut Fifth Congressional District,[57]
and The Coalition: Americans Working for Real Change was the National Association of Manufacturers in the New Mexico Third Congressional District.[58]

Steve Rosenthal, a primary labor strategist involved in recent campaigns, de-
cries the lack of interest-group disclosure. He says, "There is a real problem with
no disclosure. These groups pop up all around the country—citizens for this,
and citizens for that, and Americans for whatever—running ads in districts and
claiming to be mass based when the fact of the matter is nobody knows who
they are."[59] When Mr. Rosenthal was reminded that labor had hidden behind the
innocuous label "Coalition to Make Our Voices Heard" in Connecticut in 1998,
he said, "Frankly we've taken a page out of their book because in some places
it's much more effective to run an ad by the 'Coalition to Make Our Voices
Heard' than it is to say paid for by 'the men and women of the AFL-CIO.' "[60]
Mr. Rosenthal accurately captures the reason why groups will continue to hide
their identity—it improves the chances of persuading voters.

INTEREST-GROUP AIR WAR

As in the 1994 and 1996 election cycles, interest groups used television and radio
to campaign for and against congressional candidates. Paul Herrnson observes
that "new technology has encouraged a major change in the focus of most congressional election campaigns. It has enabled campaigns to communicate more
information about candidates' personalities, issue positions, and qualifications
for office."[61]

Thomas Patterson and Robert McClure found that television advertisements
do not affect voters' impressions of the candidates, but the advertisements do
affect voters' perceptions of campaign issues and candidates' platforms.[62] There
were several examples of television ads from interest groups that helped set the
agenda in 1998 races, including labor ads on Social Security in Iowa and Illinois,
League of Conservation Voters ads on environmental issues in the Nevada Senate
race and New Mexico Third Congressional District race, and pro-term-limits ads
in the Utah Second Congressional District race. Not only is setting the agenda
important in terms of persuading voters, but it also has the benefit of forcing
candidates to talk about issues of concern to interest groups. Interest groups do

not hesitate to remind candidates of the role their election ads played in the candidate's victory.

Cable television and radio permit interest groups to target their message to segments of voters. For example, if an interest group wanted to reach mostly men they could advertise on ESPN; women, Lifetime; mature audiences, History Channel; blacks, BET; and higher income levels, CNN.[63] One African American mobilization in 1998 followed this strategy in its advertising on BET and particular radio stations with a predominantly African American listening audience.[64]

Timing of Election Advertisements

The timing of candidate- and election-centered interest-group ads is critical. Herrnson argues that there are motives for interest groups spending their money both early and late.[65] Interest groups will spend their money early in a campaign season to affect the national and district-level agendas. Interest groups tend to spend money late in a campaign to supplement candidates' campaign ads with their own message of support or to catch opponents off guard. In 1998, the Sierra Club ran most of its ads early, before Labor Day, after which campaign season really begins. Its philosophy was that it receives sufficient "bang for the buck" pre–Labor Day when air costs are lower and when it could make the environment a part of the national agenda. The Sierra Club continued with its candidate campaigns two weeks before the election with a large get-out-the-vote drive in twenty states, targeting a quarter of a million people.[66]

Although campaign advertisements in general increased substantially in the last three weeks of the 1998 campaign, interest groups were the heaviest hitters in the final weeks, with nearly three-fourths of their election campaigning occurring during that time period. Some groups waited too long to enter the fray. In the Kentucky Senate race, for example, Campaign for America attempted to place an ad in the Lexington Market in the last two weeks of the campaign only to have most of its $60,000 check returned because the station's time was sold. In the Nevada Senate race one television station permitted groups and parties to bid for an 11:00 P.M. time slot shortly before the election, with the final bid at five times the normal rate. Data obtained from Strategic Media, which included costs of ads by the week, reflect this trend of increasing demand for air time and exorbitant rates (see fig. 3.2). Interestingly, there is evidence that the costs of interest-group campaign ads rose significantly in the last three days before the election.

The use of outside money in 1998 illustrates that parties and interest groups have multiple or separate agendas, ranging from helping elect their candidates to pressing their agendas. Some groups indicated that they would continue to press their agendas through ads, even if tracking polls showed that they were hurting the candidate when they presumably were trying to help. Other contests showed that despite a candidate's request that an interest group not join the campaign,

Figure 3.2   TV Ad Expenditures by Week: Interest Groups and Political Parties

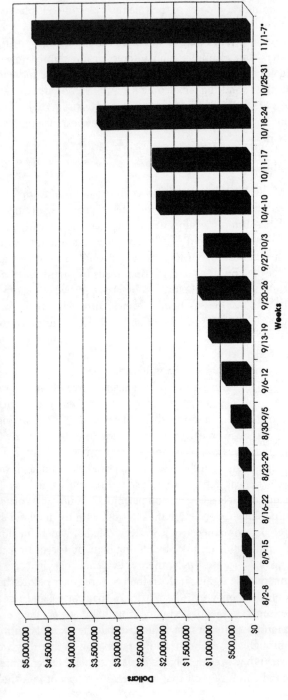

Source: Data from Strategic Media Services.
*Estimated for the whole week from 1–3 November data.

the outside campaign goes ahead. Interest groups may also retaliate against legislators for votes in Congress by mounting issue-advocacy campaigns.

CONCLUSION

Generic issue advertising and issue advertising pegged toward legislation is, in our view, quite different from interest groups running campaign ads designed to influence voters to support or oppose a candidate. Such advertising is thus termed election advocacy. While not fitting the Supreme Court's definition of express advocacy, defined as any public communication that directly advocates the defeat or election of a particular candidate, interest-group election advocacy is clearly intended to influence the outcome of an election. Groups can and do make compelling voting-related messages without "express words of advocacy for election or defeat, such as 'vote for,' 'elect,' 'support,' 'cast your ballot for,' 'Smith for Congress,' 'vote against,' 'defeat,' 'reject.' "[67]

Interest groups and their media consultants understand that they can influence elections without expressly calling for the election or defeat of a candidate. Interest-group electioneering affects candidates' political agendas. This is an important departure from what has been a candidate-centered electoral system where candidates set the campaign agenda and campaign planning anticipates the issues and charges likely to be raised by their opponent.[68] The campaign activity by interest groups and parties means that candidates now face multiple opponents and a more diverse and unexpected set of issues.

For candidates, the involvement of outside groups is, as one candidate put it, "a double-edged sword."[69] Candidates may benefit from the attack on their opponents, but they may also be harmed if the ads are too negative or if these groups bring baggage with them. It is clear from our research that outside groups influence the outcome of campaigns. The National Rifle Association (NRA) endorsement of Democrat Strickland in the Ohio Sixth Congressional District generally helped him with social conservatives. The support of the League of Conservation Voters helped Udall in the New Mexico Third Congressional District win back voters who likely supported the Green Party in the previous special election in which the Green Party candidate, Carol Miller, got 14 percent of the vote. The American Medical Association PAC ran a very hard $450,000 campaign for Fox (R-PA 13), an amount equal to more than a third of Fox's war chest, the ante may have been misplaced in the air rather than ground war, leading to Fox's defeat.

For voters in competitive races, the new world of campaigns is a barrage of broadcast ads by candidates, parties, and groups. Not only does the frequency of the ads make it hard to tell who is saying what, but the interest-group and party ads are indistinguishable from the candidate ads. One result is voter confusion. But this confusion is understandable. Even Strategic Media, the firm hired to monitor twenty television markets active in our sample races, miscoded several interest-group political advertisements as candidate ads and coded party ads as candidate ads. Voters are no more immune to this confusion than corporations that specialize in media coding and tracking. While federal election law requires differentiation and credit for candidate and noncandidate advertisements, voters find such a distinction meaningless. Confusion also can result when an interest-group spokesperson in ads supporting one person speaks at a fund-raiser for the opposing candidate, as happened with NRA spokesman Charlton Heston in the Ohio Sixth Congressional District.

Despite the importance of electioneering by interest groups, their campaign activities are not well covered by the local and state media. More broadly, the media gave less attention to the 1998 elections than past midterm elections. Getting clear information on who the groups are and how much they are spending is difficult. For voters, the result is many efforts to persuade them but with little understanding of the source of that persuasion. When asked, the public overwhelmingly favors requiring interest groups to disclose their sponsorship of such ads.[70]

The implications of this campaign activity by outside groups and parties are therefore more negative campaigning, voter uncertainty about who is saying what in the campaign, and candidate loss of control of the content of campaigns. The large amounts of money spent on interest-group election activity not only drive up the overall costs of campaigns, as parties and candidates assume the need to respond to the interest-group attacks, but also the high levels of spending may benefit groups with the resources to spend on electioneering, while hurting those who lack the money to get involved.[71] Our data from 1998 suggest that successful groups have enhanced power because of the role they played in helping their friends in competitive races.

NOTES

1. See *Buckley v. Valeo,* 424 U.S. 1 (1976).

2. Steve Rosenthal, lunchtime discussion panel at the Pew Press Conference, "Outside Money: Soft Money & Issue Ads in Competitive 1998 Congressional Elections," National Press Club, Washington, D.C., 1 February 1999.

3. Cited in Tom Konda, "Ads on Issues Go Back Decades," *New York Times* Letter to the Editor, 1 November 1993, A22.

4. Darrell M. West and Burdett A. Loomis, *The Sound of Money: How Political Interests Get What They Want* (New York: W. W. Norton & Company, 1998), 51.

5. Dan Rostenkowski, "Hortonizing the Health Debate," *Washington Post,* 19 August 1994, A27.

6. Kathleen Hall Jamieson, " 'Tax and Spend' vs. 'Little Kids': Advocacy and Accuracy in the Tobacco Settlement Ads of 1997–8," 6 August 1998, 1.

7. Ibid.

8. "Health Benefits Coalition," *Issue Ads @ APPC,* 12 January 1998, at <http://appc-penn.org/issueads/profiles/hbc.htm>, 20 July 1999.

9. "Business Roundtable, Flatline Ad," *Issue Ads @ APPC,* 8 December 1998 at <http://upenn.edu/appc/issueads/profiles/brtable>, 20 July 1999.

10. *Buckley v. Valeo,* 424 U.S. 1 (1976).

11. In 1980, Common Cause and the FEC challenged the legal parameters of independent expenditures by conservative organizations who had made independent expenditures for Ronald Reagan's presidential campaign. A federal court rejected the FEC's argument, claiming it would be an unconstitutional limitation on the First Amendment right of free speech. The decision was appealed to the Supreme Court and failed. See *Common Cause v. Federal Election Commission,* 692 F. Supp. 1397 (D.D.C. 1988). Campaign finance issues once again emerged on the Court's agenda in 1985 when the Supreme Court struck down a stipulation limiting independent expenditures by PACs. The National Conservative PAC and Fund for a Conservative Majority had spent millions of dollars supporting Reagan's 1984 campaign and were being sued by the FEC (see *Federal Election Commission v. National Conservative Political Action Committee, et al.,* 105 Sup. Ct. 1459 (1985).

12. *Federal Election Commission v. Massachusetts Citizens for Life, Inc.,* 479 U.S. 238 (1986).

13. Trevor Potter, "Issue Advocacy and Express Advocacy," in *Campaign Finance Reform: A Sourcebook,* ed. Anthony Corrado, Thomas Mann, Daniel Ortiz, Trevor Potter, and Frank Sorauf (Washington, D.C.: Brookings, 1997), 229–30.

14. *Colorado Republican Federal Campaign Committee v. Federal Election Commission,* 116 Sup. Ct. 2309 (1996).

15. Mark J. Rozell and Clyde Wilcox, *Interest Groups in American Campaigns* (Washington, D.C.: Congressional Quarterly, 1999), 136–37.

16. Neil R. Peirce and Robert Guskind, "The New Right Takes Its Political Show on the Road to Win Power in the States," *National Journal,* 13 October 1984, 1918.

17. Wayne King and Warren Weaver Jr., "Nuts for Sale," *New York Times,* 9 April 1986, B6.

18. Allan J. Cigler and Burdett A. Loomis, *Interest Group Politics* (Washington, D.C.: Congressional Quarterly, 1998), 203.

19. Martin Schram, "The 1982 Elections: Negative Advertising," *Washington Post,* 30 October 1982, A1.

20. Saundra Seperstein, "Sarbanes' Strategy Turned NCPAC Attack into Votes for Him," *Washington Post,* 3 November 1982, A34.

21. Frank J. Sorauf, "Campaign Finance in the House and Senate," in *Elections in America,* ed. Kay Lehman Schlozman (Boston: Allen & Unwin, 1987), 209.

22. Frank J. Sorauf, *Inside Campaign Finance: Myths and Realities* (New Haven: Yale University Press, 1992), 40.

23. Myra MacPherson, "The New Right Brigade: John Terry Dolan's NCPAC Targets Liberals and the Federal Election Commission," *Washington Post,* 10 August 1980, F1.

24. Gary C. Jacobson, *The Politics of Congressional Elections* (New York: Longman, 1997), 71–72.

25. Ibid.

26. Charles Bullock III and John C. Grant, "Georgia: The Christian Right and Grass Roots Power," in *God at the Grassroots: The Christian Right in the 1994 Elections,* ed. Mark J. Rozell and Clyde Wilcox (Lanham, Md.: Rowman & Littlefield, 1995), 52.

27. John C. Green, "The Christian Right and the 1994 Elections: An Overview," in *God at the Grassroots: The Christian Right in the 1994 Elections,* ed. Mark J. Rozell and Clyde Wilcox (Lanham, Md.: Rowman & Littlefield, 1995) 9.

28. Ibid., 2.

29. David E. Rosenbaum, "Tax-Exempt Status Rejected, Christian Coalition Regroups," *New York Times,* 11 June 1999, A20. The Christian Coalition will divide into Christian Coalition International, a for-profit organization that will engage in political activities, and Christian Coalition of America, an organization that will concentrate on voter education, assuming the tax-exempt status of the Christian Coalition of Texas.

30. Deborah Beck, Paul Taylor, Jeffrey Stanger, and Douglas Rivlin, "Issue Advocacy Advertising During the 1996 Campaign: A Catalog," report series by the Annenberg Public Policy Center, no. 16, 16 September 1997, 10. Paul Herrnson reports that labor initially targeted seventy-five districts but increased the targeted races by thirty, for a total of 105 races, at the urging of affiliated unions. See Paul Herrnson, *Congressional Elections: Campaigning at Home and in Washington* (Congressional Quarterly, 1998), 123.

31. "Labor Targets," *Congressional Quarterly Weekly Report,* 26 October 1996, 3084; Jeanne I. Dugan, "Washington Ain't Seen Nothin' Yet," *Business Week Report,* 13 May 1996, 3.

32. Paul Herrnson, "Parties and Interest Groups in Post-reform Congressional Elections," in *Interest Group Politics,* 5th ed., ed. Allan Cigler and Burdett A. Loomis (Washington, D.C.: Congressional Quarterly, 1998), 160.

33. Elizabeth Drew, *Whatever It Takes: The Real Struggle for Political Power in America* (New York: Penguin, 1998), 76.

34. Eliza Newlin Carney, "Stealth Bombers," *National Journal* 29, no. 33, 16 August 1997, 1640–43.

35. Herrnson, "Parties and Interest Groups," 160–61.

36. Todd S. Purdum, "The East Wins and Loses a Race to the West," *New York Times,* 15 March 1998, sec. 4 and 5.

37. Todd S. Purdum, "Interest Groups Run Own Race in California" *New York Times,* 7 March 1998, sec. 4 and 5.

38. Annenberg Public Policy Center 1996 and 1998 Issue Advocacy Advertising Reports.

39. James A. Thurber and Carolyn Long, *The Battle for Money and Votes in Washington's 4th Congressional District* (Washington, D.C.: American University Press).

40. See chapter 8, 143.

41. "Issue Advocacy Advertising during the 1997–1998 Election Cycle," *Issue Ads @ APPC,* 1998, at <www.appcpenn.org/issueads/analysis.htm>, 20 July 1999.

42. Remarks by Kathleen Hall Jamieson, CQ Post Election Conference, Washington, D.C., 2 November 1998.

43. Mark Mellman, interview by Marianne Holt, telephone, 23 March 1999.

44. Stephen Ansolabehere, Shanto Iyengar, Adam Simon, and Nicholas Valentino, "Does Attack Advertising Demobilize the Electorate?" *American Political Science Review* 88, no. 4 (December 1994), 829–38.

45. Ed Brookover, interview by author, Washington, D.C., 6 May 1999.

46. See chapter 9, 162.

47. Martin T. Meehan (D-MA), Scott McInnis, (R-CO), and George Nethercutt

(R-WA) have renounced their pledge; Tillie Fowler (R-FL) is undecided; Kristin Brainerd, "Several Term Limits Supporters Recant Vows to Leave House, Saying Their Work Is Not Yet Done," *Congressional Quarterly Weekly,* 19 June 1999.

48. Sam Howe Verhovek, "Some Backtracking on Term Limits," *New York Times,* 12 April 1999, A20.

49. Dan Harrie, "Cook Dismisses Term Limit Ads as a Form of Political Blackmail," *Salt Lake Tribune,* 15 October 1998, C3.

50. According to U.S. Term Limits President Paul Jacobs, Rich denies that any threat was ever made. Paul Jacobs, interview by Jay Goodliffe, telephone, 13 April 1999.

51. Ibid.

52. See chapter 11, 201–2.

53. See chapter 5, 86.

54. Elizabeth Drew, *What It Takes* (New York: Viking, 1997), 78.

55. Darrell M. West, *Air Wars: Television Advertising in Election Campaigns,* 2nd ed. (Washington, D.C.: Congressional Quarterly, 1997), 191.

56. Darrell M. West and Burdett A. Loomis, *The Sound of Money: How Political Interests Get What They Want* (New York: W. W. Norton, 1998), 70.

57. See chapter 9, 164.

58. See chapter 8, 142.

59. Rosenthal, Pew Press Conference.

60. Ibid.

61. Paul S. Herrnson, *Congressional Elections: Campaigning at Home and in Washington,* 2nd ed. (Washington, D.C.: Congressional Quarterly, 1998), 17.

62. Larry J. Sabato, *The Rise of Political Consultants: New Ways of Winning Elections* (New York: Basic Books, 1981), 118.

63. Ray Reggie, "Buying TV Spots on Cable," *Campaigns & Elections* October/November 1997, 37.

64. Yvonne Scruggs, interview by author, telephone, 2 May 1999.

65. Herrnson, "Parties and Interest Groups," 158.

66. Margaret Kriz, "The Big Green Election Machine," *National Journal,* 24 October 1998, 2512.

67. *Buckley v. Valeo,* 424 U.S. 1 (1976).

68. Martin P. Wattenberg, *The Rise of Candidate-Centered Politics: Presidential Elections of the 1980s* (Cambridge: Harvard University Press, 1991).

69. Lily Eskelsen, interview by Marianne Holt, Salt Lake City, Utah, 5 December 1998.

70. In a 1996 Brown University poll, 76 percent of Americans favored requiring interest groups to disclose who is paying for ads, and 74 percent believe groups should be subject to the same rules as candidates. See Darrel M. West, *Air Wars,* 192.

71. See Darrell M. West, "How Issue Ads Have Reshaped American Politics" (paper prepared for the conference on Political Advertising in Election Campaigns, Center for Congressional and Presidential Studies, School of Public Affairs, American University, 17 April 1998).

4

Outside Money and the Ground War in 1998

David B. Magleby

Outside money in election cycles leading up to 1998 has been discussed in terms of broadcast advertising, especially television advertising. The advertising paid for with soft money by Bill Clinton and Al Gore in the 1996 presidential election was widely discussed as well as the election advocacy by interest groups in the 1994 and 1996 congressional elections. Most discussions of the AFL-CIO $35 million election advocacy blitz in 1996 commented on the amount and tone of broadcast advertising. Labor targeted seventy-five House Republicans, including more than twenty-four Republican freshmen, and spent as much as $2 million in campaign efforts to defeat a single House member mostly on television advertisements.[1]

The role of outside groups was also prominent in most discussions of the 1997 and early 1998 special elections in Santa Barbara, California, and New Mexico, again emphasizing the "air war" approach to voter persuasion. Both races were expensive; in excess of $3 million was spent in California's special election and almost $4 million in New Mexico. The Republican Party spent $1 million in New Mexico's First Congressional District, a record for party spending in a special election.[2] Interest groups not only contributed heavily to the candidates in these races but they also mounted independent candidate-advocacy campaigns. Groups involved in this blitz included environmental organizations, labor unions, the Religious Right, and term-limits advocates. Both political parties also spent soft money on these races.

Political scientists debate one another about the impact of campaign spending on turnout. Few dispute Campbell's early finding that the stimulus of a presidential election leads to a surge in turnout followed by a decline in voting in the next midterm election.[3] Looking at aggregate data, Cox and Munger find that turnout rises in congressional elections in midterm years when the race is competitive, when there is a simultaneous senatorial and gubernatorial race, and when campaign spending rises.[4] Other studies using individual level data find that "congressional campaign spending makes a relatively small and insignificant contribution to turnout."[5] But it is difficult to disentangle the impact of spending for competitive races on turnout, since the two independent variables tend to appear together.

Parties and interest groups have always invested in voter identification, registration, and activation, and they have always used such techniques as phone banks and direct mail to reach their targeted audience. Past research has found that political elites, like party leaders, are the primary agents of voter mobilization.[6] What has not been monitored as closely is the extent and intensity of interest-group electioneering, which began in 1994, grew in 1996, and reached extraordinary levels in the special elections of 1997 and 1998. Our research in 1998 was designed to monitor and gather data on all forms of communication with voters by candidates, parties, and interest groups, including the kinds of direct communications that have been excluded in other studies of unregulated and undisclosed campaign activities.[7]

Because of our relatively small sample size—only twelve House races—our study does not resolve the debate over the effect of campaign spending on turnout. But our study examines spending on broadcast and print advertising as well as spending to register, identify, and mobilize voters. Given the low turnout of the primary and special elections of 1997 and 1998, there was reason to believe that the ground war would be important in 1998. First, it was a midterm election with the predictable decline in turnout, the kind in which broadcast advertising has reached at least two nonvoters for every voter. This process of targeting has been defined by one congressional elections scholar as follows: "Targeting involves categorizing different groups of voters, identifying their political preferences, and designing appeals to which they are likely to respond."[8] Because of the election context, we believed that targeting and the ground war would be important in 1998. Second, ground-war tactics permit parties and groups to do election-related work without telegraphing to the opposition or the media what they are doing. While some groups want to flaunt their electioneering role, many we assumed would prefer to be more strategic in the deployment of resources. Finally, in much of the debate over campaign finance reform there has been an unanswered question about the extent to which one side or the other has an advantage in phone banks, direct mail, or other interpersonal communications.

In designing a study of how party soft money and interest-group electioneering impacted the 1998 midterm election, it was important to include these other forms of campaigning. But monitoring direct voter contacts is more difficult than tracking television, newspaper, or radio ads. One advantage of this study's methodology—involving academics in the districts or states and encouraging them to develop networks with candidates, parties, political reporters, former students, and other volunteers—is that the outside money study has at least a partial picture of the full range of campaign activity by candidates, parties, and interest groups.

Candidate and party campaigns have long included voter identification and activation. Indeed as Darrell West has written, "The classic avenue is to influence citizens at the grassroots level."[9] The strategies and approaches taken by interest groups, parties, and candidates in the ground war were important in the surprising victory for the Democrats in 1998, especially in the House of Representatives.

GROUND-WAR THEORY, TACTICS, AND APPLICATIONS IN 1998

Drawing from the literature on campaigns and elections I will describe the theory and tactics involved in direct mail, telephone contacts, person-to-person canvassing, and get-out-the-vote efforts (GOTV). Then, in each section, I will provide examples from contests that we monitored in 1998 that illustrate how this tactic was applied and to what effect.

Direct Mail

Direct mail is the tactic of sending tailored campaign messages to targeted audiences through the mail. Direct mail is also often used for fund-raising. The lists used for direct mail purposes come from registered voter lists, interest-group membership lists, contributor lists, or zip code lists permitting the communicator to target certain socioeconomic groups. The precision of the targeting varies by the type of list employed. When going after very specific targets, direct mail firms call the practice "rifle shooting," in contrast to mailing to broader lists, which consultants call "shotgunning."[10] The use of direct mail is enhanced by the now widespread availability of high-speed computers and printers, permitting a much more widespread use of the process by parties, candidates, and interest groups. The major advantage of direct mail is the communicator's ability to send a particular communication to a specific audience.[11]

Paul Herrnson sees the relatively low cost of direct mail as one of its great advantages and finds that "direct mail is one of the most widely used methods of campaign advertising in congressional elections. It is used by more than nine out of ten House and nearly all Senate candidates."[12] Another advantage of mail over broadcast is the ability to convey more information. As S. J. Guzzeta has written, "A 30- or 60-second TV or radio commercial essentially projects an impression; it takes "print," a letter or newspaper, to project substance."[13] But as more and more voters receive mail solicitations, not just about politics but for other purposes as well, voters may be less inclined to read their "junk mail" and the impact may diminish. One study estimated that three in four people who receive political direct mail actually read it.[14] Voters residing in our sample districts or states, especially if they were targeted by both sides, received a lot of mail, as many as eleven pieces in one household in the Connecticut Fifth Congressional District.[15]

The impact of direct mail can be enhanced when it is combined with person-to-person canvasses in person or on the telephone. The initial contact assesses which candidate they plan to support or if they are undecided. The second stage uses the mail to persuade the "undecideds." In campaigns motivating voters to turn out, the second stage for voters inclined to support the preferred candidate is a mailing stressing the importance of voting.

Larry Sabato argued in 1981 that direct mail has been more a tool of the right than of the left and liberals had not yet matched the right's quality or technology of the conservative firms.[16] By 1998, this generalization no longer held. In several of the most competitive U.S. House and Senate races in 1998 for Democratic candidates, party soft money–funded communications and interest groups supporting a Democrat were more effective in their use of direct mail than were the Republicans and their allied interests, even when outspent. John Haskell, who studied the Iowa Third Congressional District race between Larry McKibben (R-challenger) and Leonard Boswell (D-incumbent), found that "although union mailings were much fewer and more targeted than those undertaken by the GOP and the Christian Coalition, both of which blanketed the district almost indiscriminately, the Democrats partially made up for fewer resources by using more efficient means and as we have argued, a more coherent message."[17]

One of the Republicans' problems in 1998 may have been a misjudgment about how much to make out of the Clinton-Lewinsky scandal. In the Ohio Sixth Congressional District race between Nancy Hollister (R-challenger) and Ted Strickland (D-incumbent), the Republicans had no shortage of direct mail on such themes as Strickland's 1993 vote to increase taxes, his education policies, and his liberal politics. But in the crucial final two weeks of the campaign the Republican Party also sent out anti-Clinton mailers asking voters not to reward Clinton with their vote on election day by electing other Democrats. Strickland's allies at the NEA spent $54,865 on direct mail, radio, and television broadcasting. The direct mail campaign was conducted in late October and discussed how the incumbent Strickland was "giving our kids a quality education." The NEA's campaign was positive and low key and fit with Ohio's concerns for education in this region, because its schools are among the poorest in Ohio. Strickland's campaign sent out several high-quality mailers. Echoing the education theme, Athens County Democrats sent out a "pro-student ticket" that included Strickland.[18]

In at least two of the competitive 1998 House races the direct mail activity by interest groups far exceeded direct mail from the parties or candidates. Such a contest was the Oregon First Congressional District open-seat race between Molly Bordonaro (R) and David Wu (D), where political scientist Russ Dondero found "the primary medium used by noncandidate groups was direct mail, which flooded the district in the last two weeks of the campaign, eclipsing the candidate's targeted mail by at least a four-to-one ratio. Direct mail was used by Labor and the Sierra Club on behalf of Wu, while such efforts were used by the Oregon Family Council and the Christian Coalition on behalf of Bordonaro."[19] Dondero, who studied this race, found that Wu benefited from these outside campaigns and that although the messages did not coincide with the candidate messages, voters responded to them positively.[20] Robyn Kolodny and Sandra Suarez, who studied the Pennsylvania Thirteenth Congressional District race between Jon Fox (R-incumbent) and Joseph Hoeffel (D-challenger), also found that interest groups generated roughly twice as much direct mail as candidates and parties. The groups involved in Pennsylvania included the AMA, Organized Labor, senior citizens groups like AARP, and the National Abortion Rights Action League.

Our investigation of campaign communications in competitive congressional races in 1998 found that direct mail made up one-third of campaign contacts in the sample races, and over three-quarters of all direct mail went out in the last three weeks of the campaign. For example, in the Kansas Third Congressional District, Democratic candidate Moore identified over 30,000 voters who were Republicans or Independents but who were against concealed weapons and were pro-choice. Up to three pieces of mail went to each of these persons in the last three weeks of the campaign.[21] Interest groups roughly matched parties in the amount of direct mail sent to voters.

Absentee and Early Voting

In recent years, states have liberalized their absentee voting rules so that citizens may vote before the election even if it is only a matter of convenience. The process of requesting an absentee ballot has also been reformed so that in many states voters may request ballots by postcard. Both parties utilized an absentee ballot strategy in the competitive races the outside money study researched in 1998. Absentee ballots "have been the deciding factor in many state and local campaigns, including the extremely close race for the governor of California in 1984."[22] In the past, students of campaign strategy described only two ways of using absentee ballots: first, through contacting senior citizen centers or institutions where possible voters may have difficulty getting to polls on election day and second, responding to absentee ballot requests generated from door-to-door or phone canvassing.[23] But our study found parties mailing out absentee ballot request cards to strongly supportive voters, essentially encouraging them to vote early for the candidates endorsed in the direct mail piece.

This strategy became controversial in the Utah Second Congressional District race, when the Republican Party bypassed the normal process in which the county clerk provided the absentee ballot request forms. Instead, the party printed its own request forms and sent 60,000 of them to Republicans likely to vote and included in the mailer a slate of the Republican candidates. Shortly thereafter, the Democrats followed suit by sending out 50,000 applications for absentee ballots but did not send out Democratic candidate slates, ultimately in-creasing absentee voting over 67 percent from the last midterm election.[24] Using a similar strategy, Democrats in New Mexico increased their absentee voting rate by over 6,000. The Democrats targeted precincts where their performance was 65 percent or higher. The party also sent letters in English and Spanish from former Congressman Bill Richardson, encouraging voters to vote soon and vote Democratic; an absentee ballot application was enclosed in the letter.[25] The Ne-vada Senate race also mobilized the Democrats, with the polls opening two weeks before election day for "early voting" and a continual stream of absentee ballots from the rural areas.

Telephone Contacts

A second way campaigns, including those mounted by interest groups and parties, can communicate with voters and motivate them to vote is by telephone. As with direct mail, telephone contact can utilize computerized lists, and most modern campaigns do. Telephone banks were part of campaigns before the ad-vent of computers. To campaign professionals they are referred to as "boiler rooms" because before telemarketing firms, many of them were located in base-ments or boiler rooms.[26] The phone banks operating in the races we monitored were generally professional operations, often run out of state, and which utilized sophisticated computer and telephone technology.

The scholars monitoring the sixteen competitive races found telephone con-tact activity in each of them, and in some cases it was carried out by six or more groups. It is difficult to estimate, but some single groups spent over $30,000 on the phones in House races and much more than that in Senate races. Telephone contact by the parties was even more extensive.

An example of this kind of telemarket targeting in 1998 is the term-limits pro-ponents in Idaho's Second Congressional District race, where independent voters were targeted and urged to support term limits and vote for Mike Simpson (R), who was running against Richard Stallings (D) in the open-seat contest.[27] The use of telecommunications in congressional elections has, in the experience of one consultant, doubled every election year since 1990.[28] We found substantial telephone activity in each of the contests we studied in 1998, and in the Kentucky Senate race, the two parties combined made more than one million telephone calls.[29]

The process can be more grassroots, with people calling other voters from their homes, or more sophisticated, using banks of telephones linked to comput-ers so that information on voters can be stored and processed instantly. This latter technique can be linked to follow-up mail on specific issues or concerns mentioned by the voter or additional telephone contacts to be sure the voter actually turns out to vote. As Beaudry and Shaeffer have observed, "Calls may also be used to respond to voters' questions, thank supporters, draw in potential volunteers, or invite undecided voters to candidate coffees or other events."

Wally Clinton, a Democratic consultant, stated, "The telephone is a medium of dialogue, not monologue. That is its strength. That's what makes it work."[30] Steve Rosenthal, AFL-CIO political director, stated that labor "got an enormous response from one-on-one bank contacts, not from paid vendor contacts, but from union members talking to each other."[31]

Telephone calls are also often used in a second round of direct contacts in campaigns that want to reinforce the positions of favorable voters. In this instance recorded messages from the candidate or another person prominent for that segment of voters delivers the recorded message. This technique was used by multiple groups in the Pennsylvania Thirteenth Congressional District race between Jon Fox (R-incumbent) and Joe Hoeffel (D-challenger).

Some estimate that phone banks can reach about 50 percent more people per hour than door-to-door canvassers, and phone banks can operate later in the evening than in-person canvassers. Wally Clinton stated, "Most of today's paid operations can complete three times as many contacts in a given hour than a volunteer operation."[32]

While some complain of too much telemarketing, consultants who use the process assert that it is more effective than direct mail because it is interactive and it "cuts through the direct mail clutter and aggressive media ads. The phone is an excellent way to generate immediate awareness which leads to targeted turnout."[33]

Telephone banks generally do not begin until four weeks prior to the election, and calls are generally made during the evening between 6 P.M. and 9:30 P.M.[34] Consistent with this past research, we found that 90 percent of all phone calls were made two to three weeks prior to election day. Phone calls in our 1998 sample races made by outside groups were rarely neutral in tone. The preponderance of phone contacts in competitive races in 1998 was made in support of Democratic candidates.

Telephone campaigns can also be used for push polling, where callers masquerade as pollsters when in reality the purpose of the call is to present negative information on one of the candidates. In the Utah Second Congressional District race between incumbent Merrill Cook (R) and Lily Eskelsen (D), Americans for Limited Terms spent $30,000 on phone banks. Their four-question phone poll asked voters if term limits mattered to them and informed the voters that Lily Eskelsen supported term limits but that Cook had refused to sign a term-limits pledge limiting his service to three terms.[35] ALT President Eric O'Keefe argued that this wasn't push polling because it presented "informative and accurate" information.[36] The Ensign (R) Senate campaign in Nevada contends that supporters of Harry Reid (D) used push polling on Social Security in the days just before the election.[37]

A related tactic is called "vote suppression," where the callers hope to discourage voters likely to support the opposing candidate from voting. An unidentified group mounted a vote suppression effort in the Wisconsin First Congressional

District open race in 1998 between Paul Ryan (R) and Lydia Spottswood (D). Dennis Dresang, who studied this race, found that in violation of state laws, the callers did not identify their group, but asked: "Do you plan to vote?" If the recipient answered, "Yes," callers continued, "If the election were held now, would you vote for Ryan or Spottswood?" If recipients answered Spottswood, callers asked, "Would you still vote for Spottswood if you knew that she had voted for six property-tax rate hikes and also voted to increase her own salary?"[38]

Internet Campaigning

As Ron Faucheux, editor and publisher of *Campaigns & Elections* magazine, has written, "The Internet is not only the newest medium, it is the fastest growing and least understood."[39] In general, the Internet is seen as a versatile, innovative, and cost-effective tool. It can be used to leverage media advertisements on television and radio, recruit volunteers, raise funds, get out the vote, as well as educate people on the campaign message. The most critical aspect of the Internet as a campaign tool is the e-mail address list. Like telephone and mail contacting, using the Internet to communicate with supporters or interest-group associates has the advantage of not telegraphing messages and strategies to the opposition.

Kathryn Combs has observed that issue advocacy has already started on the Internet.[40] Nearly three-fifths of the candidates we followed had home pages in 1998 and several local parties also had web sites.[41] For example, the Nevada Democrats ran an attack-Internet site aimed at Republican John Ensign.[42] However, we found little evidence of parties, candidates, or interest groups investing substantially in the Internet as a way to reach large numbers of voters. Competitive candidates, their parties, and allied groups were much more likely to use conventional mail, phone banks, and broadcast or cable advertisements. One of the candidates who did not have a home page was Tom Udall of New Mexico. In response to an inquiry from Lonna Atkeson, one of his campaign staff said they felt a home page was a waste of campaign money because web pages "don't influence anyone."[43]

In a contest that was not part of our sample but generated extensive media coverage, the Minnesota governor's race, winning candidate Jesse Ventura made use of the Internet, where he reached a large number of voters at a very low cost. It helped mobilize voters and helped coordinate activities and voting. The best example of this was through the e-mail net with over 3,000 members on the list. They were contacted close to the election in preparation for a 72-hour get-out-the-vote drive coordinated and organized solely through the Internet. The 3,000 members were contacted to be volunteers, and 250 showed up to organize the final tour.[44]

Person-to-Person Contacts and Get-Out-the-Vote Efforts

Candidates and their supporters have long invested in walking precincts, talking to voters, and noting which voters to remind to vote on election day, but it has been the state and local parties that have traditionally managed the get-out-the-vote responsibility.[45] As Paul Herrnson has observed, "Person-to-person contact is one of the oldest and most effective approaches to winning votes."[46] This activity, called a canvass, was also a staple of political parties. To an extent, telephone canvassing and direct mail now substitute for this kind of person-to-person contact. We found that voter canvasses were not only part of candidate and party strategy but were a major emphasis of interest-group election efforts in support of candidates as well. The single most important example is the U.S. Senate race between Harry Reid (D-incumbent) and John Ensign (R). Ninety full-time shop stewards went door-to-door visiting the homes of 40,000 labor union members.[47] These voters were reminded to vote on election day, and Labor '98, the overall mobilization effort's name, had sixteen vans running to and from the polls on election day.[48] Labor organizers found that 78 percent of union members in Nevada supported Harry Reid.

A second example of an interest group that conducted its own GOTV effort in a 1998 congressional race was Planned Parenthood, whose members worked to organize a campaign in support of Joe Hoeffel (D-challenger) and against Jon Fox (R-incumbent) in Pennsylvania's Thirteenth Congressional District. In July 1998, Planned Parenthood announced a $70,000 campaign to canvass ten thousand pro-choice women who would later be targeted via mail and phones and encouraged to support Hoeffel. Local observers of the race credited pro-choice and labor organizations for helping Hoeffel's campaign message through their ground-war efforts.[49] Planned Parenthood also mounted an extensive GOTV campaign in New Mexico in 1998, with direct mail followed by phone calls urging all women, regardless of party to vote for Udall.[50] Michelle Featheringill, president of Planned Parenthood of New Mexico, believed that her group's efforts in New Mexico paid off: "A concerted effort, with that targeted a group, has to have an impact—absolutely, without a doubt."[51]

An important part of the ground war in 1997–98 was communication between organizations like the National Rifle Association (NRA) or unions like the AFL-CIO and their members. When a corporation or labor organization spends over $2,000 on internal communications, expressly advocating the election or defeat of a candidate, these expenditures must be reported to the Federal Election Commission. In the 1997–98 election cycle, the AFL-CIO reported spending $2.8 million on internal communications, more than any other group. The NRA disclosed $642,749 in internal communications and another $1.7 million on independent expenditures. The other group which invested substantially in internal communications in 1997–98 was the National Association of Realtors which spent $614,754 on this activity.[52] As we have demonstrated, the disclosed activity by interest groups is often only part of a larger campaign effort, and much of that activity is undisclosed.

GOTV and other election day activities, such as ballot security programs, were a more important part of competitive races in 1998 than in most congressional contests where the outcome is known long before election day. To get the voters to the polls, candidates, parties, and their allied groups utilized the voter canvass as well as data from their phone banks and Internet operations to identify the voters they most wanted to vote. In some states, party poll watchers monitored lists of those who had not voted and sent runners to phone banks to encourage those voters to come to the polls. Collusion between allied interest groups and candidates has long been part of effective GOTV efforts,[53] and in some of our races there was evidence that the interest groups shared lists with each other.[54]

WHO WON THE GROUND WAR IN 1998?

In 1998, Democratic Party committees and their allies in the labor and environmental movements won the ground war. Since the early 1970s, Democrats have contacted a higher percentage of the electorate than Republicans,[55] and in 1998 President Clinton and First Lady Hillary Clinton "went to considerable efforts to stimulate Democratic Constituencies."[56] Voter turnout for the Democrats surged among African Americans in targeted states.[57] For example, in 1994 blacks were 19 percent of Georgia's voters. This year they were 29 percent of the vote. Black turnout also increased in North Carolina, South Carolina, and Illinois.[58]

The effort to mobilize African Americans stemmed from the National Coalition for Black Voter Participation, which was a coalition of nonprofits, including the Black Leadership Forum, the Black Leadership Roundtable, the Jennings Randolph Institute (affiliated with the AFL-CIO), People for the American Way, and People for a Fair Chance. The leader of this effort was Dr. Yvonne Scruggs of the Black Leadership Forum. Their focus was not on registration but rather on twenty-three states where—based on voter participation data for several elections—they felt they could have an impact by mobilizing African American voters. Building on the network already established by Operation Big Vote, which has been the "legs of every voter registration effort for twenty years" and which was "at the core of the Jessie Jackson campaign in 1984 and 1988, the 1998 mobilization "used traditional and tested means of activation."[59] These included personal contacts, providing transportation to the polls on election day, announcements in churches, phone banks for reinforcement, communication via the minority press, radio, and Black Entertainment Television (BET), as well as voter intimidation hotlines. Dr. Scruggs indicated that in her view, the media and churches were most important in 1998.

While the efforts of the National Coalition for Black Voter Participation were officially nonpartisan, the implications of higher African American turnout have clear partisan consequences. The Democrats understood this and also made increasing black turnout a priority. Former Democratic Congressional Campaign Committee (DCCC) Chair Martin Frost (Texas) and Cochair Charles Rangel (New York) worked closely with the Black Caucus in the House of Representatives to plan joint campaign efforts. Long-time observer David A. Bositis of the Joint Center for Political and Economic Studies saw Martin Frost and Charles Rangel as "most influential" to the Democratic Party effort to register and get African Americans to the polls in 1998.[60] DCCC Executive Director Matt Angle stated that the Democrats "recognized that in a low-turnout year, that even a small percentage of minority or base voters in a district could have a significant impact on the election." The DCCC then "targeted those districts where they had competitive candidates" and where activating 3 to 4 percent might make a difference.[61] According to the campaign issue director for the DCCC for 1997–98, John Williams, the African American vote in 1998 was "motivated in part for Clinton's defense and in part to vote against Gingrich and local Republicans."[62] Democrats targeted young blacks by running ads on hip-hop radio with themes like "Vote—It's a Power Thing," as well as radio segments voiced by celebrities and well-liked congressmen. This power message resonated well with young African American voters who not only planned on voting but also became very active in the voter mobilization efforts, driving buses to and from polls on election day.

African Americans were also targeted in South Carolina, where the Democratic Party spent between $1 million and $1.5 million in a statewide GOTV effort. State and national party committees collaborated on mass voter-registration drives, absentee ballot applications, curbside voting sites, phone banks, and door-to-door contacts. In South Carolina, African American turnout increased from 17 percent of the overall voter turnout in 1994 to 25 percent in 1998.[62]

Republicans also mounted a ground war in competitive races, but that effort was not as effective as the Democrats' ground war, being overshadowed by the attention given the $10 million spent on television ads by the NRCC on the Clinton/Lewinsky matter in the final two weeks before the election. Representative Bob Livingston, who was elected to succeed Speaker Newt Gingrich, summed up the view of many Republicans when he said, "Relying on TV was a major tactical mistake. We got beat on the ground."[64]

It would be a mistake to believe that Republicans did not mount a major ground-war effort of their own. The RNC reports that Republican committees produced more turnout mail and phone calls than Democratic committees, campaigns, and labor unions combined.[65] In competitive races the Republican ground war did not have the same convergence of theme and message as did the Democrats'. The outside money study's data reinforce the views of some Republican critics of the 1998 campaign that the GOP lacked a focused message-driven campaign. It is also clear that in a low-turnout election like 1998, the ability to target and mobilize specific segments of the electorate as was done by labor unions and African American groups could be very important, especially when groups like Christian conservatives were not being mobilized as effectively on the other side.[66]

Our findings on the ground war in 1998 demonstrate that the role of outside money in elections is just as important in the ground war as in the air war, and perhaps more important. Part of the success of the ground war was mobilizing people who were members of identified groups active in the campaign, but part of it was the ability to apply campaign technology of targeted lists and telephone and mail to reach the voters most likely to support the preferred candidate. These lessons have not been lost on candidates, parties, and interest groups.

We found several examples of an effective synergy between air and ground wars mounted by interest groups and political parties. In the Kentucky Senate race, for example, direct mail used the same image of Democratic candidate Baesler as was used in the air-war commercial labeled by the Kentucky media as the "Hitler commercial." The broadcast ads were paid for by the Bunning campaign, while the mail was paid for by the party. Interest groups like Americans for Limited Terms, labor unions, and environmental groups also had reinforcing air- and ground-war communications.

One other implication of these findings about the ground war in 1998 is that it was almost entirely missed by the news media reporting on the election. Their coverage, as noted, was limited to begin with, but reporting on this "hidden" campaign eluded them. In competitive races late communications via the phone and through the mail can be very important, and in the absence of good political reporting, voters are left to their own devices to sort through the negative and often extreme claims. As with outside money in elections generally, there is no one voters can hold accountable for these forms of communication.

NOTES

1. John E. Yang, "Dornan's Is Among a Handful of House Seats Still in Question," *Washington Post*, 8 November 1996, A20.

2. Part of the Republican Party spending was in response to a well-funded Democratic candidate.

3. Angus Campbell, Philip E. Converse, Warren E. Miller, and Donald E. Strokes, eds., *Elections and the Political Order* (New York: John Wiley & Sons, 1966), 40–62.

4. Gary W. Cox and Michael C. Munger, "Closeness, Expenditures, and Turnout in the 1982 U.S. House Elections," *American Political Science Review* 83 (March 1989): 217–31.

5. Robert A. Jackson, "Voter Mobilization in the 1986 Midterm Election," *Journal of Politics* 55, no. 4 (November 1993): 1083.

6. Robert A. Jackson, "The Mobilization of Congressional Electorate," *Legislative Studies Quarterly* 21, no. 3 (August 1996): 425–45.

7. Mark J. Rozell and Clyde Wilcox, *Interest Groups in American Campaigns: The New Face of Electioneering* (Washington, D.C.: Congressional Quarterly, 1999).

8. Paul Herrnson, *Congressional Elections: Campaigning at Home and in Washington*, 2nd ed. (Washington, D.C.: Congressional Quarterly, 1998), 116.

9. Darrell M. West and Burdett A. Loomis, *The Sound of Money: How Political Interests Get What They Want* (New York: W. W. Norton, 1998), 54.

10. Michael Young, *American Dictionary of Campaigns and Elections* (Lanham, Md.: Hamilton Press, 1987), 47.

11. Ann Beaudry and Bob Schaeffer, *Winning Local and State Elections: The Guide to Organizing Your Campaign* (New York: The Free Press, 1986), 101.

12. Herrnson, *Congressional Elections,* 189.

13. S. J. Guzzeta, *The Campaign Manual: A Definitive Study of the Modern Political Campaign Process* (Alexandria, Va.: Campaign Publishing, 1981), 43.

14. *Campaign Insights* 8, no. 5 (1 March 1976): 5.

15. See chapter 9.

16. Larry J. Sabato, *The Rise of Political Consultants: New Ways of Winning Elections* (New York: Basic Books, 1981), 223.

17. John Haskell, "Profile of Iowa's Third District," in *Outside Money: Soft Money & Issue Ads in Competitive 1998 Congressional Elections,* ed. David Magleby and Marianne Holt (report of a grant funded by the Pew Charitable Trusts, 1999), 93–102.

18. DeLysa Burnier, personal e-mail to David B. Magleby, 3 May 1999.

19. Russ Dondero, "Profile of the Oregon First Congressional District," in *Outside Money,* 155–64.

20. Ibid.

21. See chapter 5, 84.

22. Beaudry and Schaeffer, *Winning Local and State Elections,* 106.

23. Ibid., 106–07.

24. Jay Goodliffe, "Profile of Utah's Second Congressional District," in *Outside Money,* 180.

25. Lonna Atkeson and Anthony C. Convey, "Profile of New Mexico's Third Congressional District," in *Outside Money,* 140.

26. Young, *American Dictionary of Campaigns and Elections,* 32.

27. Doug Nilson, "Profile of Idaho's Second Congressional District," in *Outside Money,* 83–92.

28. Don Powell, "Telephones as Strategic Tools," in *Campaigns & Elections,* August 1997, 22.

29. See chapter 11, 199.

30. Powell, "Telephones as Strategic Tools," 22.

31. Steve Rosenthal, lunchtime discussion panel at the Pew Press Conference, "Outside Money: Soft Money & Issue Ads in 1998 Competitive Congressional Elections," National Press Club, Washington, D.C., 1 February 1999.

32. Powell, "Telephones as Strategic Tools," 19.

33. Mac Hansbrough, "Telephones as Strategic Tools," *Campaigns & Elections* (August 1997): 22–23.

34. Edward Schwartzman, *Campaign Craftsmanship: A Professor's Guide to Campaigning for Elective Office* (New York: Universe Books, 1973), 213.

35. Americans for Limited Terms calling script for all districts, received by Jay Goodliffe, academic investigator for Utah Second Congressional District, from Eric O'Keefe, president of Americans for Limited Terms.

36. Bob Bernick, "Survey Looks Like 'Push Poll' Aimed at Cook," *Deseret News,* 22 October 1998, B2.

37. Mark Emerson, interview by Ted Jelen and David B. Magleby, telephone, 24 June 1999.

38. Dennis Dresang, "Profile of Wisconsin's First Congressional District," in *Outside Money,* 188–89.

39. Ron Faucheux, "How Campaigns Are Using the Internet: An Exclusive Nationwide Survey," in *Campaigns & Elections*, September 1998, 22.

40. Kathryn Combs, "Grassroots Lobbying and the Internet Explosion: New Opportunities for Issue Campaigning," in *Campaigns & Elections*, February 1999, 26–29.

41. We wish to thank Flavius Chircui of Georgetown University for sharing data about web sites in the 1998 campaign.

42. Eric B. Herzik, personal e-mail to David B. Magleby, 1 May 1999.

43. Sean Rankin, interview by Lonna Atkeson, Santa Fe, New Mexico, 5 November 1998.

44. David Beiler, "The Body Politic Registers a Protest," in *Campaigns & Elections*, February 1999, 42.

45. Peter W. Wielhouwer and Brad Lockerbie, "Party Contacting and Political Participation, 1954–90," *American Journal of Political Science* 38, no. 1 (February 1994): 212.

46. Herrnson, *Congressional Elections*, 16.

47. Steve Rosenthal, Pew Press Conference.

48. Michael Bowers, Tim Fackler, Nathalie Frensley, Erik Herzik, Ted Jelen, and Todd Kunioka, "Profile of Nevada's Senate Race," in *Outside Money*, 42–52.

49. Robin Kolodny and Sandra Suarez, "Profile of Pennsylvania's Thirteenth Congressional District," in *Outside Money*, 165–74.

50. See chapter 8, 144.

51. Ibid.

52. The Center for Responsive Politics, *The Big Picture: The Money Behind the 1998 Elections* (Washington, D.C.: The Center for Responsive Politics, 1999), 5.

53. Beaudry and Schaeffer, *Winning Local and State Elections*, 105–06.

54. An example of this would be the New Mexico Third Congressional District.

55. Wielhouwer and Lockerbie, "Party Contacting," 214.

56. Paul R. Abramson, John H. Aldrich, and David W. Rhode, *Change and Continuity in the 1996 and 1998 Elections* (Washington, D.C.: Congressional Quarterly, 1999), 258.

57. Charles S. Bullock, III, "High Turnout in a Low Turnout Year: Georgia's Second Congressional District, 1998" (paper written for the American University Improving Campaign Conduct Study, 1998).

58. Steven Holmes, "The Nation: Why Both Parties Wooed Black Voters This Year," *New York Times*, 8 November 1998, A4.

59. Yvonne Scruggs, interview by David Magleby and Marianne Holt, telephone, 2 April 1999.

60. David A. Bositis, interview by David Magleby, Washington, D.C., 3 December 1998.

61. Matt Angle, lunchtime discussion panel at the Pew Press Conference, "Outside Money," National Press Club, Washington, D.C., 1 February 1999, 18.

62. John Williams, interview by Marianne Holt, Washington, D.C., 19 March 1999.

63. Bill Moore and Danielle Vinson, "Profile of South Carolina's Senate Race," in *Outside Money*, 63–70.

64. Ruth Marcus, "Outside Money Wasn't Everything," *Washington Post*, 5 November 1998, A39.

65. Vic Gresham, "Why Didn't Conservatives Turnout?" *Campaigns & Elections*, February 1999, 56.

66. Christian conservatives did effectively mobilize in some races, e.g., the Kentucky Sixth Congressional District race.

5

The 1998 Kansas Third Congressional District Race

Allan J. Cigler

On 5 November 1998, Democrat Dennis Moore defeated first-term Republican incumbent Vincent Snowbarger 52 percent to 48 percent in a closely watched congressional contest. The results were surprising to many observers because the Kansas Third District, located in eastern Kansas, west and southwest of Kansas City, Missouri, was considered a safe Republican district prior to 1998. The district had been Republican for thirty-eight years and represented the type of upper-income, suburban, professional, highly educated constituency that routinely supports Republicans.

District demographics reflect the lack of diversity that is usually associated with Republican dominance.[1] Republican voters outnumber Democrats 42 to 29 percent, with another 29 percent registered as independents. Two-thirds of district voters live in Johnson County, a wealthy suburban county where per capita income is over $35,000, compared to a statewide average of just over $23,000. Caucasians make up just over 86 percent of the district. The district's minority population, largely Hispanic and African American, is concentrated in Wyandotte County (Kansas City, Kansas), a working-class area with the highest poverty level in the state (20.8 percent, compared to a statewide average of 12.2 percent). It is the most Democratic area in the state. Republican-leaning Douglas County, home to Lawrence and the University of Kansas, sits at the western edge of the district. Rural Miami County, south of Johnson County, is strongly Republican.

Democrat Moore's congressional victory in 1998 was due to a variety of factors, among the most important being the role played by a mobilized Democratic Party and its liberal allies in activating supporters through the skillful use of televised issue ads and "ground-war" efforts of a magnitude never before seen on behalf of a Democratic candidate in the district. While the candidate campaigns raised and spent around $2 million on the race, a record for a congressional contest in Kansas, interest-group and party expenditures likely rivaled that of the candidates. Many of the party/interest-group expenditures did not come under the regulation and disclosure of current federal or state campaign finance law. And it was often difficult to distinguish the two campaigns' efforts from those of their party and interest-group allies.

Despite the overwhelming Republicanism of the Kansas Third District, divisiveness among Republicans over social issues has encouraged Democrats to contest seriously a number of district elections in recent years. Starting in 1992, Christian Right groups, led by the leading anti-abortion group in the state, Kansans for Life, attempted to gain control of the Johnson County Republican Party organization by a concerted low-profile, grassroots effort.[2] The anti-abortion groups, in conjunction with a growing number of evangelical churches, developed slates of candidates and worked to turn out social conservatives at the precinct caucuses, overwhelming moderate elements, who were unorganized.[3] By 1994 the Christian Right was firmly in control of the Johnson County Republican organization, selecting a pro-life advocate as the party chair, much to the dismay of pro-choice Republicans.

In 1996, the state House majority leader, Vincent Snowbarger, won a bitter Republican primary in the district over an opponent supported by moderates and endorsed by popular U.S. Senator Nancy Kassenbaum, defeating Overland Park Mayor Ed Eilert by 4 percent of the vote (Snowbarger received 44 percent). Snowbarger then defeated a well-funded Democratic challenger, Judy Hancock, in the general election by a mere 4 percent of the vote. In the 1995–96 election cycle, Snowbarger raised less than $500,000 and was outspent by almost $400,000. Despite the financial disadvantage, as well as the lack of support in the district's press, Snowbarger won because of a concerted grassroots effort by the Christian Right, which saturated the district with Snowbarger literature and orchestrated a massive targeted get-out-the-vote (GOTV) effort. Snowbarger himself was a Christian Right adherent and a member of the Nazarene Church.[4]

THE CANDIDATES AND THEIR CAMPAIGNS

The nature of the 1998 race between incumbent Snowbarger and challenger Moore was greatly influenced by the Republican intraparty squabble. In 1998 Snowbarger faced the task of trying to unite a party deeply divided over social issues, while he was strongly linked to Christian Right elements. Not only were moderates uneasy with what they viewed as the congressman's extreme views on issues like abortion and school prayer, but the incumbent's Christian Right base was unhappy as well.

In the spring of 1998 the popular pro-choice Republican governor, Bill Graves, was challenged in his party's primary by the leading figure in the pro-life movement in the state, the sitting Republican state chairperson, David Miller.[5] According to those close to the Snowbarger campaign, the congressman was told by Christian Right leaders in the Third District that it was expected that he endorse and campaign for Miller.[6] Viewing the Miller challenge as having little chance of success, and not wanting to antagonize further moderate elements by associating himself with the confrontational style and extreme views of Miller, Snowbarger remained uninvolved in the gubernatorial primary. After Miller's defeat in August (the challenger received only 28 percent of the vote), angry Christian Right leaders told Snowbarger not to expect much help in his reelection efforts.[7] Further compounding the problem, the Miller challenge also enabled the moderates to successfully recapture the party organization in Johnson County. Snowbarger was now isolated from both party factions. As he noted after the election, "I got hit by the revenge factor from both ends of the party."[8]

Snowbarger's vulnerability had been recognized by Democrats and liberal interest groups earlier. Unlike most incumbents, Snowbarger was not skilled at fund-raising and was on record as saying he simply hated to ask people for money. Indeed, he and his staff did no fund-raising for his first six months in office, and he started 1998 with the smallest campaign war chest of all first-term incumbents. Moore probably would not have entered the race if Snowbarger's war chest had been larger at the start of the year (FEC reports show that Snowbarger only had $67,757 on hand on the last day of 1997; Moore already had $68,837 on hand).

Moore was the best-known challenger Democrats had put forward in years. Three times he had been elected Johnson County district attorney, and he had barely lost a state attorney general race in 1986. Subsequently, he had twice been elected to the board of Johnson County Community College, a prestigious position in a county that was highly supportive of public education. In recent years he had become a highly visible criminal attorney, participating in a number of cases that garnered much media coverage.

Moore's decision to enter the race was made easier by the promise of substantial party and interest-group help. The national Democratic Party targeted the district, and Snowbarger was on the hit list of such important groups as the AFL-CIO and the Sierra Club, both of which committed in the fall of 1997 to helping a Democrat capture the seat. Moore understood that he would be the number one priority for Democrats in Kansas in 1998. The three other congressional districts were clearly noncompetitive, as was the Senate seat held by Sam Brownback and the governorship held by incumbent Bill Graves.

The race between Moore and Snowbarger began early, with both candidates making comments about each other well before the August primary. The Snowbarger campaign, for inexplicable reasons (other than perhaps to see if negative ads diminished Moore's support), became involved in a noncompetitive Democratic primary by sending three separate mass mailings to registered Democrats and independents in the district prior to August (at an estimated cost of around $50,000). The postcard flyers suggested that Moore "makes a living defending murderers, rapists, drug dealers and child molesters," "lobbied to dump out-of-state trash in Kansas," and "wants to deny seniors the right to choose their own doctor." The mailings backfired, as the press condemned the negative material. Clearly, Snowbarger was worried about his likely Democratic opponent.

The rival campaign organizations, their strategies, and financial bases could not have been more different. The Snowbarger organization had a distinctly local flavor, almost an amateur quality to it. The campaign director, Snowbarger's own Washington chief of staff, Kevin Yowell, was heavily volunteer dependent, and was reported to be distrustful of out-of-the-district help. While spending an estimated two-thirds of its campaign budget on campaign advertising, the Snowbarger campaign relied on early (starting in mid-October) spots on talk radio stations and a concentrated effort on television during the final week and a half. Snowbarger projected a weak television presence and was not found in his own commercials; the incumbent once remarked, "I've got a face made for radio."[9] The campaign conducted minimal polling and neglected GOTV efforts.

The Moore operation, in contrast, was the epitome of the professionally run, out-of-state, consultant-dominated campaign.[10] Extensive polling was conducted, focus groups were used to test and design campaign advertisements, and efforts were made to mold attitudes, keep the opponent off balance, and to dictate the issue agenda. While roughly two-thirds of the campaign budget focused on television advertising, Moore operatives saved some resources until the very end for a massive GOTV effort coordinated with the party and directed at areas with a high concentration of known Democrats, large numbers of independents, and potential Republican defectors.

Moore was quite effective personally in his television commercials. One of the campaign's most successful ads, entitled "Guitar Lessons," showed Moore strumming a guitar and singing a melody of country, rock, blues, and bluegrass ditties. His rendition of a country tune was immediately followed by "My patient's bill of rights will make you kick up your heels." Turning then to rock mode, he sang, "We need to make Social Security solid as a rock." Next came a blues rendition, stressing "That's what you'll feel with Vincent Snowbarger's votes on education." Finally, in bluegrass style, he ended with "I hope you'll be pickin' Dennis Moore for Congress. Thank you." The ad was judged by the American Association of Political Consultants as the best congressional TV spot of thirty seconds or less in the 1997–98 election cycle.[11]

Strategically, both campaigns had a negative focus along the lines of national Republican/Democrat stereotypes. The Snowbarger camp was anxious to paint Moore as an economic and social liberal, out of touch with a conservative district. The Clinton scandal had little impact, despite Snowbarger's attempt to make it an issue in September, when he called for the president to resign. He soon dropped the issue when it did not resonate with either the press or the public. Social issues such as abortion were little discussed in order not to further anger Republican moderates. The fundamental thrust of Snowbarger's campaign was to link Moore's criminal law practice to the challenger's being soft on crime and to assert that Moore would be traditional, big-government liberal, eroding local control over such things as education. Connecting organized labor to the Moore campaign was also a prominent Snowbarger theme in the heavily pro-business Third District (Kansas is a Right-to-Work state). Snowbarger attempted to paint himself as anything but an extremist, parading out Governor Graves and ex-Senators Dole and Kassebaum to endorse him as a moderate, in ads paid for by the Snowbarger campaign.

The Moore effort focused on issues such as Social Security, health care, education, and public safety, attempting to portray Snowbarger as an extreme ideologue with an antigovernment bias. Moore television ads and direct mail flyers chastised Snowbarger for wanting to end "Social Security as we know it," wanting to limit health care choice for senior citizens and children, holding positions against special-education funding, and advocating the right of citizens to carry concealed weapons. Moore, who is pro-choice, also avoided talk about abortion; he did not want to activate the Christian Right, which had been so influential in the prior Snowbarger victory.

The candidate organizations raised and spent similar amounts. According to FEC data, the challenger raised $1,010,145 and spent $986,688 in the 1997–98 election cycle, while the Snowbarger campaign raised $1,008,912 and spent $1,003,113 (see fig. 5.1). The sources of campaign funds roughly paralleled national Republican/Democratic patterns. PACs contributed $346,683 to the Moore effort, almost two-thirds ($229,750) coming from organized labor, especially the AFL-CIO and affiliated unions. The other two-thirds of Moore's money came from individual contributions, especially Moore's friends within the trial lawyer community. As might be expected of an incumbent, Snowbarger received well over half of his funds ($537,113) from PACs, concentrated among leadership PACs and business interests generally, particularly PACs concentrated in the real estate, general contractor, and financial sectors. The various national party committees contributed maximum or close to maximum amounts to the respective campaigns.

THE POLITICAL PARTY BATTLE

The political parties were very active in this election, perhaps more crucial to the final outcome than any of the interest groups involved. The parties differed significantly as to tactics and the extent of their efforts. The advantage went to the Democrats.

Democratic Ground Wars

Although the national Democratic Party sent a number of flyers to registered Democrats in the district and contributed the maximum allowed by law to

Figure 5.1   Kansas Third Congressional District Candidate Financial Activity in the 1998 Election Cycle

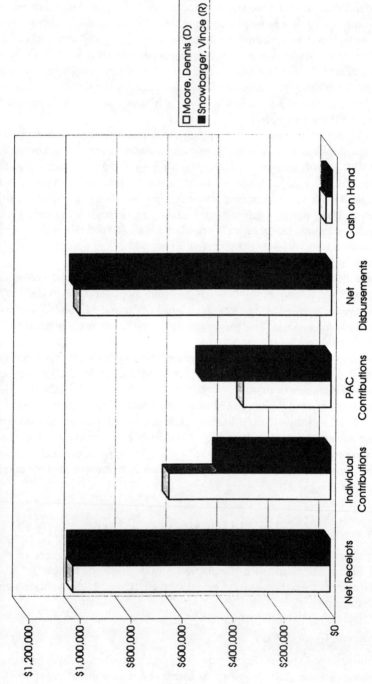

Source: Data from FEC press release, *FEC Reports on Congressional Fundraising for 1997–98,* 28 April 1999.

Moore's campaign coffers, the various national party organizations were not active on Moore's behalf on radio or television. The state party's efforts, however, were crucial to Moore's victory, using as a conduit the Kansas Coordinated Campaign (KCC), a quasi-independent political organization set up as a virtual arm of the Kansas Democratic Party (KDP).[12] The KCC relied upon both hard money and soft money to support multiple candidate efforts statewide, the bulk of the resources coming from contributions to the state party rather than through transfers from the national party.[13]

The KCC was a statewide operation with a full-time staff of ten, employing a variety of campaign service vendors (e.g., direct mail and telemarketing firms) and operating with an estimated budget of over $400,000. It was designed to provide services to a number of campaigns in the state, from polling services to field organizers to voter identification and get-out-the-vote efforts. The organization, which was partially funded by the various campaigns themselves, was designed to pool resources to avoid duplication, especially on ground-war efforts, freeing the individual campaigns to concentrate their resources upon their own media efforts.

During the campaign the KCC was overseen by the executive director of the KDP, Brett Cott, who used the Topeka party headquarters as the base of operation to save on overhead. The KDP's field director also served as the KCC field director, and four of the nine field organizers lived and worked in the Third District, starting immediately after the August primary. Since none of the other congressional races or statewide campaigns were considered competitive, the KCC used most of its resources in the efforts to unseat Snowbarger, virtually acting as an extension of the Moore campaign organization. During the first two months of the general election campaign, the KCC was active in the district, recruiting volunteers for Moore's campaign as well as identifying voters who might wish to "advance" vote.[14]

It was the sophisticated targeting efforts of the KCC, combining information from National Committee for an Effective Congress (NCEC) reports with that of the Voter Tracker 2.0 file, that were probably most helpful to the Moore campaign. The NCEC prepares precinct-by-precinct reports that reflect past election patterns, enabling report users to identify areas of partisan strength and weakness as well as precincts where voters have a tendency to split tickets. Such precinct level data provided the initial basis for GOTV efforts.

The other tool used in targeting was a recently developed Voter Tracker 2.0 file. Outside consultants were hired by KCC to construct a voter file using information from the secretary of state's office, which was then enhanced with phone and household matching in a manner such that no household received more than one piece of mail, freeing the campaigns from conducting their own mass canvasses or blanket mailings. As the KCC field director, Chris Gallaway, noted, "The voter file takes a lot of the guesswork out of campaigns. We're no longer delivering our message to voters based just on where they live, but on things like age, sex, party affiliation and voter history. The old days of going into a precinct because six out of ten are Democrats and knocking on every door because you still come out ahead are over. Now, we just go talk to those Democrats."[15]

For the Moore campaign, which felt it had to have a strong turnout among Democrats as well as defections from Republicans, targeting information was crucial. Older voters throughout the district, for example, were sent campaign material focusing on Social Security and health care, while women of child-raising age were sent material focusing upon Snowbarger's support for concealed weapons and his opposition to state-funded health care measures for pregnant women. Material dealing with Snowbarger's anti-choice position on abortion was sent to pro-choice Republican women.

Because of the partisan complexion of the district, special attention was paid to identifying and then cultivating likely Republican defectors. Using paid phone vendors, the KCC identified 31,576 "wedge" voters, who, while Republican or independent, were against concealed weapons and pro-choice on abortion. Up to three pieces of mail were sent to these voters during the last three weeks of the campaign, reminding them of Snowbarger's positions on such issues. An even more specialized group, made up of 3,640 pro-choice voters who had said they were "undecided" during phone interviews in early October, received the same piece of mail three times during the last two weeks of the campaign, emphasizing Snowbarger's issue stances.

Generic GOTV efforts orchestrated by the KCC were crucial as well. Nearly 53,000 district households received two different pieces of GOTV mail reminding them to go to the polls and vote Democrat during the final week of the campaign. In Kansas elections there are usually no poll watchers present. In 1998, Democratic poll watchers (but not Republicans) could be found in many precincts throughout the district, recording the names of Democrats who had yet to vote by 3:00 P.M. Poll watchers would then go home to call those partisan and likely Moore supporters who had yet to cast their ballots. In Douglas County party volunteers made over 6,000 calls on election day, some only forty-five minutes before the polls closed.

Overall, the ground-war efforts engineered by the KCC complemented the Moore campaign strategy. Indeed, Moore's campaign manager, Chris Esposito, regularly went to Topeka throughout the campaign to raise money for the party, which was later channeled to the KCC.[16] According to Esposito, the KCC

allowed the Moore campaign to spend a maximum amount on television. The KCC's money spent on phones, advance ballots, and mail saved the Moore campaign thousands of dollars. In retrospect, Snowbarger would have beat [*sic*] Moore without paid field organizers to execute the KCC field plan. However, the KCC provides campaigns with the ability to save and spend more money. For example, Moore raised and spent $1,000,000 and the KCC raised and spent $400,000 on campaign activities. Without the KCC, Moore does not benefit from an additional $400,000.[17]

Republican Air Wars

Republican Party efforts on behalf of Snowbarger were entirely different. The state and local party apparatus, due to internal conflicts within the party, played virtually no role. The state party, for example, raised less than $123,000, the majority from out of state, from late July until election day.[18] The state party organization was still controlled by Christian Right elements (the executive director of the state party during the general election had been Miller's campaign manager during the primary). Republican moderates were encouraged to give their funds directly to individual candidate organizations.

At the local level, some Republican moderates worked to elect Republican Graves and Democrat Moore. Four recently elected precinct chairpersons endorsed Moore; their names were prominently displayed in the challenger's newspaper advertisements.[19] There was no Republican equivalent to the KCC and little in the way of party-sponsored ground-war efforts or door-to-door activity. "We could never get a lit drop [literature distribution] off the ground," noted Kevin Yowell, Snowbarger's campaign manager, after the election.[20]

On the other hand, the national Republican Party organizations, especially the Republican National Committee (RNC), sensing the difficulty Snowbarger was facing, came to the incumbent's aid during the last month of the campaign with a series of hard-hitting ads.[21] The RNC's initial commercials began to be aired on October 3, before any of the Snowbarger campaign television ads were shown. The ads claimed that Moore was "soft on crime" because of his opposition to "truth in sentencing laws" and reinforced a major theme of the Snowbarger campaign. The reason for Moore's opposition, suggested the ad, was the challenger's "career of defending violent criminals." Moore's campaign manager attempted to get area television stations to pull the ads, which he claimed distorted the candidate's position. The ads continued to air.

During the last weekend of the campaign the RNC spent over a quarter of a million dollars in a negative TV blitz attempting to link Moore to Kennedy liberals and labor money as well as continuing the soft-on-crime theme. Overall, the RNC spent over $439,414 on the Third District race, airing 532 ads in five weeks on four Kansas City, Missouri, television stations. The RNC also sent out two flyers to registered voters in the district. The first dealt with Social Security, claiming that the party in Congress "has balanced the budget and set aside $1.4 trillion to preserve Social Security," while Democrats have "not a penny set aside to preserve Social Security." The second, entitled "Stop the Revolving Prison Door," continued the assault on Moore for being "soft on crime." In neither ad was Representative Snowbarger mentioned.

The National Republican Congressional Committee (NRCC) did no advertising on local television but did underwrite a number of mass mailings in the district. The most hard-hitting, which registered voters received the last week of the campaign, was entitled "Kids don't get rewarded for bad behavior." The ad urged voters to vote Republican in order not to "reward Bill Clinton" on November third. Again there was no mention of Snowbarger in the ad.

Interest-Group Influences

The relative lack of competitive races in 1998, coupled with the perceived vulnerability of incumbent Snowbarger, made the Moore/Snowbarger race a hotbed of interest-group activity, especially for groups of the political left. Most activity was in the form of issue ads or independent expenditures, but ground-war activity by liberal groups was also present.

By far the most consistently active interest throughout the campaign was organized labor. AFL-CIO ads against Snowbarger, depicting Republicans as seeking to undermine Social Security and health care by their proposed tax cuts, started to appear in late September, even before the commercials of the two campaigns (124 ads were run, starting on September 23). Such ads set the campaign agenda in a manner quite compatible with the Moore campaign strategy. Indeed, the AFL-CIO ads, while "officially" not coordinated with the Moore campaign, seemed almost to be lead-ins to the Moore commercials in early October. For example, one union ad invited viewers to call Snowbarger and protest the Republican stance on Social Security and health care; approximately fifteen minutes later a Moore commercial aired about Moore's support for Social Security and health care choice.

The most encompassing union efforts were less visible. Especially impressive were the activities of the labor-sponsored '98 Project, a coordinated, grassroots presence directed toward mobilizing liberal support in the district.[22] The organization, which had at least two paid operatives in the district since early in 1998, was a registered 501(c)(4) tax-exempt organization based in D.C. It operated on what it called "soft-money" contributions, and hence was prohibited from engaging in overtly partisan political activities such as fund-raising and attending party or candidate-strategy or organizational planning meetings. But there is a vague line between partisan and nonpartisan.

The group, keeping a low profile and disguising its labor connections in a strongly pro-business district, was influential in activating a number of progressive interests to become involved in the election. Besides flyers sent by the '98 Project itself, a series of mass mailings by groups such as the National Council of Senior Citizens was orchestrated by the "project coordinators." The mailings were careful not to endorse Moore or to say vote against Snowbarger, instead urging flyer recipients to voice their concerns about Social Security, the environment, or about the incumbent's vote against funding required to maintain food programs for pregnant women and children in need. Targeting efforts were quite sophisticated (the flyer dealing with food programs for women and children went only to women in the 25-to-45 age category). In stealthlike fashion, '98 Project operatives were often behind the scenes recruiting individuals to write letters to the editor or to attend town meetings with Representative Snowbarger. Needless to say, the communications painted the congressman in an unfavorable light.

Other union activity was more visible. The state AFL-CIO, based in Topeka, was responsible for a number of mass mailings. The last weekend of the campaign, labor unions in Kansas City, Kansas, underwrote a massive GOTV effort, involving both in-person contact and phone banks. The effort appeared to work, especially in traditionally low-turnout Wyandotte County.[23]

Other pro-Democrat interest groups played a more minor role. The Sierra Club underwrote some television and radio advertisements and sent an expensive mass mailing to a targeted group of registered voters in the district. During the last week of the campaign the Sierra Club also placed phone calls in the district. In early October the group said it planned to commit $65,000 in the effort against Snowbarger.[24] After the election, it claimed to have spent $100,000. Because much of their expenditures need not be reported, groups may tend to exaggerate their expenditures if their candidate is successful.

The League of Conservation Voters also was active in the race, with Robert Redford speaking for the group in a radio commercial, saying the group was endorsing Moore. The advertisement was paid for by the Moore campaign.

Other groups made efforts on behalf of Moore, but they palled compared to labor efforts. Organizations like the Kansas National Education Association (KNEA), Handgun Control (Sara Brady came to town for a Moore fund-raiser), a local anti-Christian Right group—the Mainstream Coalition—supported by many moderate Republicans, and various antidiscrimination groups such as the Human Rights Campaign did send flyers or voters' guides primarily to their members.

On the Republican side, there was less interest-group activity. Christian Right activists, still angry with Snowbarger's refusal to back David Miller in the gubernatorial primary, did not engage in the grassroots efforts that were so instrumental in Snowbarger's 1996 triumph. Members of conservative churches reported receiving one Christian Coalition voter's guide dealing with a multitude of races, including the Moore/Snowbarger contest. In parts of the district a local socially conservative group called Citizen United Political Victory Fund left anti-Moore flyers in doors the weekend before the election. The Eagle Forum did a mailing in the district, but it appears to have been limited to a narrow core of registered voters. Charlton Heston, movie actor and president of the National Rifle Association (NRA), appeared at a fund-raiser for Snowbarger, but the group did not get involved in the campaign as it had in 1996.

Snowbarger did get help from a number of pro-business/anti-labor organizations. *National Journal* rated Snowbarger the sixth most conservative member of

Congress during his first term, a fact widely circulated among business groups by Snowbarger fund-raisers. Perhaps most helpful to his cause were television ads sponsored by the Business Roundtable. The ads were apparently aimed at countering the negative, anti-Snowbarger AFL-CIO ads that had started running in late September. The business group ran 126 ads, costing $96,607, starting on October 6. The ads were among the very few positive ads aired by any interest groups in the race, proclaiming that Snowbarger was a strong friend of education and children. A few flyers from pro–right-to-work groups, such as Candidate Survey '98, appeared as well. The Associated Builders and Contractors, Control for Free Enterprise, and the Business Council ran a number of radio ads during the last three weeks of the campaign, accusing Moore of being a captive of organized labor and hostile to business interests.

Perhaps the most bizarre incident in the campaign occurred in early October, when a secretive, hastily organized group called Citizens' Committee for a Clean America ran radio, television, and newspaper ads clearly designed to discourage the involvement of another interest group in the race. The ads, entitled "Let's Play 'Follow the Dirty Money'," claimed that Koch Industries, a Wichita-based oil company, made its money from polluting the environment and was the financial force behind Triad Management Services.[25]

Triad, a political consulting firm, was responsible for aiding Snowbarger's 1996 efforts by spending $287,000 in negative television and radio ads against the congressman's opponent in the four days prior to the election. The ads were widely criticized by the local press because no one could determine whose interests were represented by the group and because Snowbarger's opponent had no time to respond. Though Triad listed the Moore/Snowbarger race as one of the twenty-four "most-competitive" races in 1998, the group was not active in this year's race.[26]

Overall, the ads by interest groups in the race reinforced the desired campaign themes of the candidates they supported. The targeted direct mail flyers were particularly impressive. The early ads by labor, especially those dealing with Social Security, put Snowbarger on the defensive from the beginning of the television campaign, forcing his media specialists to design ads denying that he wanted to kill the revered entitlement program and preventing him from getting out a more positive message.

CONCLUSION

A variety of factors converged in the 1998 Kansas Third District race that enabled a Democrat to win the seat for the first time since the late 1930s. Despite the Republican partisan advantage, Snowbarger was clearly hurt by the split in the Republican Party, the lack of a positive message, the lack of attention paid to fund-raising early on, and his willingness to let his opponent set the issue agenda.

But in the close contest, the key to the outcome was that the Democrats did a far better job than did Republicans of activating their core supporters and attracting independents and defections from the opposing party through the coordinated efforts of the Moore campaign, the state party, and Democratic-allied interest groups. While the Republican governor Bill Graves received 75 percent of the vote in the November election, Snowbarger's 48 percent suggested that Democratic turnout and Republican defections and independents were crucial components of Moore's victory.

This case study clearly shows that interest-group activity outside the confines of FEC regulations can affect campaigns, be it through air waves or ground wars. Most bothersome is that voters associate such activity with the campaigns themselves, paying little attention to the source. Almost all outside group advertisements on radio, television, or through direct mail in this race were negative.

Particularly for Moore, the interest-group ads closely resembled the themes desired by the official campaign, reinforcing rather than setting a separate campaign agenda, saving the candidate a great deal of time and money in the process. Neither candidate spent much time disassociating himself from the ads by interests or parties on their behalf.

Overall, the major interest group influence in this race was through mass mailings and GOTV efforts, rather than through the electronic media. Some observers believe that Moore "owes labor" for his victory, a factor that could cause him problems should he vote with labor on such issues as "fast track"[27] in this pro-business district.[28] Besides the role of organized labor, the big interest-group story in this race was the fact that the Christian Right was demobilized, robbing Snowbarger of the grassroots effort he sorely needed in a close contest.

The role of the parties may have been even more crucial than that of the interest groups. Both Republicans and Democrats continue to learn how to exploit their role as service vendors to candidates through expansive interpretations of vague terms, like *soft money* and *coordinated*, found in the campaign finance laws at both the national and state level. Even tax-exempt groups, like '98 Project, can become virtual arms of a candidate's campaign. State Democratic efforts through the vehicle of the Kansas Coordinated Campaign provided the Moore campaign with the GOTV resources and the freedom to concentrate on the television campaign. And while RNC television ads may have appeared too late to do Snowbarger much good, the shear magnitude of the national party effort was impressive.

NOTES

1. Thelma Helyar, ed., *Kansas Statistical Abstract 1997* (Lawrence, Kans.: Institute for Public Policy and Business Research, 1998).

2. Allan J. Cigler and Burdett A. Loomis, "Kansas: The Christian Right and the New

Mainstream of Republican Politics, in *God at the Grassroots*, ed. Mark J. Rozell and Clyde Wilcox (Lanham, Md.: Rowman & Littlefield, 1995), 202–22.

3. The growth of evangelical churches and Christian Right political activity is most evident in southern Johnson County. See Peter Beinhart, "Battle for the 'Burbs,' " *New Republic* 18 (October 1998): 25–29.

4. Cigler and Loomis, "Kansas" 216–17.

5. Cigler and Loomis, "After the Flood: The Kansas Christian Right in Retreat," in *Prayers in the Precincts: The Christian Right in the 1998 Elections* (Washington, D.C.: Georgetown University Press, forthcoming spring 2000).

6. Tim Carpenter, "Snowbarger Takes Blame for Loss," *Lawrence Journal World,* 18 November 1998, A1.

7. Ibid.

8. Ibid. There were probably reasons beyond the decision not to endorse Miller that contributed to the Christian Right's disillusionment with Snowbarger. Some in the movement had expected Snowbarger to be the "point man" on social issues in Congress and were disappointed in a number of his votes. According to Kevin Yowell, Snowbarger's campaign manager and chief of staff, Snowbarger's support for extending most-favored-nation (MFN) trading status to China was troubling to some in the Christian Right, given China's abortion policies. Yowell, interview by author, telephone, 4 June 1999.

9. Steve Kraske and Scott Canon, "Seeds of Bitterness Sown in 3rd District Long Before Election Harvest," *Kansas City Star,* 5 October 1998, A1.

10. For an in-depth analysis of decision making in the Moore campaign, see Burdett Loomis, "Kansas 3rd District: The 'Pros from Dover' Set Up Shop," prepared for "Money, Media and Madness: Inside the 1998 Elections" conference, sponsored by the Center for Congressional and Presidential Studies, American University, 4 December 1998.

11. Tim Carpenter, "Moore Ad Wins Honor," *Lawrence Journal World,* 22 January 1999, 3B.

12. Material on the activities of the KCC was gathered in a variety of ways, including interviews conducted via e-mail with various party and campaign officials after the election. Some of these individuals are directly quoted in this chapter. Jack Martin assisted with the interviews. Some of the specific data come from the December 1998 *Demogram,* the communication organ of the Kansas Democratic Party <http://www.ksdp.org>.

13. It appears that most of the party money used in 1998 came from hard-money sources. Fully 29 percent ($120,000 out of the $419,000 raised) came from one individual, Bill Koch, who had his eight West Palm Beach, Florida, corporations contribute the maximum amount under state law, $15,000 each to the Democratic Party, during the general election campaign. See John Hanna, "Demos: A Koch and a Smile," *Topeka Capital-Journal,* 2 November 1998, B1. Only about $70,000 in combined DNC/DCCC federal transfers of funds was given to Kansas state/local party committees in the 1998 election cycle. In 1996 the Kansas Democratic Party was accused of irregularities in the use of soft money transferred from the national party office (some state legislative candidates who received national money were told to contribute a portion to the state party, a technical violation of the law). This year, according to at least one party official, in order to avoid even the appearance of irregularity, the party wanted to go the hard-money route.

14. Kansas now has a procedure, separate from absentee voting, where individuals may elect to cast their ballots prior to an election. The KCC sent applications for an advanced

voting ballot to those Democrats identified as unlikely to turn out to vote but likely to vote Democratic if they voted (based on their participation in the past two primary and general elections). A week or two later a phone call was made asking whether or not an advanced voting application for a ballot had been received. Nearly 42,000 advanced voting applications were sent to voters in the Third Congressional District. The list of these voters was constructed using the targeting methods described later in this chapter.

15. Chris Gallaway, personal e-mail to author, 7 December 1998.

16. At least some of the money raised for the party came from contributions both by groups and individuals who had already contributed the maximum amount to the Moore campaign. Several unions were on both lists, as were individuals such as Bill Koch.

17. Chris Esposito, interview by author, e-mail, 7 December 1998.

18. Hanna, B1.

19. John Altevogt, "Responsibility Requires Loyalty," *Kansas City Star*, 2 December 1998, B6.

20. Jim Sullinger, "Snowbarger Reflects on Loss at Polls," *Kansas City Star*, 11 November 1998, B1.

21. Throughout the campaign, Snowbarger's campaign manager was in daily contact with the NRCC, but had few dealings with the RNC, and was surprised to see that the RNC was the sponsor of campaign commercials on the candidate's behalf. He speculated that the NRC and the NRCC were cooperating on targeting competitive districts, and RNC funds were used for the ads for "accounting reasons." Yowell, interview.

22. Sponsoring organizations of the '98 Project include unions, such as the AFL-CIO, the American Postal Workers Union, the International Brotherhood of Teamsters, as well as groups such as Clean Water Action and the National Council of Senior Citizens. According to the group's brochures, its purpose is to "expand the visibility, credibility and voice of the local progressive community" by "working with local activists to build relationships among groups and individuals who share common goals." '98 Project operatives were involved in fifteen House and Senate races in 1998.

23. Nearly 43 percent of registered voters in Wyandotte County, a traditionally low-turnout area, participated in the election, the highest percentage in an off-year election in the past two decades.

24. Jim Sullinger, "Sierra Club to Campaign Against Vince Snowbarger," *Kansas City Star*, 10 October 1998, C3.

25. Citizens' Committee for a Clean America, a nonprofit corporation under California law, was incorporated just days before it ran the anti-Koch Industries ads. Most observers believe it was created and funded by Bill Koch, disaffected brother of Koch Industries owners Charles and David Koch, in order to embarrass the brothers, who he believes cheated him out of the family fortune. Triad Corporation is reputedly funded by Koch Industries. See Lori Lessner, Tom Webb, and Bill Bartel, "Anti-Koch Ads Shrouded in Mystery," *Wichita Eagle*, 25 October 1998, A1.

26. Snowbarger himself was not anxious for Triad to enter the race. In mid-July the incumbent wrote a letter to Triad (with copies to the Moore campaign and the district's newspapers) asking it to refrain from participating, arguing that, while he appreciated the group's help in 1996, he was uneasy with independent advertising. He indicated that it was difficult for voters to distinguish between a candidate's ads and those sponsored by independent organizations. He recalled that in 1996 during the final weeks of the cam-

paign, of the seven radio ads run on his behalf only two came from the campaign itself, confusing voters as to the source.

Not only were voters confused by the source of the Triad-sponsored ads in 1996, so was the Snowbarger campaign itself. According to Kevin Yowell, Snowbarger's 1996 and 1998 campaign manager, at one point during the 1996 campaign Snowbarger operatives found one of Triad's ads "too negative and offensive," having the potential to hurt Snowbarger. An attempt was made to contact Triad to get the ad pulled from TV, but the group could not be located and the ad continued to run, much to Snowbarger's dismay. Yowell, interview.

27. Fast track is the ability of the president to negotiate trade bills that Congress cannot amend but may only pass or fail.

28. Steve Kraske, "Dennis, This Victory Has a Price," *Kansas City Star*, 8 November 1998, B2.

6

The 1998 South Carolina Senate Race

Bill Moore and Danielle Vinson

The 1998 South Carolina Senate race between incumbent Ernest F. Hollings (D) and Bob Inglis (R) proved to be fertile ground for studying the strategies and effects of outside spending by parties and interest groups in campaigns. The state is also undergoing rapid change as retirees and new industries enter the state. An estimated 140,000 people migrate to South Carolina each year, primarily from the Northeast and Midwest. Poverty is still commonplace, with 19.9 percent of the state's population living below the poverty line. A disproportionate percentage of those living in poverty are African Americans, who in 1994, constituted approximately 30 percent of the state's population and 25 percent of the state's registered voters. African Americans are strongly Democratic, but their turnout rate has traditionally been below their white counterparts.

During the 1990s, South Carolina became more Republican. In 1992, Republican presidential candidate George Bush received 60 percent of the white vote and 48 percent of the total vote, compared to 39.9 percent for Bill Clinton. This was the second highest percentage of the vote received by Bush in the fifty states. In the same election Democratic Senator Ernest Hollings barely survived a challenge by Republican Tommy Hartnett. Hartnett, who had been out of politics since an unsuccessful race for lieutenant governor in 1986, held Hollings to 50 percent of the vote.[1]

South Carolina's shift to the Republican Party received another boost in 1994, when Republican State Representative David Beasley narrowly defeated Democratic Lieutenant Governor Nick Theodore in the governor's race. This marked the third consecutive Republican gubernatorial victory in the state. In 1994, the Republicans also won six of the other seven statewide constitutional offices. In 1996, Bob Dole carried South Carolina with 51.3 percent of the vote to 45.1 percent for Bill Clinton. An exit poll revealed that a majority of the state's voters identified themselves as Republican, reinforcing the perception that South Carolina was becoming the deep South's most Republican state.[2] Going into the 1998 election, Ernest Hollings, the senior southern Democrat in the United States Senate, was considered vulnerable because of his narrow reelection in 1992 and the increased Republicanism in South Carolina.

But the 1998 election was also about more local concerns and a competitive governor's race. Despite the state's booming economy, Republican Governor David Beasley had alienated many voters in the state because of his ties to the Christian Right and his opposition to a state lottery. In addition, during his reelection bid, Beasley targeted South Carolina's electronic gaming industry for extinction. This decision ended up impacting significantly not only the governor's race but the U.S. Senate race as well.

THE CANDIDATES AND THEIR CAMPAIGNS

In the 1998 U.S. Senate race, the contrasts between the two candidates could not have been greater. Ernest F. Hollings, a Charlestonian, had served in public office in South Carolina for fifty years and had been in the U.S. Senate for thirty-two years. Other than the comptroller-general, Hollings was the only statewide-elected Democrat in South Carolina and one of only seven Democrats in the U.S. Senate from the eleven states of the old Confederacy.

Hollings' opponent, Bob Inglis, was a thirty-nine-year-old, conservative, three-term congressman and father of five from Greenville, a burgeoning metropolitan area infused with new foreign investment and fervent Christian conservatism. While Hollings' campaign was based on the importance of seniority and his ability to bring federal grants and projects to South Carolina, the theme of the Inglis campaign was "A New Senate." Inglis advocated giving more authority to the states and opposed federal grants. He also advocated term limits; he promised to serve only six years in the House and only two terms in the Senate. He tried to present himself as a moral, idealistic individual and contrasted himself with Hollings, whom Republican Party operatives and several newspaper reporters accused of being aloof and arrogant.[3]

Money and the Campaigns

One significant contrast between the two candidates was Bob Inglis' refusal to accept political action committee funds because he felt that PAC money had no place in politics. Some members of Inglis' campaign disagreed with this philosophy, and the financial records of the campaign suggest it had a significant impact on this race. Between July 1 and September 30, 1998, the Hollings' campaign raised $674,379 while Inglis only raised $459,588. Two thirds of Hollings' contributions came from out of state compared 6 percent of Inglis' funds. A total of

$559,775 of Hollings' contributions came from PACs in 1998.[4] An analysis by the Center for Responsive Politics showed that 26 percent of Hollings' previous contributions had come from PACs while 70 percent came from individuals. In contrast 82 percent of Inglis' funds came from individuals while 17 percent came from other sources.[5]

Perhaps more significant than the contributions were the expenditures by the two campaigns. Between July 1 and September 30, 1998, the Hollings' campaign reported expenditures of $1,800,000, more than four times Inglis' expenditures of $404,000.[6] Much of this was spent on media advertising. The Hollings' campaign was able to advertise freely during the election, whereas Inglis had to conserve his limited resources. Hollings had a virtual monopoly on advertising during this period, since neither Inglis nor the state Republican Party was concentrating on the media during this phase of the U.S. Senate race.

The final report of the two campaigns shows that the Hollings campaign outspent the Inglis campaign by more than a two-to-one margin (see fig. 6.1). Hollings spent $4,968,456, while Inglis spent $2,143,278. Henry Eichel of the *Charlotte Observer* noted that the combined expenditures of the two candidates made the U.S. Senate race the eleventh most expensive contest and that Hollings ranked eleventh in raising money while Inglis ranked thirty-eighth among all the U.S. Senate candidates in 1998 in terms of aggregate spending.[7]

POLITICAL PARTY CONTRIBUTIONS

Although Hollings was able to raise more than twice what Inglis raised, the money contributed by the national parties and their Senate campaign committees favored the Inglis campaign, which received nearly twice what Hollings did from these sources (see fig. 6.2). However, most of these funds from the national Republican party organizations were in the form of soft money and thus out of Inglis' direct control, creating problems that are examined more closely in the next section.

The Democratic Senatorial Campaign Committee contributed $919,075 federal (hard) and $312,500 nonfederal (soft) monies to the Democratic Party of South Carolina, while the National Republican Senate Committee contributed $282,800 federal (hard) and $946,134 nonfederal (soft) funds to the South Carolina Republican Party. The NRSC had earlier stated it had planned on spending $2,000,000 on this race.[8] In fact, Bob Inglis heard on election day that the NRSC had spent $5,000,000 on his race.[9] However, he had no idea on where or how the money was spent, and the FEC data do not support the NRSC's assertion. The state Republican Party also received $258,357 federal and $946,134 nonfederal monies from the RNC; this raised Inglis to 540,000 hard dollars and 1.9 million soft dollars, more than double what Hollings got in combined party money. The South Carolina Democratic Party received $34,578 federal and $17,500 non-

Figure 6.1   South Carolina Senate Candidate Financial Activity in the 1998 Election Cycle

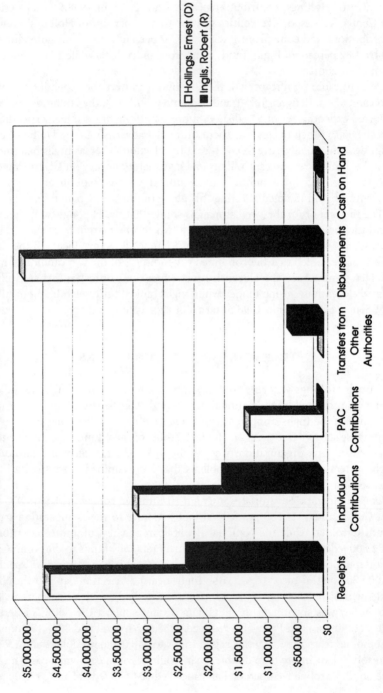

Source: Data from FEC press release, *FEC Reports on Congressional Fundraising for 1997–98*, 28 April 1999.
Note: Candidate self-support and closing debt data omitted.

Figure 6.2 South Carolina: Soft-Money Transfers from National to State Party Committees, 1 January 1997 to Year End 1998

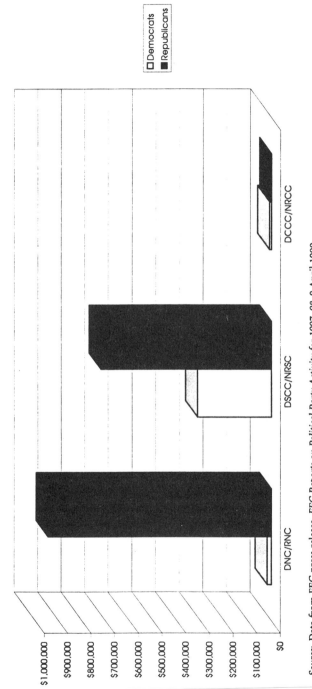

Source: Data from FEC press release, *FEC Reports on Political Party Activity for 1997–98,* 9 April 1999.

federal funds from its Democratic counterpart. Overall, South Carolina Republicans got over $2.4 million from their party committees, compared to about $1.3 million from national party committees to the Democrats. Other outside party funds contributed to the Democratic Party came from the Association of State Democratic Chairs Dollars for Democrats ($40,473), while the Republican Party received $121,000 from the Republican Governors' Association and $5,000 from the New Republican Majority Fund.

In late October 1998, Chris Roberts of the *State* newspaper in Columbia reported that while the four candidates for senator and governor had raised a total of $14.1 million, millions more had been funneled through the parties. Roberts estimated that the two parties spent at least $3 million in soft monies on these races.[10] Data from the Federal Election Commission show that Roberts was conservative in these estimates. The South Carolina Democratic Party reported expenditures of over $4 million, while the South Carolina Republican Party reported expenditures of slightly more than $3 million (see table 6.1).

Soft-money contributions to the state parties in South Carolina by private groups or individuals are presently not subject to disclosure and regulation; thus, it was impossible to document these outside groups' contributions to the parties. In fact, the campaign organizations of the candidates and the parties were more willing to provide information to the media and interested citizens about their opponents than themselves. For example, *USA Today* reporter Jim Drinkard noted that the South Carolina Republican Party Chair Henry McMaster told reporters that AT&T, Sprint, and MCI each contributed $50,000 to the state Democratic Party upon Fritz Hollings' request.[11] Hollings is on the Commerce Committee, which decides policy concerning the telecommunications industry.

Ironically, the group that probably had the most impact on the U.S. Senate race, according to Bob Inglis and officials from both parties, was never directly involved in the U.S. Senate race. This was the electronic gaming or video poker industry. This industry had expanded rapidly in South Carolina during the 1990s. In 1997, its revenue in the state from 28,000 machines totaled $2.1 billion, while its licensing fees only totaled $58,000,000.[12] When Republican Governor David Beasley proposed a ban on video poker in 1998, the industry responded with large contributions to the Democratic candidate for governor, Jim Hodges, and more importantly to the state Democratic Party. Democrats are not telling

Table 6.1   **South Carolina State Party Receipts and Expenditures, 1998**

Item	Republican Party	Democratic Party
Total Receipts	$4,040,528.30	$3,137,150.39
Total Disbursements	$4,019,223.00	$3,098,582.00
Total Federal Disbursements	$1,312,776.00	$1,408,413.56

Source: Data from FEC Reports of Receipts and Disbursements, 1998.

the exact dollar amount contributed, but this money was in the hundreds of thousands of dollars and helped finance the party's GOTV effort. In addition, one video poker operator, Fred Collins of Greenville, conducted his own campaign against the Republican governor. Collins, who owns approximately 5,000 video poker machines, put an estimated $500,000 into billboards, newspaper ads, and radio spots alone. In addition, he marshaled his own get-out-the-vote campaign that he claims transported 8,000 voters on election day.[13] Although these efforts were limited to the governor's race, the Democratic Party and its statewide candidates were the primary beneficiaries.

Republican Party Campaign

Both parties ran mostly negative campaigns. According to South Carolina Democratic Party Executive Chair Brent Weaver, this was to be expected, since soft money cannot be used to run ads on behalf of the candidates.[14] One media consultant for the Republican Party agreed that it was safer to use attack ads to avoid accusations of coordination with the candidate when soft money was involved. Although both parties went negative, the contrast between their campaigns was stark. The state Republican Party ran an attack campaign against Hollings that clashed with Inglis' pledge to be courteous and often left Inglis disassociating himself from his party's tactics.[15]

The South Carolina Republican Party's television ads consisted exclusively of negative attacks on Hollings. All of these ads were produced by a firm in Washington, D.C., and were sent to the state party for distribution. The first of three ads attempted to portray Hollings as an opponent of welfare reform and out of touch with the state. To illustrate the point, the ad included a video of a jet landing and a limousine pulling up beside it, presumably to show how Hollings traveled, though the ad never said so explicitly. It also showed a video of Hollings in his last campaign saying, "The hell with everybody. I'm free at last." The quote was taken out of context and had nothing to do with welfare reform, but it did create an image of Hollings as arrogant. A second ad criticized Hollings for voting for pay raises for Congress and increasing his own pension. The ad used a computer-generated unflattering cartoon image of Hollings in a Hawaiian print shirt enjoying a tropical drink on the beach.

The direct mail ads were equally negative, highlighting Hollings' votes to raise taxes and increase spending, followed by the recurring theme, "Isn't 32 years of this long enough?" One mailing was designed to get people to vote Republican and tried to tie in national issues. On an application for an absentee ballot sent out by the state party, a cartoon showed a Democratic Donkey with its arm around Bill Clinton with the caption, "Looking for an *honorable* party?"—an indirect reference to the Clinton/Lewinsky scandal and pending impeachment. Another mailer told voters to send Clinton a message on election day by voting Republican.[16]

While the state party's ads and mailings did reinforce some of Inglis' themes that Hollings was out of touch with the state, the tactics the party used to do this completely contradicted Inglis' call for a courteous campaign. He spent much of his time after party ads began to run trying to distance himself from the state Republican Party's commercials. In fact, during a debate between the candidates in Columbia, the moderator showed the Hawaiian shirt ad and asked the candidates to respond. Hollings said the ad was "ludicrous," and Inglis, in a very awkward moment, had to agree that the ad was ridiculous and expressed his frustration with the state party's efforts.[17]

The national Republican Party took a less direct approach than the state party in the campaign. It was not as negative and more in line with the tone of the Inglis campaign. The RNC mailings compared Democratic and Republican records on the budget and Social Security. The coordinated television ad with Inglis had a mixture of testimonials from people praising Inglis and criticizing Hollings, mostly for being in office so long and contributing to pork barrel spending. Though critical of Hollings, these ads were more in line with Inglis' courtesy pledge. They drew comparisons between the two candidates and included real people rather than paid actors or a disembodied voice attacking the incumbent.

Democratic Party Campaign

In contrast to the state Republican campaign, the state Democratic Party's efforts were largely coordinated with the Hollings' campaign, and even when the party acted independently, it complemented Hollings' efforts. Most of the television ads were attacks on Inglis' record on issues such as Social Security or education. One ad recalled votes Inglis had made against education, each followed by a school-age child asking, "Mr. Inglis, why did you cut education funds?" Some ads were rebuttals to the state Republican Party ads against Hollings. These response ads attributed the negative attacks on Hollings to Inglis rather than the state Republicans, making Inglis look hypocritical in light of his courtesy pledge.

The direct mail paid for by the South Carolina Democratic Party was indistinguishable from that of the Hollings campaign in both themes and style. Both were glossy color brochures focusing on benefits to senior citizens, education, and the environment. The big difference in the party mailings was that they tended to be negative issue ads against Inglis and never mentioned Hollings. They ended with the imperative, "Call Congressman Inglis and tell him to stop voting against seniors," or education, or the environment, depending on the subject. Hollings' own mailings were comparative and included Hollings' accomplishments on the issues on which the party had attacked Inglis. In these ways, the party complemented and reinforced Hollings' own efforts.

The soft money contributed to the parties, especially the Democratic Party, played a significant role in the election. Television and radio advertising in the four major markets in South Carolina (Charleston, Columbia, Florence, and Greenville-Spartanburg) constituted the major expenditure by the two parties on the U.S. Senate campaign. *State* newspaper reporter Chris Roberts quoted state Democratic Chair Dick Harpootlian as saying the Democrats spent over $900,000 on anti-Inglis ads.[18] State Republicans did not spend as much. Lee Bandy of the *State* reported on 28 October 1998 that the South Carolina GOP had spent $1.3 million in an effort to unseat Hollings, including $728,000 in soft money. Bandy estimated that the Democratic Party had spent $1.7 million, of which $934,000 was soft money.[19] South Carolina Democratic Party Chair Brent Weaver estimated that the party spent between $1 million and $1.5 million on activities that impacted the Senate race.

A second major expenditure of the state Democratic Party was the get-out-the-vote (GOTV) effort. The Democratic Party, through the DNC, launched a massive GOTV campaign, operating under the assumption that one of the biggest challenges in the final weeks of the 1998 campaign was voter apathy and under the fear that this could result in the lowest voter turnout in our country's history. To help the Hollings/Hodges coordinated campaign prepare and energize their volunteers for the critical GOTV campaigns the final four weeks, the DNC organized GOTV workshops with a number of targeted states around the country, including South Carolina.

There were several initiatives involved in the GOTV campaign. To combat poor organization, the Democratic Party in South Carolina began to hold regional meetings throughout the state in order to assist with electoral challenges and create a stronger relationship between the state party and the county parties and activists. County parties were provided with political precinct manuals that gave direction on being efficient and effective. Regional training sessions on running better campaigns were also held.

Throughout the state, mass registration drives and assistance for voters to utilize absentee ballots and curbside voting were provided. Voter targeting enhanced these efforts. County parties received manuals to better enable them to motivate the base voting population. Targeting allowed resource allocation to the most important activities, such as registering favorable voters, persuading the undecided, and getting voters to the polls on election day. For example, one postcard paid for by the state Democratic Party was sent to people living in HUD-subsidized housing in the Greenville area. The front said, "It's your neighborhood, and Congressman Bob Inglis doesn't care what happens to it!" The back continued, "Vote to save your neighborhood!" and explained that Hollings had helped Greenville get HUD grants for twenty-five years, while Inglis twice had cosponsored legislation to get rid of HUD.

African Americans were given particular attention. The state Democratic Party contracted with a professional firm to do a phone bank to call all registered African Americans in the weeks prior to the election. Campaign staff visited black churches to enlist their help in mobilizing the African American community.

According to Scott Henderson, the upstate director for the coordinated Democratic campaigns GOTV effort, African American registration and mobilization were accomplished largely through nonparty organizations such as the churches, the NAACP, and other community organizations, which made their members and communities aware of the new, easier voter registration laws and the importance of voting.[20] After some criticism by black campaign staffers that the Democratic candidates were ignoring black voters, the state Democratic Party ran ads on black radio stations encouraging voter registration and the need to vote. According to sources in the Inglis campaign, some Democratic ads that claimed that more black churches would burn if Republicans were elected were run on black radio stations.[21] On election day, people were paid by the Democratic Party to go door to door in African American neighborhoods reminding people to vote and offering rides to the polls.

At all levels the party tried to give voters, especially African Americans, a link to the party and its candidates. The state party conducted regular polls and used a focus group during the campaign. Automated software that reached voters by using the voice of First Lady Hillary Clinton was instrumental in making voters feel a connection with the election. In different counties, the Democratic Party sponsored social get-togethers, walks for candidates, and sign drops. Phone banks were conducted to canvass voters and enlist their support. In the final days of the election, registered-voter listings were utilized to contact voters, reminding them of the importance of their vote and offering assistance in getting to the polls on election day.

The state Democratic Party worked very closely with the video poker industry on GOTV efforts. Employees of some convenience stores that had video poker machines were told that they would lose their jobs if the Republicans won because a ban on video poker promised by the Republican governor would cost the stores too much revenue. Many of these employees were given election day off to volunteer to make phone calls for the Democrats to get people to the polls.

To finance these efforts, the state Democratic Party distributed money to the forty-six county organizations to supplement funds raised by the local parties. These amounts varied from $250 to Anderson County to $25,020 to Charleston County. Altogether, the state Democratic Party distributed approximately $230,000 to county organizations. Henry Eichel of the *Charlotte Observer* noted that without the money, the GOTV effort by the Hodges and Hollings campaigns could not have been successful.[22]

In contrast, the state Republican Party concentrated its direct contact more on direct mailings, with printing and postage being cited as major expenses. One of its earliest mailings was targeted at people who had voted in recent Republican primaries, and it encouraged them to vote by absentee ballot by including a detachable postcard preaddressed to the voter's county election board requesting absentee ballot information. The state party also did some phone bank activity, though it did not appear to be as widespread as the Democratic efforts.

Party Effectiveness

Overall, candidates on both sides agreed that the Democratic campaign had been much more effective than the Republican campaign. The consensus among observers both within and outside the campaigns is that the Republican ads directed at Hollings were badly done and relatively ineffective. The images and the sound bites in these ads were so at odds with reality and so clearly out of context that many found them unbelievable and hard to follow. And while Republican Party officials claim that their polling showed that the ads helped Inglis, the negative news coverage they generated and the anecdotal evidence that Inglis himself encountered suggested that they were not much help. Friends of his campaign told him they did not like the ads. And he explained that he considered asking the party to pull the ads, but he was concerned that the FEC would interpret that as coordination between the candidate and the party. In contrast to the Republican ads, one person on the Inglis campaign staff declared that the Democratic Party ad where the children questioned Inglis' education record was "probably the most effective ad in the entire campaign." These ads may help to explain Hollings' strong female support. Voter News Service exit polls showed that Hollings received 55 percent of the female vote compared to 43 percent for Inglis.[23]

The Democratic Party's and Hollings' ads targeting senior citizens and the issues of health care and social security were most effective. Exit polls showed that in terms of those who considered health care the most important issue in the Senate campaign, 71 percent voted for Hollings' while only 23 percent voted for Inglis. The figures on Social Security were nearly identical. Two other issues where Hollings did significantly better than Inglis among the voters were the economy (60 percent versus 40 percent) and education (50 percent versus 44 percent). Inglis' advantage was greatest among those voters who considered most important the Clinton/Lewinsky matter (82 percent voted for Inglis) and taxes (73 percent voted for Inglis).[24]

The success of the Democratic Party in statewide elections in 1998, however, is linked most closely to its registration efforts and its ability to turn out newly registered voters (see table 6.2). In 1994, there were 370,351 African Americans registered to vote. They constituted 24.7 percent of the state's registered voters. In 1998, however, African American registration had increased to 552,066, better than a 49 percent increase from four years earlier. In comparison, white registration had increased during the same four-year period from 1,122,585 to 1,469,697, an 8.3 percent increase. As a result, the African American percentage of registered voters increased from 24.7 to 27.3 percent of the state's registered voters. While some credit for the increased registration must go to the Motor Voter statute, table 6.3 shows that the GOTV effort was important. Only 117,197 people registered through the nine state agencies in South Carolina that set up registration operations. Of those, only 53,380 (45.5 percent) actually voted.

Table 6.2   South Carolina Voters: Registration and Turnout, 1992–98

	Year	Registered Voters	Number Voted	Percent Registered Who Voted
All Voters	1992	1,397,923	1,236,209	80.4%
	1994	1,499,589	951,901	63.5%
	1998	2,021,763	1,098,484	54.3%
White Voters	1992	1,149,519	949,572	82.6%
	1994	1,122,585	748,699	66.9%
	1998	1,469,697	817,195	59.3%
Nonwhite Voters	1992	381,524	286,637	75.1%
	1994	370,351	202,502	54.7%
	1998	552,067	281,289	50.1%

Source: Data from South Carolina Election Commission reports 1992, 1994, 1998.

This helps to explain the decline in registered voter turnout among both African Americans and whites in 1998. The percentage of nonwhites who voted decreased from 54.7 percent in 1994 to 50.1 percent in 1998. However, the number of African American voters increased by almost 79,000. White turnout, however, decreased even more, from 66.9 percent in 1994 to 59.3 percent in 1998. While the number of white registered voters increased by 347,112 between 1994 and 1998, the increase in the number who actually voted was lower than their nonwhite counterparts. As a result, nonwhite voters who constituted 21 percent of the votes in 1994, made up 25.6 percent of the voters in 1998. Three of the top five counties in turnout had a majority of African American voters. For example, Hampton County, which ranked first in turnout, gave Hollings 79 percent of its vote. Statewide, African Americans clearly made the difference in the U.S. Senate race. Exit polls conducted by the Voter News Service show that Hollings received 92 percent of the black vote but only 40 percent of the white vote.[25] The combined efforts of the churches, the NAACP, and other community organizations brought this crucial vote together, particularly in a race where Hollings won by only a 7 percent margin (52.7 to 45.7).

Table 6.3   Status of Motor Voter in South Carolina, 1998

	Registered	Voted	Percent Registered Who Voted
Motor Voter	117,197	53,380	45.5%
Nonmotor Voter	1,697,580	1,150,106	67.8%

Source: Data from South Carolina Election Commission.

INTEREST-GROUP CAMPAIGNS

There were at least fifteen outside organizations that became involved in various stages of the South Carolina Senate race. Eleven were national organizations such as the League of Conservation Voters (LCV) and the Christian Coalition. Four were local organizations such as the South Carolina Education Association (SCEA). Nine of the outside groups supported Inglis directly or indirectly by attacking Hollings, while five supported Hollings. One group, Good Common Sense, took no position on the candidates.

The groups used a variety of tactics to influence the election. All of the local organizations endorsed one of the candidates or parties and used direct mail or newspaper advertising to publicize their positions. The South Carolina credit unions ran a full-page ad in all the major newspapers around the state the weekend before the election to endorse Hollings, and the Committee for South Carolina's Freedom (a group that was more active in the governor's race against video poker and gambling issues) ran a small ad in newspapers encouraging people to vote for Republican candidates and listing those running for statewide office. The Democratic Club of Beaufort sent out a direct mail piece on Hollings' behalf, comparing Inglis' and Hollings' records on Social Security. And the SCEA sent two direct mailings—one encouraging people to vote for Democrats and another specifically comparing Inglis and Hollings on education issues that showed Hollings supported SCEA's positions and Inglis did not.

The involvement of the national organizations ranged from simply running candidate advocacy ads to supplementing the candidates' and parties' GOTV efforts with phone banks and direct mail. Americans for Job Security ran an ad in several major markets attacking Democrats and Hollings for raising taxes and being against working people. Similarly, Campaign for Working Families, a political action committee founded by social conservative Gary Bauer, ran a radio ad in one major market of the state in which Bauer praised Inglis for being pro-life and pro-family. Other groups mailed out scorecards listing the two Senate candidates and their records on particular issues. The Christian Coalition and the National Rifle Association sent similar voter guides to their members, though neither made an explicit endorsement. The National Right to Life PAC, working with several local right-to-life groups, ran some radio and newspaper ads, sent literature to voters, and did phone banks endorsing Inglis and the Republican gubernatorial candidate as the pro-life choices. After endorsing Inglis publicly, the National Federation of Independent Business carefully targeted its own South Carolina members through phone banks, newsletters, and direct mail, encouraging them to vote for Inglis.

The LCV had perhaps the most sophisticated strategy of the groups involved directly in the Senate race. The League coordinated its effort with the Hollings' campaign. Therefore, the limit to its contributions was $5,000. This money was spent on what was described as "earned media." There were no issue ads or television ads in the South Carolina area, and everything was reported to the FEC. To start the ball rolling in South Carolina, a press conference was held in which the organization named Bob Inglis to the "Dirty Dozen." Hollings attended the conference. The nature of this campaign was rather negative because the organization did extensive polling and found that people expected their politicians to vote for the environment. When people discovered that the politicians did not, they took action. Inglis was the last person named to the national list called the "Dirty Dozen." His environmental rating, tabulated by the LCV, dropped to 15 percent during 1998. Because the LCV looked for tight races where the environmental issue may make a difference, the organization placed some of its funds in the South Carolina area. The organization believed that a third-party verification of the positions of candidates on the environment helped the voters to decide. It did a mailing the week before the campaign, highlighting Inglis' environmental record.

Determining how much these groups spent independently on the campaigns was almost impossible. Except for the National Right to Life PAC and LCV, FEC reports were not broken down sufficiently to see what was spent on the South Carolina race. And all the organizations were reluctant to give dollar amounts or even general breakdowns on what percent of their money was spent on which activities. According to the FEC, National Right to Life spent $3,652 on radio ads, $2,438 on newspaper ads, and $1,930 for postage. LCV contributed the $5,000 maximum directly to Hollings, and whatever amount was needed to do its mailing the last week of the campaign. Most of the other groups appeared to spend less than $15,000.

Themes of Interest-Group Campaigns

The themes of the groups' efforts varied as much as their methods. Surprisingly, at least in light of independent spending by the parties, many of the groups stayed positive by endorsing a candidate and urging their members or voters in general to support that candidate without attacking the opponent. Others were somewhat mixed because they offered comparisons of the candidates' voting records. Several were particularly negative. For example, LCV's direct mailing stated, "Voting *against* Bob Inglis is one of the best ways you can protect the environment." It never mentioned Hollings. Similarly, Americans for Job Security attacked Hollings on taxes without actually endorsing Inglis.

In most cases, the groups' issues or themes and tone complemented the candidate they were designed to help. SCEA and LCV pushed issues that Hollings dealt with in his own commercials and direct mail. And the Campaign for Working Families radio ads not only focused on issues Inglis emphasized but also adhered to his guidelines for a courteous campaign. The ad focused positively on Inglis' record, and the spokesperson in the ad, Gary Bauer, identified himself rather than having some disembodied voice attack Hollings, as the South Carolina Republican Party ads had done.

The motivations for the groups to get involved appeared to be mostly an attempt to reward the candidate who supported the group's goals or to punish the one who had opposed legislation important to the organization. LCV's attacks on Inglis were clearly retaliation for his votes, while Americans for Job Security did the same to Hollings. For the groups who wanted to support Inglis, independent spending was a necessity because he refused to take PAC money. Most of the national groups targeted this race because it was expected to be close.

There were two groups that appeared to want to shape the agenda. Americans for Limited Terms was not very strategic in its involvement, choosing to run ads praising Inglis for his position on term limits during the primaries when Inglis faced token opposition, but deciding to stay out of the general election completely, even though the race was close and Hollings made an excellent target. The organization Good Common Sense spent at least $75,000 on television ads that argued for tax cuts and merely urged voters to contact Inglis and Hollings without actually endorsing either candidate.

Effectiveness of Interest-Group Campaigns

There is little evidence that the groups who were directly involved in the Senate race were very influential in the election. Most groups, especially those supporting Inglis, tended to target voters who already favored the group's choice, thus changing few minds. For example, right-to-life supporters were already likely to support Inglis, as were the people most likely to listen to Gary Bauer. And although groups did little to move the agenda beyond the candidates' own themes, Inglis did lament his inability to coordinate with his allies. He noted that while he was appreciative of the efforts by organizations supporting him, he had found evidence in the polls that some of their tactics had not always aided his cause even when their messages were in line with his. The example he cited was a mailing and radio ad that endorsed his pro-life positions. The problem was that the ad also endorsed David Beasley, the incumbent Republican governor, who ultimately lost his reelection bid. Inadvertently, the ad linked Inglis to Beasley's sinking ship.

CONCLUSION

The soft monies available to the parties were an important feature of the 1998 Senate race in South Carolina. These funds resulted in numerous candidate attack ads. In addition, the funds allowed the parties to coordinate and finance other activities. Such funds also allowed the Democratic Party to become financially competitive with its Republican counterpart for the first time in many years. Those funds were important in increasing the registration and turnout of the traditional Democratic core and resulted in the Democratic Party not only retaining the U.S. Senate seat but in winning three constitutional offices, including governor.

The contrasting strategies of the two parties show both the advantages and the problems with outside spending. The Democratic Party's coordinated campaign efforts, both through the media and on the ground, complemented its candidate's campaign. In contrast, the Republican Party's ad campaign appeared to undermine its candidate and at times dictate an agenda that clashed with the candidate. And the Republican ground effort was not extensive enough to make up for Bob Inglis' lack of resources.

The 1998 campaign and the soft-money issue did result in a call for change in campaign financing in South Carolina. In an 11 December 1998 editorial, the *State* newspaper called for reform in South Carolina's campaign finance laws, noting that in the past the Republican Party had been flush with cash, while in 1998 the Democratic Party had benefited more. The editorial suggested that limits should be placed on party expenditures: $50,000 for statewide races and $5,000 for others. In addition, candidates should be required to report the occupation of their donors and to post these reports on the Internet weekly or daily during the final month of the campaign.[26] Although this does not address the problem of federal campaigns or unlimited contributions, it does illustrate recognition of the problem of soft money in American political campaigns today.

NOTES

1. Cole Blease Graham Jr. and Bill V. Moore, *South Carolina Politics and Government* (University of Nebraska Press, 1994), 80–86.

2. Lee Bandy, interview by William Moore, telephone, Columbia State, 2 August 1999. Data cited were collected by Dr. Earl Black and communicated to Lee Bandy after the 1996 election.

3. Albert Eisele, "Ol' Fritz Battles Bob Inglis' Charge of 'Old Time Politics,' " *The Hill*, 28 October 1998.

4. Steve Picante, "Hollings Tops Campaign Fund Race," *Charleston Post and Courier*, 16 October 1999, B6.

5. Ibid.

6. Ibid.

7. Henry Eichel, "True to Form, N.C. Produces a Costly Senate Campaign," *Charlotte Observer*, 5 December 1998, A18.

8. Inglis staff person, interview by authors, Columbia, South Carolina, 9 October 1998.

9. Bob Inglis, interview by authors, Greenville, South Carolina, 8 April 1999.

10. Chris Roberts, "Follow the Money," *The State*, 24 October 1998, A1.

11. Jim Drinkard, "Loopholes in Campaign Law Are Gifts That Keep on Giving," *USA Today*, 26 October 1998, A1.

12. South Carolina Department of Revenue, "Video-Gambling," *Charleston Post and Courier*, 6 September 1998, A10.

13. Clif Leblanc and Douglas Pardue, "Gaming Group Closes Door on Collins' Plan to Speak," *The State*, 8 April 1999, B5.

14. Brent Weaver, telephone interview by authors, 1 December 1998.

15. Dan Hoover, "Inglis Disagrees with, but Won't Disavow Attack Ad on Hollings," *Greenville News*, 2 October 1998, 1B.

16. Sarah O'Donnell, "Hollings Airs Frustrations about Opponent Inglis," *The Herald* (Rock Hill, South Carolina), 15 October 1998, 1A.

17. Televised debate between Hollings and Inglis, 24 October 1998, aired statewide on South Carolina educational TV.

18. Chris Roberts, "Midlands Political Ads," *The State*, 3 November 1998, A6.

19. Lee Bandy, "National GOP Hurls Cash Against Hollings," *The State*, 28 October 1998, D4.

20. Scott Henderson, interview by Danielle Vinson, Greenville, South Carolina, 2 June 1999.

21. Bob Inglis, interview by Danielle Vinson, telephone, Greenville, South Carolina, 8 April 1999.

22. Henry Eichel, *Charlotte Observer*, interview by authors, telephone, 8 January 1999.

23. "Exit Poll Results," *The State*, 4 November 1998, A11.

24. Ibid.

25. Ibid.

26. Editorial, "We Must Improve Campaign-Finance Laws," *The State*, 11 December 1998, A10.

7

The 1998 Nevada Senate Race

Tim Fackler, Nathalie Frensley, Eric Herzik, Ted G. Jelen,
Todd Kunioka, and Michael Bowers

The 1998 Nevada Senate race, in which incumbent Democrat Harry Reid defeated Republican Congressman John Ensign after a controversial recount, was
closely fought and well financed. The race was decided by a mere 428 votes after
a lengthy statewide recount and scrutiny of possible voting irregularities in
northern Washoe County. It was the most expensive Senate race in Nevada history,[1] indeed, on a per vote basis, the race was among the ten most expensive
Senate races in U.S. history.[2] As Mark Emerson, Ensign's chief of staff, put it,
"[The race] was so close because it was a clash of two titans and both knew what
they were doing."[3] Both parties spent heavily in the race, generally in close cooperation with candidate organizations and some key interest groups. State party
advertising dollars were heavily devoted to attacks on the opposing party's candidate, allowing the candidates to remain on a slightly higher road a few weeks
longer. National advocacy groups, most notably labor and conservation groups,
pushed their national agendas but managed, to a surprising extent, to spend their
efforts and money in ways that resonated with local meaning. Despite these efforts, voters responded by producing a turnout substantially lower than normal.
According to a representative of the Reid campaign, turnout was about 52 percent of "active" registered voters and 46 percent of all registered voters, which is
rather low for a western state such as Nevada.[4]

A PROFILE OF THE STATE

Nevada is a competitive two-party state, dominated socially, economically, and
politically in the latter half of the twentieth century by gaming interests. Party
ties are relatively weak in Nevada, as evidenced by Ross Perot's getting over 26
percent of the Nevada vote in 1992, and Nevada's unique ballot option "none of

these candidates" routinely attracts votes as well.[5] At the same time, more than 80 percent of voters register under a major party label, with roughly equal numbers of Democrats and Republicans. In the Senate race this year, for instance, more than 4 percent of votes cast went to neither of these candidates and two minor-party candidates. Split-ticket voting appears to be common. For example, Democratic U.S. Senate candidate Harry Reid rolled up 22,000 more votes than Republican John Ensign in Clark County, while the Republican gubernatorial candidate, Kenny Guinn, out-polled the Democratic candidate Jan Jones by more than 14,000 votes.[6]

Nevada is politically divided into two regions: a largely rural, conservative, GOP-dominated north, in which, apart from the casino industry in the Reno area, mining and ranching are the principal industries, and a highly urbanized, Democratic-leaning Clark County, which contains more than two-thirds of the state's population.[7] Clark County is the destination of most of the state's newcomers. As a result, voter turnout is generally depressed in the Las Vegas area, where even established incumbents must wage an uphill battle for name recognition. Though outnumbered, the north remains competitive because it contributes a disproportionate share of the vote, although far short of a majority, in statewide elections. In 1998, Clark County voters accounted for 56.4 percent of all votes cast statewide, well below the county's share of the population, and had the lowest rate of any county in the state.[8]

Linking Nevada's various subpopulations is an individualist political culture: the state as a whole is, of course, sin tolerant but also unusually tax averse and relatively tolerant of minor political corruption. Like other western states, gun control and environmental liberalism are relatively unpopular issues.

Despite the fact that Nevada is a right-to-work state, organized labor is also a strong presence, particularly in Clark County. The Hotel Employees and Restaurant Employees Union (HERE), more commonly known as the culinary workers' union, is a particularly potent political force in Clark County politics. The rapid population growth, with a corresponding demand for new housing, has increased the importance of trade unions in the construction industry.

The state has experienced enormous population growth in recent years, to the apparent advantage of the GOP. Politically active immigrants (especially in Clark County, which contains Las Vegas) appear to be older, mostly white, and more Republican leaning than the longer-term residents. According to U.S. Census figures, the state's median age is rising, from thirty-three in 1990 to thirty-five in 1997, while the population of Nevada's population that is fifty-five and older has increased almost 50 percent during the same period. Other studies using figures for Clark County, which contains the majority of the state's population and fastest rates of growth, portray an even grayer Nevada: the median age in Clark County is almost forty-six, while 25 percent of new Clark County residents in 1997 were fifty-five or older. While turnout rates in Clark County average roughly 56 percent of the eligible electorate, rates in local retirement communities run almost 90 percent.

Residents of Hispanic origin are the fastest growing segment of Nevada's population (currently 12.9 percent), but their registration and voting rates average less than 20 percent. Among the small (7.5 percent) and more slowly growing African American population, rates approximate those of whites. According to exit polls, the proportion of black voters in 1998 was 9 percent.[9] Nevada also contains a small but rapidly growing Asian population (3.3 percent).[10] Thus, while in percentage terms the number of whites is slowly shrinking (currently 87.4 percent) the raw numbers of new white residents still vastly outnumber immigrants from other groups.

Gender is important to Nevada politics. Women in the state have a comparatively high political profile, with many prominent women from both parties occupying and seeking leadership positions. Moreover, while population estimates indicate slightly more men than women residing in the state, significantly more women than men are part of the active electorate. For example, Current Population Survey registration and voting figures for 1996 indicated that women on average registered and voted at rates more than 10 percentage points higher than men do. Less dramatically, a 1998 exit poll reported 52 percent women in its sample.[11]

THE CANDIDATES AND THEIR CAMPAIGNS

The Senate race pitted two-term Democratic incumbent Senator Harry Reid against two-term U.S. Representative John Ensign. Reid served in the state assembly and as the state's lieutenant governor before losing narrowly to Paul Laxalt in the 1974 Senate race. He lost a contest for mayor of Las Vegas in 1976 before assuming the chair of the Nevada Gaming Commission. When Nevada received a second House seat in 1982, Reid ran and won. In 1986, he won the Senate seat vacated by Laxalt's retirement. Reid's service on the Gaming Commission provided him with an enduring network of associations in the casino industry. Reid remains a loyal, but by no means liberal, Democrat. A devout member of the Church of Jesus Christ of Latter-day Saints (LDS), Reid has regularly maintained conservative positions on some issues, such as abortion, winning him the endorsement of Nevada Right to Life in this election.

John Ensign, the son of a prominent gaming executive with experience as a casino manager himself, grew up in northern Nevada. Ensign was only in his second term as U.S. Representative from the First Congressional District (Las Vegas), his first elective office. He had defeated an incumbent in a heavily Democratic district to become a member of the Class of 1994, helping usher in the Gingrich Revolution. He survived a heavy independent attack from organized labor in 1996, establishing his credentials in Nevada's candidate-poor Republican

Party as a dynamic, young conservative campaigner with a knack for fund-raising. An Evangelical Christian with strong ties to the religious right, Ensign is a member of Promise Keepers, an ecumenical Christian men's group that emphasizes "traditional" gender roles within the family. He is also a veterinarian, a qualification he repeatedly contrasted with Reid, a lawyer and professional politician. Ensign's voting record is distinctively conservative, and he proved to be a younger and more dynamic candidate than Reid.

Although a child of the more conservative north, Ensign was virtually unknown outside his urban southwest Nevada district. In contrast, Reid was well known, having carried the largest northern county (Washoe) in his previous Senate bids and having worked hard on a regional water settlement and preservation of Lake Tahoe. Thus, Reid's statewide name recognition provided a sufficient buffer for him in the generally conservative Republican northern counties, which Democrats did not expect to carry anyway, forcing Ensign to devote considerable attention to Republican Washoe and the northern counties while holding his own in Democratic Clark County.[12]

Media

Nevada is a relatively inexpensive state in which to campaign, in part because two media markets cover the entire state and because TV time is comparatively cheap and cost-effective. Television was the medium of choice in both the north and south. With prices ranging between $50 and $300 in the north and roughly $100 to $3,000 in the south for thirty-second spots, competition heated up toward the end of the campaign. As stations hit the saturation point with political advertising, prices sometimes were bid up dramatically and the media profited handsomely. A story in the *Las Vegas Sun* noted that, as a result of the election campaign, advertising grosses were "35 percent higher than the amount collected in 1996," or "two to three times more than projected." This windfall, according to General Manager Rolla Cleaver of the NBC affiliate KVBC, the largest station in the Las Vegas market, was due principally to the Senate race: "It's made this year better than anything we had ever dreamed of. This race is one of the critical ones nationally, so both parties have stepped up to try to win this thing. Tons of Democratic and Republican money have come in."[13]

The comparatively low cost of television advertising in Nevada caused some observers to believe that the extent of the "air war" had reached a point of diminishing returns and may even have been counterproductive. As media consultant David Weeks told us, "The clutter on television during the last few weeks of the campaign really prevented our message from getting through as clearly as we would have liked. Voters had a tough time figuring out which ads were run by the candidates, which by the parties, and which by independent groups."[14]

The Campaigns

Neither candidate faced a real challenge in the primary. However, both the Reid campaign and the state Democratic Party on Reid's behalf began running advertisements early in the spring of 1998, in order, in the words of one party leader, "to reintroduce Harry to the voters."[15] Positive, "pro-Reid" spots were run by the senator's campaign, while the party ran "voter education" ads critical of Congressman Ensign's voting record. With thousands of new residents moving to the state each month since his last campaign in 1992, Reid, despite his incumbent status, began the 1998 campaign needing to build positive name identification.[16] Given Ensign's electoral base in the south and his ideological affinities with the north, many observers felt that the north held the key to victory in the race. As it turned out, the outcome reflected recent voting trends. Ensign carried fifteen of the state's seventeen counties, but Reid's margin in Clark County proved enough to reelect him, despite losing by 2,182 votes in the state's second population center in Washoe County.

The Reid campaign emphasized three major themes: protecting Social Security, opposing high-level nuclear waste storage in Nevada, and promoting Reid's clout and seniority in the Senate. In advertising funded by his own campaign, Reid largely talked about what he has done as Nevada's senior senator for seniors, for the environment, and for Nevada's schools. Backed by party advertising in the general election and citing an Ensign vote to authorize temporary storage of nuclear waste at the Nevada Test Site, Reid proved particularly effective at raising questions about Ensign's trustworthiness on this and other issues. Indeed, the state Democratic Party ran a number of ads carrying the message that "you can't trust Ensign," which several Republican campaign and party representatives regarded as quite effective.[17]

The Ensign campaign emphasized the importance of limited government, low taxes, tough approach to crime, and local control of schools. Republican soft-money advertising hammered Reid as someone who spoke one way in Nevada but voted differently in Washington on issues of taxation, education, legislation protecting seniors, and preservation of Social Security entitlements. The Reid campaign regarded the tax issue as particularly effective for Ensign; as one Reid spokesman told us, "He [Ensign] beat the crap out of us on taxes."[18] Both the Ensign campaign and the Republican Party emphasized the tax issue aggressively. As one GOP ad stated, "That old card shark Harry Reid sure talks a good game. . . . Call that card shark Harry Reid. Tell him on taxes and negative ads . . . start dealing straight."[19]

Both camps sought to carve out positions supportive of Social Security and funds for education while opposing nuclear waste. In the highly valenced issue environment of Nevada politics, the campaign was largely fought over which candidate was more committed and in a better position to benefit Nevada. Ensign frequently found himself forced to respond to Reid's attacks on his positions on nuclear waste, the environment more generally, education, and Social Security. Additionally, he made an apparent significant misstep when he scheduled an October 23 Las Vegas fund-raiser featuring Senate Majority Leader Trent Lott (R-MS) along with senators Larry Craig (R-ID), John Ashcroft (R-MO), and Jim Jeffords (R-VT), collectively billed as "The Singing Senators" in announcements of the event. When Lott's and Craig's active support for a high-level nuclear waste dump in Nevada was publicized, the event was hastily canceled.

Both campaigns felt it necessary to respond to the attacks of the other. Thus, Reid ran an ad in which he denied having voted to tax Social Security or having voted himself a pay raise, while Ensign felt it necessary to address his support for the environment and Social Security. This indicates the candidates felt that some attacks on them had an impact. For example, a media consultant for the Ensign campaign told us that he regards the attacks on Ensign's environmental record as one of the pivotal factors in the election's outcome, and virtually all of the Ensign and GOP representatives with whom we spoke regarded these attacks as extremely unfair. Similarly, Senator Reid ran several ads responding to Ensign's attack on Reid's Social Security record, including one in which he stated: "Beware. Be careful, Congressman Ensign. This sleazy commercial can come back and bite you."

ROLE OF MONEY IN THE CAMPAIGN

Political Party Contributions

As with other highly competitive 1998 elections, party spending generally was the leading category in noncandidate spending. The state parties coordinate—at least tacitly—expenditures and activities among candidate organizations and outside interests. Although we were not privy to decisions by parties, candidates, or outside interests to coordinate activities, several pieces of circumstantial evidence lead us to emphasize the coordinating function of Nevada's party organizations.

Familial, social, and political connections are important, particularly in Nevada's political culture. For example, David Cherry, a media operative for the state Democratic Party with whom we communicated, now works in a similar capacity for Reid in Washington. In 1998 Cherry's father Michael Cherry was running a successful union- and Strip-backed (Las Vegas Casino backed) campaign for an important state district judgeship. Then–state Democratic Party Chairman Paul Henry had worked as senior legal counsel for Reid when he chaired the Senate Environmental and Public Works Committee before coming to Nevada and winning the chairmanship of the state party. Henry's replacement as party chair, elected in spring 1999, is Reid's own son, Rory, a lawyer for the Lady Luck Gaming Corporation. Though we had less access to the Republican side, Ensign is son of a top Circus Circus (now Mandalay Bay) executive, one of the largest casino corporations in the state. The state's chief political pundit, moderate- to liberal-leaning Jon Ralston, whose newsletter is widely read in Nevada gaming and political circles, is married to another Circus Circus executive. In such overlapping relationships, even if direct communications could be suspended, indirect communications through contributors, reporters, pundits, and other go-betweens—nearly impossible to track or to police—permitted coordinated activity.

Cooperation was also evident between the candidates, parties, and groups in the campaigns. Union organizing efforts required a high degree of coordination and cooperation. Investigator Tim Fackler observed the election day get-out-the-vote (GOTV) effort at a Las Vegas union hall, where a union phone bank operated on one side of a large room along with several long tables where union representatives kept tabs on volunteers hanging reminders on the doors of Democratic-leaning registered union households. On the other side of the room representatives of the Reid campaign and the Democratic Party were coordinating similar efforts on the part of another group of volunteers. The state Democratic Party chair, the political director of the AFL-CIO, other senior union representatives, and senior Reid operatives held a number of meetings at the hall during the day. A number of politicians put in appearances to watch the efforts under way, most notably Nevada's other senator, Democrat Richard Bryan.

Although we did not have occasion to observe Republican campaign operations in quite the same way, state Republican Party contribution and expenditure reports provide evidence of the role of parties in coordinating campaigns. The Republican Party received more than thirty contributions for candidates themselves, totaling just under $110,000. Reciprocal giving and receiving reflects at minimum a well-developed sense of shared purpose necessary to successfully coordinate activities.

Finally, the return addresses of the Reid campaign and the Democratic Party were identical street addresses though different suite numbers. These observations on cooperation and coordination may not meet legal tests for coordination. But they show in the highly permeable world of campaigns and elections how much overlap there is between candidate campaigns and those waged by political parties and interest groups.

Since Nevada is a self-contained media market, with inexpensive broadcast advertising rates, most of the campaign was conducted on television and radio. The war of party attack ads began during the primary season and quickly escalated, with each side responding to the other's ads. By the primary election, figures from the secretary of state's office indicate that the Democratic Party had spent about $700,000 on television ads, while the Republican Party had spent more than $1 million. These expenditures presaged what was to come. Half of the twenty spots that the Democratic Party aired in the north in the general election were first run during the primary; the same was true for two-thirds of the Republican's ads in northern Nevada. The general division between positive candidate-funded ads and negative party-funded ads, described by Marianne Holt in chapter 2 of this volume, appeared during the primary and held throughout the campaign.

Since neither candidate faced real primary opposition, party primary advertising in the Senate race was devoted to setting the agenda for the general election campaign.[20] During the general election campaign, the parties expanded their other activities. Each party established statewide direct mail efforts, conducted polls, and hired staff. Print advertising, traditional campaign items such as buttons, posters, and billboards, and even radio played little role in the parties' campaigns. As the figures in table 7.1 indicate, the medium of choice for the parties was television, which is quite understandable in a state with well-defined media markets and relatively inexpensive advertising rates. Of Republican Party expenditures, 52.8 percent went to television advertising while the Democratic Party spent 48.2 percent. Direct mail was a distant second for both parties, and the Democratic Party also invested substantially in radio advertising.[21]

Much of the air war involved attacks on selected portions of the opponent's record. For example, the GOP ran an ad urging voters to "call Harry Reid and

Table 7.1   Nevada State Party Disbursements and Contributions

Disbursements by Category	Nevada State Democratic Party	Nevada Republican Party Central Committee
Office	753,880	87,706
Related to Volunteers	7,227	2,090
Travel	57,837	33,174
Television	2,438,127	2,858,180
Newspaper Advertising	539	2,611
Radio	105,456	0
Billboards	0	0
Printed Signs, Novelties, etc.	6,430	1,254
Direct Mail	491,306	987,649
Paid Staff	502,469	195,011
Consultants	311,974	228,219
Polling	111,000	80,010
Special Events	83,324	78,215
Value of In-kind Services	0	3,398
On-line Services	11,310	2,576
Other Miscellaneous Expenses	174,732	845,296
Total Disbursements	**5,055,611**	**5,405,389**
Total Contributions	**4,823,102**	**5,141,090**

Source: Data from reports filed with the Nevada secretary of state for the period 1 October 1997 to 19 December 1998.

tell him to stop taxing Social Security." Similarly, the Democrats ran an issue ad criticizing Ensign for voting to relax federal food inspection standards and urged voters to "call John Ensign and tell him to stop risking our children's health." While these commercials were quite negative, they dealt largely with questions of public policy. Both campaigns felt it necessary to respond to the attacks of the other.

Party organizations spent more than $10 million on the Nevada senate race, more than half of it on television advertising; Reid and Ensign's combined spending on TV advertising was $8.4 million.[22] Both parties saw the race, as winnable and made it a top-priority race, with the National Republican Senate Committee (NRSC) transferring over $1.5 million in soft and hard dollars to the state party and the Democratic National Senate Committee (DNSC) transferring over $1.4 million to the state party, according to FEC reports.

Nevada law requires parties to disclose the source and amount of all contributions in excess of $100. Similarly, the recipient and amount of all expenditures must be reported as well. Table 7.1 summarizes expenditures by Nevada's Democratic and Republican parties for all races and activities during the 1998 election cycle.[23]

Although reporting is not enforced by legal sanctions, the major parties appear to do a thorough job of reporting contributions and expenditures. They clearly have the resources to hire staff to meet the requirements of the law. Moreover, the party reports serve an important signaling function. Although these reports are typically not digest for the public by the press, party and campaign personnel use these reports as a "map" of the competition.

These reports identify the source of almost all contributed dollars. Of the contributions reported in figure 7.1, the Republicans received less than 2 percent and the Democrats less than 1 percent of their totals in contributions of less than one hundred dollars. The bulk of the contributions came from national party committees and gaming-related sources. In turn, the greatest share of national party contributions came from the Democratic Senate Campaign Committee and the NRSC ($1.3 million and $2 million, respectively, according to reports filed with the secretary of state. Only small amounts came from party organizations in other states ($125,000 to the Democrats and $30,000 to the GOP).

It seems reasonable to assume that, at the minimum, the contributions from the national party Senate committees were spent on behalf of the Senate candidates. Although these data do not allow us to draw direct links between party contributions, expenditures, and the Senate campaigns, the preeminence of the U.S. Senators in Nevada politics, as well as substantial evidence of coordination in other statewide races, suggests that the vast majority of money spent benefited the Senate candidates indirectly.

While most of the expenditures are reported in gross categories that provide little insight into the operations of the state parties, close examination of the substantial discrepancy between Democratic and Republican miscellaneous expendi-

Figure 7.1 Nevada Senate Candidate Financial Activity in the 1998 Election Cycle

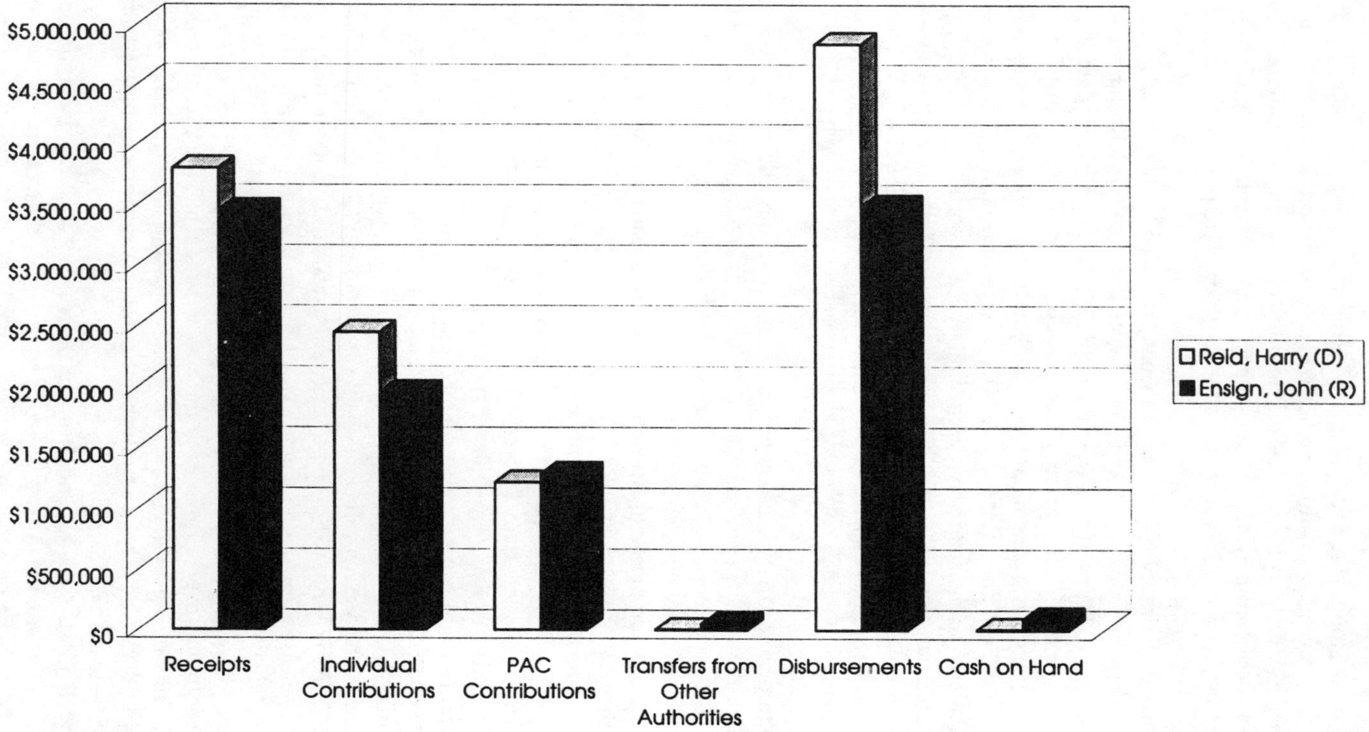

Legend: □ Reid, Harry (D)   ■ Ensign, John (R)

Categories (horizontal axis): Receipts, Individual Contributions, PAC Contributions, Transfers from Other Authorities, Disbursements, Cash on Hand

Vertical axis: $0, $500,000, $1,000,000, $1,500,000, $2,000,000, $2,500,000, $3,000,000, $3,500,000, $4,000,000, $4,500,000, $5,000,000

Source: Data from FEC press release, *FEC Reports on Political Party Activity for 1997–98,* 9 April 1999.

Figure 7.2 Nevada: Soft-Money Transfers from National to State Party Committees, 1 January 1997 to Year End 1998

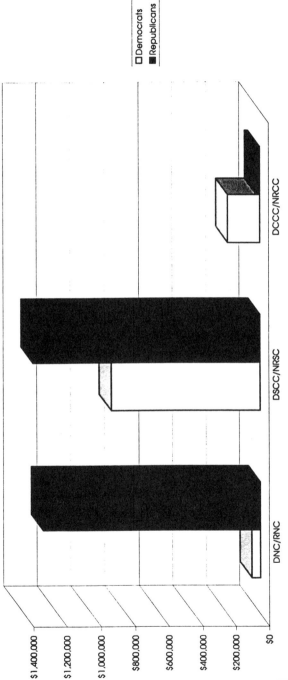

Source: Data from FEC press release, *FEC Reports on Congressional Fundraising for 1997–98,* 9 April 1999.
Note: Candidate self-support and closing debt data omitted.

tures provides the basis for some plausible inferences into the complexity of party choices and activities. The basic story is that for various purposes, the Democrats had a "grassroots" cadre of activists into which they could tap, while the Republicans were forced to spend more money hiring their campaign "ground forces."[24]

THE ROLE OF INTEREST GROUPS

Labor

Interest groups were also important to the campaign, but often their identity went unknown. Ensign chief of staff Mark Emerson explained, "No voter out there knows [who the interest groups are], because I didn't even know." The coordinated efforts of organized labor, labeled "Labor '98," appeared decisive to many observers inside and outside of both parties and campaigns.[25] Rather than spending large sums of money under the direction of the national AFL-CIO, local union leaders collaborated with each other, national leaders, the Nevada Democratic Party, and the Reid campaign to mount a massive GOTV effort. The real union contribution to the Nevada Senate race cannot be accounted for in dollar terms. According to a key union strategist, the effort cost less than $300,000.[26] Aided by experienced national organizers and by hundreds of volunteers, organizers visited about 40,000 households during the fall. Each household was contacted at least three times by phone, mail, or personal visit. While it is difficult to judge the effectiveness of the effort in terms of votes, judging from the extent of the effort, the number and commitment of the organizers, and the enthusiasm of the rank and file, it was crucial to Reid's victory.

Labor targeted Nevada for reasons beyond the Reid/Ensign Senate race. The Silver State was one of several states in which anti-union forces were pushing a paycheck protection initiative like the one that went before California voters in June 1998. Paycheck protection measures require union members and other people to designate each year whether they want part of their wages to go to charities or union political purposes. The intent is clearly to reduce the treasure chest of union money and to force unions to spend millions opposing the initiatives rather than supporting candidates. On the California initiative, unions spent roughly $25 million to defeat the measure.[27] Faced with a similar initiative in Nevada, organized labor countered by collecting signatures for its own initiative and initiating litigation. As a result of union efforts and fears among candidates on the Republican ticket—notably John Ensign and gubernatorial candidate Kenny Guinn—that paycheck protection on the November ballot might spark a voter backlash at the polls, state Republican Party leaders decided not to file the signature petitions that had been collected, and despite much internal wrangling, union leaders withdrew their counterpetition. Having geared up to fight pay-check protection, Unions then focused their efforts on the Reid reelection.[28]

Researchers from our team along with David Magleby, principal investigator for the entire project, were permitted to visit the Labor '98 headquarters set up in temporary trailers behind a union hall in Las Vegas. There the full labor strategy unfolded. All Nevada labor households (more than 40,000) were contacted in their homes by campaign representatives. Labor members were canvassed for their vote intentions, and those supporting or leaning towards Reid were sent subsequent mailers on Reid and the environment, Social Security, education, Reid's support for women, and links between Ensign, Adelson, and Grover Nor-quist, who was characterized as a conservative advisor on labor issues to Newt Gingrich.[29] Numerous fliers emphasized Adelson's threat to working families in a variety of ways and compared Ensign and Reid's records on workers' rights, particularly on health care, retirement, open shop laws, and paycheck protection. All voter canvass data were computerized for use as the database for election day get-out-the-vote activity. The effort was well organized and dedicated. Labor vans were still taking voters to the polls at 6:45 P.M., as the polls were about to close. Our interviews with the Labor '98 leaders demonstrated an understanding that this race would be close, that union members were angry about the anti-union rhetoric and spending by Sheldon Adelson, and that the election would be decided by which side did a better job mobilizing votes. The evidence over-whelmingly indicates that organized labor exceeded its ambitious goals in its identification and mobilizing efforts.[30]

GOP observers told us that they regarded labor's GOTV efforts as quite effec-tive for two particular reasons. A state factor that was important is the fact that Nevada permits "early voting." For two weeks prior to election day, voters can cast ballots at public facilities such as shopping malls. This enabled labor's orga-nizers to check and recheck the effectiveness of their efforts. Second, this window of opportunity for an elaborate GOTV effort may have benefited from a national trend as well. According to Ensign Chief of Staff Mark Emerson, the early voting period coincided with news stories from Washington in which then House Speaker Newt Gingrich was threatening the possibility of another government shutdown, due to disagreement between the Congress and the White House on the terms of a budget agreement. Emerson believes that this negative news com-ing from the nation's capitol depressed Republican turnout during the precise period when labor was most active.[31]

Labor was particularly active in Clark County because of the $2 million issue-advocacy campaign waged by casino owner Sheldon Adelson against three Clark County Commission candidates (two incumbents and one open-seat candidate) supported by the unions. Labor made Adelson the theme of a campaign poster and mailers depicting two babies with a monstrous Adelson looming threaten-ingly in the background captioned, "Working families have a choice in the elec-tion. Our kids or him." Adelson's heavy personal investment in issue ads against the commissioners did not succeed, as all three handily won their races. The ads backfired because they allowed union organizers to personify a villain in almost monstrous form with which to rally their troops.

Gaming

Compared to Adelson's high-profile attacks targeting Clark County Commission candidates, the rest of the gaming industry was notably subdued in the Senate race. While gaming interests contributed heavily to both candidates and parties, they were more concerned with contests in Missouri, South Carolina, and particularly California, where an initiative on the ballot threatened to permit Las Vegas–style casino gambling on Native American reservations.[32] The close ties of Reid and Ensign to the gaming industry also meant that gaming interests did not take sides. Instead, individual casino corporations backed their preferred candidate, gave money to both, or contributed strategically to national party organizations.

Records from the Nevada secretary of state's office and the FEC support this story. Hard-dollar contributions from gaming interests appear to have been fairly evenly distributed. Likewise, total contributions by gaming interests directly to the state party organizations were roughly equal.[33] However, soft-money contributions from gaming interests and representatives to national party organizations favored Republicans.[34] Between direct contributions to the state parties from gaming interests and soft-money transfers from the national parties, which apparently received much of the money from Nevada gaming interests, the state parties received the majority of their contributions from gaming interests (see fig. 7.2).[35] While gaming interests did not neglect the Democratic Party, their largess to the state Republican Party was considerably larger. According to FEC reports, both the outflow of soft-money contributions from Nevada, much of it from gaming-related interests and individuals, and the inflow of state party soft-money receipts appeared to favor the Republicans. Finally, the Republican tilt of Nevada's dominant industry was also evident in federal hard-money contributions. Reid outraised and outspent Ensign in the hard-money race and raised more money from gaming than did Ensign in the period since 1993. But in the last two years of the six-year cycle, Ensign raised more money from gaming-related PACs and individuals.[36]

League of Conservation Voters

The League of Conservation Voters (LCV) and the Sierra Club, opposed on environmental grounds to the storage of high-level nuclear waste at Nevada's Yucca Mountain, contributed to the Democratic Party's air war on the issue of nuclear waste. The LCV targeted Ensign as one of their "Dirty Dozen" congressional candidates for his voting record on environmental issues.[37] They ran two television spots in the north and two similar spots focusing on southern Nevada environmental flashpoints, spending more than $311,000 on these and related activities targeting Ensign, according to FEC independent expenditure reports. These ads dovetailed with Reid's own campaign thrust, highlighting his superior record on environmental issues while attacking Ensign. Indeed, a source in the Reid campaign told us that the LCV's advocacy allowed the interest group to do most of the heavy lifting on the issue of nuclear waste, and permitted Senator Reid to take a relatively high road in raising questions about Ensign's environmental record. The LCV, however, did not explicitly endorse Reid, though it did endorse the Democratic candidate for Nevada's first congressional district, Shelley Berkley. The Sierra Club chapters endorsed Reid newspaper ads and mailers, which were sent statewide to all Sierra Club members.

National Rifle Association

The National Rifle Association ran several issue ads on the radio endorsing Ensign in Clark County during the final two weeks of the campaign. NRA Chair Charlton Heston made a widely reported appearance in Las Vegas, strongly endorsing Ensign and attacking Reid on the first day of the general election campaign.[38] Heston made several subsequent appearances in Nevada, most of which appeared devoted to fund-raising. The NRA expended a greater effort in the more conservative and rural north, devoting most of its resources to radio. Expenditure levels by the NRA in the north are difficult to determine because virtually all radio stations in the region omitted these ads in their political file and refused to release information about time buys. The ads also ran on a full range of radio stations—from rock to easy listening as well as talk radio. The Federal Election Commission estimated NRA independent spending for Ensign at $81,247.[39]

Others

The trucking industry, upset with Reid for supporting legislation that would have banned triple-trailer trucks, spent nearly $300,000 on television ads in Nevada, roughly one-third of this in the north.[40] Rather than tell voters who they were, the truckers hid behind the name "The Foundation for Responsible Government (FRG)." Rather than discuss their policy difference with Reid on triple-trailer trucks, they ran mostly positive ads late in the campaign, discussing Ensign's position on health care and taxes. In the south, the ads received little attention in the vitriolic advertising environment in the waning weeks of the campaign. In our view, an interest group campaigning under a name not connected to that group and running ads on topics not related to their economic activity is a new and alarming precedent.

Eric Herzik, who monitored the northern Nevada campaign, identified radio ads by a group not observed in the south, which named itself the Committee to Save Social Security and Medicare (CSSSM). Their ads favored Reid. Because radio stations excluded these buys from their political files, the financial extent of the effort is unknown. Like the NRA, the CSSSM ads came in the last weeks of the campaign, primarily on easy-listening and talk radio stations.

Minor interest-group players included the tobacco industry, which ran ads early in the campaign on Ensign's behalf. A bipartisan Committee for Good Common Sense, an antitax group, ran similar messages toward the end of the general election campaign. Some newspaper ads were run by Hispanic groups (for Reid), and by local realtors and a Mormon credit union (for Ensign). In Boulder City, a private citizen named Paul Fisher, owner of Fisher Pen Company, ran several densely written newspaper ads on behalf of Reid. The Christian Coalition also attempted to mobilize members of churches in the Las Vegas area, but this activity appears to have been focused more on the race for the House seat vacated by Ensign. According to Representatives of both campaigns, Reid's publicly acknowledged religiosity as well as his pro-life record appear to have inoculated him against attacks by cultural conservatives.[41]

MEDIA COVERAGE OF OUTSIDE INTERESTS

With few exceptions, media coverage of labor efforts, party activities and expenditures, and the involvement of outside groups was extremely limited. Indeed, one local newspaper late in October ran a story bemoaning the lack of political coverage on television.[42] The article quotes several local media managers discussing the generally low television budgets for political coverage, lower even than a decade before. The effect of political advertising, alluded to previously, should not be overlooked either. Television stations, in order to put more ads on the air during a campaign in which the airwaves were saturated, took time away from news operations, trimming already limited time budgets for news. Even print coverage was comparatively sparse. Typical stories focused on "truth in advertising" or provided tabulations and cursory analyses of recent releases of data from the FEC, the Nevada secretary of state's office, or in a few cases the Center for Responsible Politics. Party fund-raising and expenditures received some coverage, notably from *Sun* reporter Steven Kanigher, who has incisively reported on campaign finance issues in Nevada for a number of years.[43] Efforts by outside interests, most notably organized labor, received almost no coverage throughout the campaign. What coverage of labor organizing there was appeared late or followed Reid's declaration of victory.[44] The only other outside effort targeting the Senate race to receive attention, and only because the group sought publicity with a press release, was the League of Conservation Voters' "Dirty Dozen" campaign, which included Ensign among its targets.[45] Adelson's $2 million barrage of ads targeting three Clark County Commission races generated considerable attention in the last weeks of the campaign. Though it played a key role in labor-mobilizing efforts, the media did not draw any connection to the Senate race. In an election this close, it is difficult to gauge the effectiveness of interest-group activity. The turnout drive of organized labor, however, was decisive in an election with relatively low levels of voter participation. Ensign benefited from an increasingly Republican electorate, an attractive image, and a popular Republican gubernatorial candidate. He therefore might well have won without the strong efforts of the AFL-CIO.

CONCLUSION

In a close election, it is easy to argue that many considerations affected the outcome. In our view, two factors were ultimately decisive: the ground war, the nuclear waste issue, and, to a lesser extent, soft-money spending by candidates and parties. First, the ground war conducted by organized labor was extremely important. This personal contact style of mobilization remained under the radar until very late in the campaign. This contrasted with the somewhat less intense efforts of the Ensign campaign on the ground. An Ensign spokesman told us that they had used a simple phone bank GOTV strategy on election day itself and had attempted to piggyback their efforts to increase GOP turnout on the more extensive organization of (successful) GOP gubernatorial candidate Kenny Guinn. As Emerson noted, "We lost because the grassroots did not go deep enough."[46]

Second, the nuclear waste issue allowed Reid to campaign as a protector of the environment in Nevada, but without the usual baggage (government regulation, federal control and ownership of lands, restrictions on property rights) that generally renders environmentalists unpopular in this part of the country. Environmental groups clearly helped Reid on this issue by attacking Ensign and forcing him onto the defensive, a tactic bitterly denounced by several representatives of the GOP and the Ensign campaign. Thus, in terms of interest-group support, Reid likely owes his victory to the mobilization of two traditional Democratic constituencies: organized labor and environmentalists.

Not as important to the outcome was the massive soft-money spending by both parties. Candidate and party money was effectively equal in amount and tone, with neither candidate nor party having much of an advantage. For months, Nevada voters saw political commercials, more than half of them paid for by the parties. The NRSC and Ensign ads insulated Ensign somewhat on Social Security but could not shift the agenda for the nuclear waste issue on which Ensign became vulnerable.

In general, the massive candidate, party, and independent expenditures did not appear to contribute much to the outcome. As we have noted, the relatively inexpensive electronic media in Nevada made it possible for campaign communications to saturate the airwaves, and, as Ensign media consultant David Weeks noted, to drown out specific, nuanced communications between candidates and voters.

It is also not clear why the media were not more attentive to the role of independent expenditures (and especially to the role of organized labor) during the campaign. We hypothesize that there were too many other, simpler, stories to cover during the fall of 1998, including Sheldon Adelson's highly personal attacks on Democratic members of the county commission, as well as the highly personal nature of attacks levied by candidates for governor and U.S. representative. While the Senate election was largely contested (quite fiercely) over matters of public policy, the same could not be said of other races in Nevada. Charges of personal corruption, malfeasance, and dereliction tended to dominate television and newspaper coverage of other races in the state. While preparations for labor's GOTV efforts were hardly invisible, they may have lacked the immediacy necessary to put organized labor in the media spotlight.

Further, it seems likely that attention to the efforts of interest groups may have been inhibited by the fact that some interest groups channeled their soft-money expenditures through the political parties. Environmental groups such as the Sierra Club and the League of Conservation Voters provide good cases in point. Generally, due to the individualistic political culture of Nevada and to the unpopularity of federal environmental regulations, environmentalism is a rather unpopular cause in Nevada. The environmental groups appear to have feared a countermobilization or a backlash if their advocacy of the Reid candidacy became too visible, so these groups attempted to influence the election via party contributions. On the Democratic side, this sort of strategy made it relatively easy for candidates, parties, and interest groups to provide congruent messages. According to Ensign media consultant David Weeks, such congruence was much more difficult for the Republicans. As Weeks put it, "We really couldn't put out a clear message, because of all the clutter created by independent expenditures. . . . If some group pulls the campaign in a different direction, it makes it difficult to develop a strategy."

Essentially, the Reid-Ensign race for the United States Senate was a party-based election in which a well-liked but not wildly popular incumbent was nearly defeated by an attractive, media-savvy challenger in a state with a changing partisan balance. Given the changing nature of the electorate and the dynamics of the governor's race, we regard Reid's narrow victory as something of a mild upset.

NOTES

1. As Jeff German put it, "Republicans and Democrats both have reason to smile in the aftermath of Tuesday's mudslinging election, the costliest in Nevada history" *Las Vegas Sun,* "Day of Close Calls, Labor Muscle," 4 November 1998, 1A. FEC reports indicate Reid and Ensign combined spent more than $8 million.

2. See "Reid-Ensign among the Most Expensive Senate Races Ever," *Las Vegas Review-Journal,* 23 November 1998, 3. Citing a Common Cause study, this article ranks Reid and Ensign number one and two in per-vote costs among 1998 Senate races, distantly followed by Al D'Amato of New York. Reid's per-vote cost was $22.02 and Ensign's $13.14 compared to D'Amato's $11.66. Figures were based on a partial study, made available by Common Cause at <www.commoncause.org/publications/april1999/congelect_srchart.thm>.

3. Mark Emerson, interview by Ted Jelen and David Magleby, telephone, 22 June 1999.

4. According to estimates computed from data provided by the Nevada secretary of state, the 1998 turnout (as a percentage of registered voters) was approximately 49 percent, which compares unfavorably to turnout in other off-year elections (75.0 in 1982, 71.9 in 1986, 64.4 in 1990, and 61.7 in 1994). As a percentage of eligibles, turnout in 1999 was 32.6 percent, as opposed to other elections (49.5 in 1970, 44.1 in 1974, 36.7 in 1978, 35.9 in 1982, 33.7 in 1990, 40.1 in 1994). *Statistical Abstract of the United States* (various volumes) and *Book of the States* (various volumes).

5. Richard M. Scammon and Alice V. McGillivray, *America Votes 20* (Washington, D.C.: Congressional Quarterly, 1993); "1996 Presidential General Election Results," *FEC,* 1996, at <http://www.fec.gov/pubrec/presge.htm>, 16 August 1999.

6. "Results of the 1998 U.S. Senate Recount," Nevada Secretary of State, 9 December 1998, at <http://sos.state.nv.us/nvelection/1998recount/>, 11 June 1999. Of Reid's total, 64.3 percent came from Clark County while only 53.7 percent of Ensign's votes came from Clark. Turnout figures, also available from the secretary of state's website, were reported in the *Las Vegas Review-Journal,* "Nevada Politicians Turn Off Voters: Only 49 Percent Turn Out," 5 November 1998. In Washoe County, which contains Reno, the only other major metropolitan area in the state, 52 percent of those registered voted. Statewide turnout outside of Clark County was 54.4 percent of registered voters (or approximately 41.8 percent of the voting age population).

7. "Nevada Senate," *CNN,* 1998, at <Cnn.com/ELECTION/1998/NV/S/exitpoll.html>, 15 December 1998.

8. Population figures are from estimates produced by the Nevada state demographer's office, available at <http://www.scs.unr.edu/demographer/>.

9. Since 1998 census estimates are not yet available, registration and voting figures are from the U.S. Census reports "Voting and Registration in the Election of November 1996 (P20-504)" and "Voting and Registration in the Election of November 1994" (PPL-25RV), available at <http://www.census.gov/population/www/socdemo/voting.html>. Current population figures are from estimates produced by the Nevada state demographer's office, available at <http://www.scs.unr.edu/demographer/> and from the Census Bureau at <http://www.census.gov/population/>. A newspaper report early in the general election race painted an even more radiant picture of the size and growth of Nevada's Hispanic population as well as growth among smaller minority groups, also citing "Census Data" through 1997. See "Census Charts Change in Las Vegas," *Las Vegas Sun,* 10 September 1998.

10. Ibid.

11. Registration and voting by gender for 1996 is from the U.S. Census report "Voting and Registration in the Election of November 1996 (P20-504)," available at <http://www.census.gov/population/www/socdemo/voting.html>. For exit poll results for a sample of

1001 Nevada residents, see "Nevada Senate," *CNN*, 1998, at <Cnn.com/ELECTION/ 1998/NV/S/exitpoll.html>, 15 December 1998. Notably, preferences for Reid or Ensign did not differ statistically by gender.

12. The conservative leanings of Nevada outside of Clark County are evident in registration figures as well as 1998 county vote returns. Twelve of Nevada's seventeen counties, including Washoe, reported more Republicans than Democrats registered, according to figures from the Nevada secretary of state's website, at <http://sos.state.nv.us>. In the 1998 balloting, Reid won only Clark County and sparsely populated Mineral County, the latter producing only 1,176 votes for Reid.

13. "Nevada Media Industry Big Winner in Election," *Las Vegas Sun*, 3 November 1998, 1C.

14. David Weeks, interview by Ted Jelen, telephone, 24 June 1999.

15. Paul Henry, interview by Ted Jelen, telephone, November 1998.

16. In 1998, Reid faced as many as 250,000 new voters who had entered Nevada since his last Senate race in 1992, along with tens of thousands of new voters who had come of age in Nevada since 1992. "Geographic Mobility/Migration," *U.S. Census Bureau*, 1999, at <http://www.census.gov/population/www/socdemo/migrate.html>.

17. Emerson, interview.

18. Rory Reid, interview by Ted Jelen and David Magleby, telephone, 21 June 1999.

19. B. Drummond Ayres, "Nevada Senate Race Is Gaining in Importance," *New York Times*, 23 August 1998.

20. Unlike some states such as Connecticut, where party bylaws or even state laws limit the assistance parties can provide candidates in primary races, in Nevada, particularly for statewide offices, the parties frequently settle on a candidate before the primary and provide strong political banking. In addition to the Senate race, the Republicans did this in the governor's race. This pattern of de facto nomination, labeled "anointment" by Nevada pundit Jon Ralston, is not uncommon.

21. Note that these are combined figures, not expenditures specifically linked to the Senate race. For reporting on the importance of television see, for example, "Nevada Media Industry Big Winner in Election," *Las Vegas Sun*, 3 November 1998, 1C.

22. All state campaign finance reports required by Nevada law can be found at the secretary of state's website, at <http://sos.state.nv.us/Contributions.asp>.

23. This table is based directly on party contribution and expenditure reports available at <http://sos.state.nv.us/Contributions.asp>. The expenditure categories are those employed by the secretary of state under Nevada law.

24. The largest chunk of Republican expenditures ($369,047) was reported for the first reporting period (1 October 1997 through 19 August 1998) before the 1 September primary. At least half of that amount appears to have been spent on the grassroots campaign to put "paycheck protection" on the ballot. Sizable expenditures were made from February through May to a firm called National Voter Outreach, and smaller sums during the same period went to a firm called Strategic Telecommunications. In addition, $53,075 was given to candidates during this period ($10,000 to Al D'Amato of New York, $10,000 to John Ensign, $13,075 to State Senator Mark James, and additional sums to several out-of-state candidates for the U.S. House of Representatives. Further, various northern Nevada county Republican Party committees received small sums. During the second reporting period (20 August through 21 October 1998) Republican expenditures totaled about

$300,000. Again, much of this money appears to have been spent to purchase a grassroots operation. For example, Campaign Telecommunications received $57,321. Majority Strategies based in Ohio—apparently a multipurpose consulting firm—received $75,479 in miscellaneous expenditures. Majority Strategies was also paid $185,279 for direct mail and $7,000 for consulting. In addition, a total of $110,000 was spent on direct mail on behalf of fifteen different candidates for the state assembly. Also included was a $50,000 contribution to the Republican Party of Hawaii. Period three (23 October to 3 December) saw much less activity in the miscellaneous category for the GOP. Most notably, the party paid $37,000 to the Colorado Republican Party, and $25,000 to the Republican Party of Missouri.

Conversely, the state Democratic Party reported less spending under the miscellaneous category, and examination of these expenditures is much less revealing. In period one, $11,500 (out of a total of $17,915) went to the Utah State Democratic Party. In period two, the South Dakota Democratic Party was paid $7,000 and the Missouri State Democratic Party was paid $123,250. The payment to Missouri was made on 10 September. On 11 September the Nevada Democratic Party received a contribution of $85,000 from the Missouri Democratic Party. According to former Nevada State Democratic chairman Paul Henry, these party exchanges are part of the secondary market in hard- and soft-money quotas for coordinated expenditures.

25. Emerson, interview.

26. Danny Thompson and Vince O'Brien, interview by Tim Fackler, Las Vegas, Nevada, 3 November 1998.

27. "Proposition 226: Political Contributions by Employees, Union Members, Foreign Entities, Initiative Statute," California secretary of state's office, at <http://www.ss.ca.gov/prd/bmprimary98_2/prop226-2.htm>, 6 June 1999.

28. See Jon Ralston, "The Short Unhappy Life of the Paycheck Protection Act," *Las Vegas Review-Journal*, 21 June 1998. Danny Thompson, political director of the Nevada AFL-CIO, interview with Tim Fackler, Las Vegas, Nevada, 3 November 1999.

29. Grover Norquist is head of Americans for Tax Reform (ATR), an influential conservative interest group. Norquist's name was raised by labor leaders since ATR has been active in the "paycheck protection" referendum campaigns in California and Nevada.

30. Information for this account comes from interviews with and data provided by various state and national labor representatives as well as newspaper accounts. See "Labor Helps Rally Votes for Reid," *Las Vegas Review-Journal*, 5 November 1998, 6A; and "Labor, Adelson Draw Battle Lines for 2000," *Las Vegas Sun* 5 November 1998, 1A.

31. Emerson, interview.

32. To the bitter but losing battle against Proposition 5, which threatened largely unregulated competition for Las Vegas gaming interests' largest market, southern California, Nevada-based gaming interests contributed nearly $30 million. Proponents put up nearly $67 million, making this the most expensive ballot proposition battle in the nation's history. For contribution and expenditure data, see "Proposition 5: Tribal-State Gaming Compacts. Tribal Casinos. Initiation Statute," California secretary of state, at <http://www.ss.ca.gov/prd/bmprimary98_final/Prop_5.htm>, 24 July 1999.

33. The Nevada Democratic Party received about $880,000, while the state Republican Party received about $870,000 from gaming interests. It should be noted, however, that about 40 percent of contributions to the Republicans came from Sheldon Adelson during

the spring of 1998 in his effort, through the Republican Party, to put paycheck protection on the November ballot.

34. Analysis of 1997–98 FEC soft-money data indicates that the various national Republican finance committees (the RNC, NRSC, and NRCC) took in roughly $1.5 million in soft-money contributions from Nevada gaming interests, while national Democratic finance committees (the DNC, DSCC, and DCCC) took in only about $270,000 out of a total of almost $2.4 million contributed by Nevada sources. Though we lack insider knowledge of exactly where Nevada contributions wound up, state records of party receipts from the national committees and FEC records of transfers to state committees suggest that soft-money contributions from Nevada along with hundreds of thousands more found their way back to Nevada, to the considerable advantage of the Republican Party. Data are from the FEC at <http://www.fec.gov>, the Nevada secretary of state's office at <http://sos.state.nv.us>, and from FECInfo, at <http://www.tray.com>.

35. Rough estimates with available data indicate gaming interests accounted for slightly more than 50 percent of Nevada Democratic Party receipts and about two-thirds of state Republican Party receipts. Of course, if we were to add contributions from development companies, unions, promoters, Nevada public officials, or private individuals with ties to or interests in the gaming industry, very few contributions to Nevada's parties would not be linked firmly to the interests of gaming. In addition to previously mentioned data sources, these estimates draw upon data from the Center for Responsive Politics website, at <http://www.opensecrets.org>.

36. Ensign took in about twice as much as Reid: $86,000 from gaming- and tourism-related PACs to Reid's $58,000, and $205,000 from individuals to Reid's $91,000. These figures were tabulated from FEC data on PAC and individual contributions, available at the Center for Responsive Politics website at <http://www.opensecrets.org/1998elect/dist_detail/98NVS8detail.htm>. Overclassification no doubt misses some gaming-connected money, because we are unable to classify all individuals.

37. "1998 Dirty Dozen Campaign News," League of Conservation Voters, 1998, at <www.lcv.org/dirtydozen/pr_923.htm>.

38. See "Heston Helps Ensign Take Shots at Reid," *Las Vegas Review-Journal,* 3 September 1998, 1A.

39. Found at <http://www.fec.gov>. Search "View Contributions," then "Query System," "Committee Search," "NRA," "NRA Political Victory Fund," "Committees and Candidates Supported or Opposed."

40. David Barnes, *Transportation Topics,* Washington, D.C.: TT Publishing, 22 November 1998, 1 and 27.

41. Reid campaigned quietly among Latter Day Saints (LDS) members in the Las Vegas area. The LDS population of southern Nevada is sizable (some estimates range as high as 130,000) but tends to be quite conservative and Republican. Interviews by Tim Fackler with Reid campaign operatives suggest that their strategy was to counter the "liberal" label with which Reid is often tagged locally while trying to win at least a few LDS votes on the argument that an LDS vote for Reid was an Ensign vote lost.

42. See "Even Key Nevada Races Lack Big Media Coverage," *Las Vegas Sun,* 27 October 1998, A1.

43. See Steven Kanigher, "Parties Prove Big Spenders in Campaign Stretch Drive," *Las Vegas Sun,* 13 October 1998, A1.

44. See "Jones Picks up Labor Support, Momentum in the Campaign," *Las Vegas Sun,* 17 September 1998, A3; "AFL-CIO Boss Sweeney Leads Charge for Labor '98 Political Campaign," *Las Vegas Sun,* 20 October 1998, B3; "Jones, Guinn Court Labor's Vote," *Las Vegas Review-Journal,* 15 September 1998, B1.

45. See "Conservationists Take Aim at Ensign," *Las Vegas Review-Journal,* 24 September 1998, B6.

46. Emerson, interview.

8

The 1998 New Mexico Third Congressional District Race

Lonna Rae Atkeson and Anthony C. Coveny

In an election year with relatively few competitive contests, the New Mexico Third Congressional District stood out as a potential takeover by the Democratic Party. From the district's inception in 1982, Democrat Bill Richardson had represented the district. Due to unique circumstances surrounding the special election in 1997, the district's representative was now a conservative Republican. The Democrats and numerous interest groups wanted to retake the district and believed that the right candidate and a well-funded campaign would return the district to their column. Republicans, on the other hand, knew they needed to fend off the Democratic assault in hopes of maintaining or expanding their majority in the House of Representatives. The active presence of a third-party candidate and a barrage of interest groups made the race even more unpredictable.

Part of the reason that Democrats and liberal interest groups found the district an attractive place for a Democratic takeover was the obvious ideological and partisan mismatch between the district and its newly elected Republican representative. The Third Congressional District of New Mexico encompasses the northern part of the state. The voting population is heterogeneous, with about 35 percent of the population Hispanic, 55 percent Anglo, and the remaining 10 percent American Indian.[1] The district is heavily Democratic, with nearly three-fifths (59 percent) of registered voters identifying themselves as Democratic and slightly over one-fourth (28 percent) registering as Republican.[2] Because the district is largely rural, many areas of the district are experiencing high unemployment. The overall unemployment rate in rural New Mexico is about 8.8 percent.

BACKGROUND FOR THE 1998 ELECTION

Given these characteristics, it was surprising that the Republicans were able to win the seat in a 1997 special election. Since its inception in 1982, the Third

Congressional seat had always been held by a Democrat (Bill Richardson) and always by safe margins. In 1996, Richardson easily beat the Republican candidate Bill Redmond (67.2 to 30.5 percent). But in early 1997, Richardson resigned to take a post at the United Nations, creating the need for a special election. This unique election environment allowed for a party turnover, with Republican Bill Redmond winning the seat with 43 percent of the vote. Three factors were key to his special election success: first, a weak Democratic candidate with high negatives, who was believed to have manipulated the nomination process (candidates were chosen through party chairs and not in a traditional primary setting); second, low voter turnout (35 percent);[3] and third, Green Party candidate Carol A. Miller, who received 17 percent of the vote.[4] Carol Miller's candidacy gave an additional choice to traditional Democratic voters who had difficulty supporting the party nominee.

Republicans were ecstatic and Democrats were dumbfounded by the special election outcome. Given the strong Democratic bent of the district and its traditional Democratic hegemony, the Third Congressional District of New Mexico was a prize that the Republicans wanted to keep and the Democrats wanted back. This made the district a top priority for both parties in 1998 and led to a heated general election contest. The partisan change in the district also drew in a number of interest groups doing candidate/election advocacy and several groups engaging in independent expenditure campaigns. All in all, the interest-group and party, television, and radio advertising combined exceeded candidate spending by $112,000. Interest groups and political parties were also key players in an ongoing ground war to mobilize their constituencies. Both spending and mobilization by these players were crucial in influencing the dynamics of the campaign, what issues voters considered, and how the candidates responded.

CANDIDATES AND THEIR CAMPAIGNS

By the beginning of 1998, the two main contenders for the Democratic nomination were Tom Udall, New Mexico's attorney general, and Eric Serna, who lost to Bill Redmond in the 1997 special election. In the June primary, Udall received 44 percent of the primary vote, compared with Serna's 36 percent. Meanwhile, incumbent Bill Redmond and Green Party candidate Carol Miller ran unchallenged for their parties' nominations.

Given the three-candidate general election race and Miller's reputation for taking Democratic votes in the special election, the Udall campaign's primary strategy was to woo back Democratic voters.[5] Udall's campaign therefore centered around traditional Democratic issues, including social security, education, jobs, veterans' benefits, and health care. Udall also emphasized his record as attorney general on issues like drugs, drunk driving, pollution, tobacco, and child welfare.

Incumbent candidate Bill Redmond attempted to use his eighteen-month record to enhance his electoral chances. The Redmond campaign had to get out their base of support on election day, as well as persuade many Democratic voters to again cross over and either vote for Bill Redmond or vote for Green Party candidate Carol Miller. In order to solidify and motivate his base, Redmond talked about traditional Republican issues like taxes, while attacking Attorney General Tom Udall's record on crime. To encourage Democratic defection, Redmond also focused on traditional Democratic issues and his congressional record on jobs and education. For example, he took credit for bringing 5,000 new jobs to northern New Mexico and assisting in creating a program that provided the federal government's surplus computers to schools. Redmond also worked hard throughout his term to gain passage to a land grant bill that would specifically help many Hispanic northern New Mexicans. Last, Redmond engaged in traditional incumbent activities like town meetings and communicating with key constituencies in the district.

Green Party candidate Carol Miller had little money to support her candidacy. Her strategy was largely to play up her outsider status and point fingers at the other two candidates for being traditional politicians. In debates with the other two candidates held all over northern New Mexico and on public television, Miller focused on her credentials as a political activist and as an average voter in touch with the community.

Money in the Campaign

The competitiveness of the election helped Redmond and Udall raise significant amounts of money. In a stark break from precedent, Udall, the Democratic challenger, raised more money than the incumbent Republican, spending over $200,000 more than Redmond (see fig. 8.1). Nevertheless, the $1.35 million that Redmond received far outdistanced his prior fund-raising. The possibility that he could win as the incumbent enabled him to attract nearly twenty times the financial backing he received in his 1996 challenge to Bill Richardson (in 1996, Redmond received only $235 in PAC contributions). Both candidates aired numerous television and radio ads, commissioned polls, ran phone banks, and engaged in direct mail tactics.

The origin of the campaign funds received by the candidates shines additional light on the nature of the election, with both receiving money from traditional Democratic and Republican sources. Redmond had the financial backing of banking institutions (American Bankers Association, Mortgage Bankers Association, Nationsbank), agriculture and livestock (Dairy Farmers of America, National Cattlemen's Beef Association), the NRA (and Gun Owners of America), oil companies (Exxon, Occidental Petroleum Corporation), and medical organizations (AMA, American Dental). Udall, by contrast, received money from teachers' organizations (NEA, American Federation of Teachers), labor (United

Figure 8.1 New Mexico Third Congressional District Candidate's Financial Activity in the 1998 Election Cycle

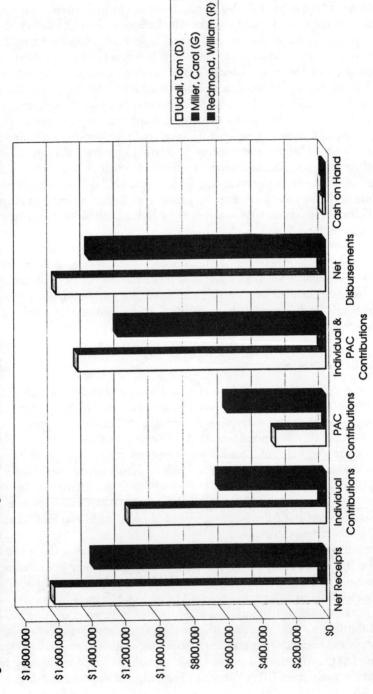

Source: Data from FEC press release, *FEC Reports on Congressional Fundraising for 1997–98,* 28 April 1999.
Note: Candidate self-support data omitted.

Transportation Union, Laborer's Political League, AFL-CIO), government employee unions (American Federation of State, County and Municipal Employees), and environmental groups (New Mexico Conservation Voters Alliance, Sierra Club).

Another distinction lies in the proportion of money each received from individuals, PACs, and other committees. Whereas Redmond received nearly 50 percent of his funds from PACs and other committees, Udall received over 75 percent of his campaign money from individuals (see fig. 8.1). Udall's individual contributions were collected through fund-raising events, mailings, and personal solicitations.[6] Several high-profile actors and political figures, including Robert Redford and Hillary Clinton, made themselves available to the Udall campaign for fund-raising events.

Udall's large war chest enabled his campaign to stay "on message" throughout the general election and respond to assaults by Redmond and the Republican Party. Given that the main objective of the Udall campaign was to woo back disgruntled Democrats, its ability to stay on message was seen as a top campaign priority. At the same time, ample funding permitted the campaign to respond directly to attacks by creating comparative spots, or positive spots, about Udall. For example, when the Republican Party attacked Udall's crime-fighting record as attorney general, the Udall campaign fought back by airing an endorsement ad that highlighted police organizations.

BEYOND THE CANDIDATES: THE ROLE OF INTEREST GROUPS

Several interest groups and the political parties played an active role in this campaign. Interest groups that were pro-Redmond and/or anti-Udall included the National Association of Manufacturers (NAM), which worked through a branch organization called The Coalition: Americans Working for Real Change; the Christian Coalition, and the National Rifle Association (NRA). Interest groups that were anti-Redmond and/or pro-Udall included the League of Conservation Voters (LCV), the New Mexico AFL-CIO, Planned Parenthood, the New Mexico National Organization of Women, the Sierra Club, People for the American Way, the Central Albuquerque United Auto Workers, and Neighbor to Neighbor. Many of these groups engaged in multiple strategies in order to both persuade voters and to get out the vote. Most groups did not run traditional independent expenditure campaigns, but ran issue advocacy campaigns that included get-out-the-vote efforts. Table 8.1 is a listing of all the groups and their campaign activities.

Two interest groups stand out for special attention because of their large, extensive, and costly campaigns. These are the AFL-CIO and the LCV. Both groups used television as a medium to communicate their message about the candidates to the public. Both groups believed they had an opportunity to make a difference

Table 8.1 Interest-Group Activity in New Mexico District Three by Type

Interest Group	TV	Radio	Mail	Phones	Other
New Mexico AFL-CIO	X		X	NA*	Person-to-person, work site
League of Conservation Voters	X		X	X	Person-to-person, GOTV
Neighbor to Neighbor	X		X	X	Sound truck
Central Albuquerque United Auto Workers			X	NA	
Planned Parenthood of New Mexico			X	X	
New Mexico NOW			X	NA	
Sierra Club			X	NA	Newspaper ads, person-to-person GOTV
The Coalition	X		X		
National Rifle Association		X	X	X	
Association of Builders and Contractors		X			
People for the American Way	X				
National Committee to Preserve Social Security and Medicare			X	NA	
Christian Coalition					State voter guide
Choice PAC					State voter guide

Source: Data from the Outside Money data set.
*Not available.

and influence the outcome of the election in the Third Congressional District through constituency persuasion and mobilization. Each group, however, took a different approach. The AFL-CIO engaged in a more modern issue advocacy campaign, while the LCV engaged in a negative anti-Redmond independent expenditure campaign.

The AFL-CIO's Campaign

The AFL-CIO ran two television issue ad spots, spending more than any other interest group, totaling $183,380. These commercials were shown a total of 427 times. The first commercial focused on tax cuts that were paid for by raiding the Social Security trust fund, and the second commercial focused on HMOs. Both ads had tag lines indicating voters should "call" their representative. Although neither of these ads directly relates to union issues, both social security and health care are issues of general importance to union members. These commercials appeared fairly early in the campaign, between September 10 and October 9, and were meant to influence the issue agenda during the campaign. According to Matthew Taylor, state AFL-CIO field director, the ads were shown early in order to "kick up some interest in the campaign."[7] The Udall Campaign felt that the Social Security ad was the most beneficial because it was in line with their overall campaign theme.[8] Although the health care ad was also in keeping with traditional Democratic issues, it was less effective, according to the Udall campaign, because of the district's poverty, which makes health insurance a luxury that many voters do not have.

The AFL-CIO of New Mexico also produced three colorful direct mail pieces. The topics covered were health care, education, and a reminder that Tom Udall was the pro-labor candidate. In addition to these direct mail pieces from the New Mexico AFL-CIO, local chapters also produced their own mail and leaflets for distribution to local members.[9] The AFL-CIO performed direct education of its members and their families with door-to-door outreach, phone banks, and work site leaflets.[10] Finally, the AFL-CIO made a direct contribution to the Udall campaign of $10,000.

The League of Conservation Voters

The League of Conservation Voters (LCV) ran an independent expenditure campaign. As part of this effort they ran a thirty-second anti-Redmond ad that aired 138 times. The LCV was second in television spending, with $129,645. According to LCV project director, Gregory Green, Redmond was on the LCV's Dirty Dozen list for his votes against approving the San Juan River for consideration as an American Heritage river and for his vote to postpone the U.S. Environmental Protection Agency's clean air standards for four more years. The ad was shown early in the campaign, from October 1 through 11, and the last week of the campaign. Initially, the ad displayed a saguaro cactus in its opening scene; unfortunately for the LCV, this cactus does not grow in New Mexico. Although this mistake was embarrassing to the LCV, and was corrected immediately, it generated a great deal of media attention for the ad and the LCV. The ad received newspaper coverage in approximately eighteen New Mexico newspapers and also some television news coverage.

Despite the embarrassing faux pas, the LCV felt their ads effectively got New Mexico voters thinking about the candidates' positions on environmental issues. A poll taken at the end of the election found 46 percent of voters recalled the ad.[11] According to LCV pollsters, "The charge about Redmond's antienvironment record was the strongest single charge against Redmond, creating serious doubts for 32 percent of voters. In contrast, the environment was the second strongest positive message for Udall, trailing only education."[12] Compared to earlier LCV polling, this was a marked change in attitudes toward Redmond and Udall.[13]

The LCV also spent money on direct mail, phone banks, person-to-person persuasion, and get-out-the-vote efforts. Its main strategy was to return the Democratic base to Udall and to reduce Green Party candidate Carol Miller's vote.[14] In keeping with this strategy, the LCV sent out letters signed by a state representative in both English and Spanish appealing to voters to vote against Redmond and for Udall. The LCV also targeted New Mexico Senate District 25 for special treatment (i.e., more phone calls, more canvassing) because many of Miller's votes were found there and voters in that district were seen as potentially persuadable.[15] Overall, LCV spent more on this House race than any other House race across the country, with expenditures totaling $252,000.[16]

The local LCV chapter members also actively supported Udall. They did one mailing that communicated their endorsement of Udall and sent out 4,800 absentee ballot request forms.[17] They also sponsored a fund-raiser for Tom Udall, which he attended, that raised about $4,000.[18] In addition, they conducted a volunteer get-out-the-vote drive and paid the half-time salary of a single staff member in Udall's campaign.[19]

Other Groups' Contributions

The National Association of Manufacturers (NAM) purchased airtime for one commercial, mostly on cable, costing $3,315. The group tagline on this commercial, however, was not NAM, but The Coalition: Americans Working for Real Change. The Coalition: Americans Working for Real Change is an umbrella organization for over thirty business organizations. The commercial was pro-Redmond and focused on his support of families and lowering taxes. NAM purchased and ran 310 ads from October 12 through November 3. The Coalition: Americans Working for Real Change also sent out a pro-Redmond mailer that focused on Redmond's record on taxes, education, Social Security, and health care. Besides NAM, the People for the American Way were the only other group to buy television time. These pro-Democratic ads ran October 6 through 13 and at the end of the campaign, from October 29 through November 2.

In addition to these groups running television ads, the NRA engaged in radio ads that named all three of New Mexico's Republican congressmen.[20] This standard Charlton Heston ad played all over the country with slight modifications to accurately identify local Republican candidates. The NRA ads ran late in the campaign, from October 26 through November 2. According to FEC records, the NRA's pro-Redmond independent expenditure campaign spent $40,640. The NRA also delivered funds directly to the Redmond campaign, making donations totaling $5,950 in 1997, for the special election, and $8,900 in 1998. In addition to the NRA, the Association of Builders and Contractors also purchased radio time. Its ad was also pro-incumbent Redmond and pointed out how the New Mexico Congressional delegation helped keep New Mexico tax- and business-friendly, supporting job creation. It spent $8,480 and ran 97 ads between October 15 and 21.

Beyond the radio and television ads, several interest groups actively engaged in issue advocacy and get-out-the-vote efforts via direct mail, phone banking, and person-to-person contact. The Sierra Club, for example, sponsored a grass-roots literature drop and a direct mail campaign that compared Redmond and Udall on environmental issues. They mailed 25,000 pieces of mail to voters who appeared on lists provided by local environmental groups.[21] They also sponsored a press conference in front of New Mexico's capitol. This, however, was not covered well by the local media. The Sierra Club organizers believed that this was because their press conference corresponded with Hillary Clinton's visit to New Mexico. The simultaneous scheduling of both events shows that the candidate campaign and the interest group were not coordinating their campaign efforts. The Sierra Club also made a direct contribution to the Udall campaign of $3,500.[22]

Several other groups also used direct mail. The United Auto Workers mailed an anti-Redmond piece on senior issues. The National Committee to Preserve Social Security and Medicare also sent out direct mail supporting Udall. It also endorsed Udall at a press conference attended by the local media. Neighbor to Neighbor, a Washington-based public-interest group that focuses on domestic human rights and economic justice, also sent out about 10,000 anti-Redmond pieces, costing about $5,000, focusing on health care and HMOs.[23] According to Shelley Moskowitz, a Neighbor to Neighbor representative, the group targeted the Redmond-Udall race because it felt that the large Hispanic population in the Third Congressional District was not well represented by the incumbent candidate.[24] It spent an additional $20,000 on voter registration drives, a Spanish-language public service announcement on Spanish radio, and a sound truck and phone banks that included volunteers and paid personnel.[25] These activities were targeted in areas of low voter turnout in the cities of Española and Santa Fe as well as in a number of Native American pueblos.

New Mexico's National Organization for Women sent out two anti-Redmond pieces. These leaflets were not approved by the National NOW offices, but were sponsored and paid for by local NOW activists.[26] The first mailer contrasted Redmond's support for funding nine new B-2 bombers with his vote against "vital funding for new breast cancer research."[27] Redmond took this attack very personally and responded with a letter from his wife that discussed the loss of his mother to breast cancer when he was twelve. In his response, he indicated that he only opposed the legislation described by New Mexico NOW because he favored another bill that gave even more money to breast cancer research. The second leaflet discussed Redmond's votes to cut legal aid to abused women.

Planned Parenthood of New Mexico (PPNM) engaged in two independent expenditure campaigns, one pro-Udall and the other anti-Redmond. These independent expenditures were financed by the Planned Parenthood National Federation as one of six targeted races in the country where Planned Parenthood felt it could make a difference. Although financed by the national organization, all ads were approved and implemented at the state level. According to Michelle Featheringill, president and CEO of PPNM, it did several direct mail pieces as well as voter identification, voter persuasion, and GOTV effort. The direct mail pieces compared Redmond's and Udall's views on women's issues, including abortion, contraception, family planning, and medical decisions. Featheringill believed "these were issues people would vote on. They will cross party lines—especially women voters." For this reason, the PPNM targeted all women who had voted in the last election (regardless of party). Featheringill explained, "We take the voter who is on the fence and motivate that voter to get out and vote."[28] These mailings were followed by a phone call (utilizing paid staff) urging these women to vote pro-choice.[29] The group's total spending was $46,478 ($25,508 pro-Udall and $20,970 anti-Redmond). According to Featheringill, the efforts of PPNM paid off: "A concerted effort, that targeted a group, has to have an impact—absolutely, without a doubt."[30]

Overall, the bulk of interest-group activity favored Udall. Of the fourteen groups we followed during the campaign only four were pro-Redmond. The other ten often did both anti-Redmond and pro-Udall activity.

While interest groups feel good about their roles in the campaign and about getting out their message to voters, candidates and their campaigns seem more ambivalent. The problem lies in the message sent by interest groups. Interest groups have a narrow agenda, while campaigns are trying to build a coalition. Ads and activities from interest groups sometimes do not reinforce the most important campaign themes. At times ads can be so off message that they drive some voters away. For example, Terry Brunner, New Mexico Democratic Party campaign coordinator, mentioned an early ad done by an environmental group that focused on the reintroduction of the Mexican gray wolf to southern New

Mexico.[31] Many ranchers in the area were opposed to the reintroduction and, therefore, calling attention to the issue could only hurt Democratic candidates. Sometimes groups are on message, resonating with the issues that candidates want to focus on; other times groups are off message, producing ads that may ultimately injure the candidate they want to help. Because of their limited agenda, groups do not necessarily consider the bigger picture but are more focused on representing their issue agendas and their constituents.

BEYOND THE CANDIDATES: THE ROLE OF THE POLITICAL PARTIES

Like interest groups, the political parties also played a role in the New Mexico election. Both political parties indicated that they did not explicitly discuss or directly correlate their campaign themes with the candidates.[32] However, both political parties indicated that such discussions were completely unnecessary because they knew their candidates and easily maintained consistent principles with them.[33]

Given the district's demographics, it was clear that the Democrats would want to win the seat back and therefore would commit numerous resources to the race. The Republican Party of New Mexico, therefore, invested a large amount of capital from hard- and soft-money sources into the Redmond-Udall race in order to "make sure that there was a counterposition to Udall and the Udall machine."[34] Their investment was necessary because they wanted to ensure that Redmond had a good showing in the general election. Republican ads played early and often; beginning prior to Labor Day and going through election day. Both the New Mexico Republican Party and the Republican National Committee (RNC) aired numerous ads, with the RNC spending $45,170 on television ads and the Republican Party of New Mexico spending $288,465 (551 were on network television and 1,440 were on cable). The RNC did both pro-Redmond and anti-Udall ads. As part of their national endeavor to elect Republicans, dubbed "Operation Breakout," the RNC ran an ad critical of Udall's support of Goals 2000, a federal program that provides grants for school programs and reforms. The RNC also ran pro-Redmond ads that covered his record on education and bringing jobs to the district. Both issues were consistent with the Redmond campaign agenda.

The Republican Party was the first to air negative ads against Udall. John Dendahl, the New Mexico Republican Party chair, believes that it is the primary responsibility of the party to do the negative comparison pieces, allowing the candidate to stay positive, or at least stay positive longer.[35] In the case of Udall, the Republicans believed that he had a dismal record as attorney general and they aggressively formulated a strategy that would communicate that to the voters. The party also wanted to emphasize Redmond's record and how much he had accomplished serving his constituency in his short eighteen-month term. Soft money was used from the RNC and the NRCC to fund the issue ads.[36] All ads were approved by the state party apparatus.[37] Soft money was also used to support down-ticket candidates in the state of New Mexico, providing an opportunity for Republican Party building.[38]

The national Democratic Party had much less money to put toward 1998 congressional campaigns than Republicans did. Because the Democrats had less money and because the poll numbers throughout the campaign showed Udall in the lead, the Democratic Party did not feel the need to pump large sums of money into the race.[39] According to Fred Harris, chairman of the New Mexico Democratic Party, "We never had a bad poll in this race."[40] Indeed, Tom Udall was ahead in the polls, from his clinching of the Democratic nomination to election day. Toward the end of the campaign, from October 20 through November 2, the Democrats did, however, run one anti-Redmond television ad. This ad ran 197 times and cost the party $129,816, less than one-third of the amount spent by Republicans. They also produced an anti-Redmond radio ad. Thus, the Democratic Party ran only issue ads against Redmond and no ads supporting Udall. The ads originated with the DNC and the DCCC, which provided the soft money necessary to purchase TV time.[41] All ads originating with the DNC and the DCCC passed the desks of Fred Harris and Terry Brunner (the campaign coordinator for the state party) for content approval. After approval, these ads and their funds went immediately to the vendors for implementation. Harris noted at least one specific case in the Third Congressional District where an ad attacking Redmond was rejected for misrepresenting his record and was sent back to the DNC for correction.[42] All party efforts in the state centered around assisting and electing candidates. The party did not engage in any other party-building activities.

Overall, the Republican Party spent nearly $700,000 on the Redmond-Udall race,[43] while the Democratic Party spent about $400,000 in the Third Congressional District.[44] These monies reflect overall spending by the parties on the northern New Mexico race. The money transferred to the state parties in figure 8.2 reflect the total transfers to the state party. The DCCC transferred the largest amount of federal money to the state parties, followed by the RNC, the NRCC, and finally the DNC. The NRCC, however, transferred the largest sum of nonfederal money to the state parties, followed by the DCCC, the RNC, the NRSC, and finally the DNC. Most of these transfers were used to purchase issue ads.

In addition to television advertising, both the Republican and Democratic parties engaged in direct mail, phone banking, and extensive get-out-the-vote efforts. The Republicans mainly relied on direct mail, sending out nearly one million pieces targeting Republicans and Democratic voters not voting in primaries.[45] Direct mail pieces were consistent with the Redmond campaign message. Because the Republican Party used volunteers on its direct mail project, it was able to use hard federal money to pay for the mailers.[46]

The Republicans adopted an interesting strategy in a three-part direct mail series. All were comparative pieces, with part one focusing on education, part

Figure 8.2 New Mexico: Soft Money Transfers from National to State Party Committees 1 January 1997 to Year End 1998

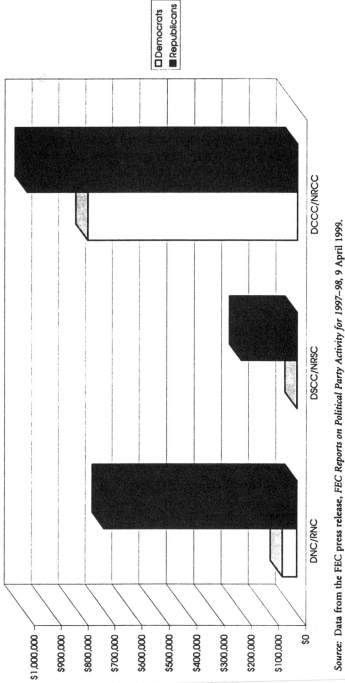

Source: Data from the FEC press release, *FEC Reports on Political Party Activity for 1997–98*, 9 April 1999.

two on crime, and part three on the environment. The difference was that while most comparative pieces focused only on Redmond and Udall, these pieces also included Carol Miller, the Green Party candidate. Both Redmond's and Miller's positions were shown positively. The strategy was clearly to take votes away from Tom Udall. The Republican Party of New Mexico also sent out several pro-Redmond pieces. These focused on his record, Social Security, GOTV efforts, education, health care, and crime. The Republicans also mobilized their constituency with phone banks, encouraging voters to vote absentee. The Republicans also used recorded calls late in the election to encourage voting. Congressman Redmond, Republican Governor Gary Johnson, and New Mexico Senator Pete Domenici, a well-liked senator by both Democratic and Republican voters, made recorded calls.

The Democrats canvassed voters for absentee ballots and did paid phone banking. The results paid off for the Democrats, who amassed approximately 6,000 more absentee ballots than usual.[47] Because their main goal was to get persuadables to vote, Democrats targeted precincts where their performance was 65 percent or above. Likely Democratic voters were also sent a letter in English and Spanish from former Congressman Bill Richardson that encouraged voters to vote Democratic and to vote as soon as possible. Enclosed with the letter was an application for an absentee ballot. A special letter from Hillary Clinton that included an absentee ballot petition was also sent out to women under 50 with a Hispanic surname. The Democrats had prerecorded calls from Hillary Clinton and from former Congressman Bill Richardson toward the end of the campaign to motivate voters to the polls. Targeted groups were those with a likelihood to vote Democratic; however, white men less than 40 years old were unlikely to get a call.

The Democratic Party of New Mexico also sent out several direct mail pieces. One was a comparison piece that focused on Medicare, Social Security, and public education. Two focused mostly on Redmond's voting record, with a final frame discussing Tom Udall. The first of these focused strictly on education, suggesting that Bill Redmond's education record was a disaster for New Mexico's children and that Tom Udall would protect public education. The second focused on Congressman Redmond's poor record on social security, Medicaid, education, and veterans' benefits. The last piece was strictly anti-Redmond, arguing that Redmond talks out of both sides of his mouth, saying he will do one thing on education, Social Security, and voting rights but will vote differently. All of these themes were consistent with candidate Udall's campaign message.

CONCLUSION

Interestingly, most of the activities engaged in by the interest groups and by the political parties went unreported in the local media. Neither print nor television news covered the extensive ground-war activities, which were a large part of the

New Mexico Third Congressional District story. This was most likely due to the difficulty in following the ground-war story. Reporters rely on information provided by others or accessible through the Internet or available through public documents. The ground-war story, the direct mail and mobilization efforts, were not easily visible and therefore not reported.

It is hard to follow the overall impact of noncandidate interest-group and party soft-money spending on the dynamics of the campaign and on the election outcomes. Candidate and party polls always showed Democratic candidate Udall in the lead, and, given the large Democratic bent of the district, it was not surprising to see Udall win a majority of the vote. Nevertheless, the Republican Party and pro-Redmond interest group clearly made a difference. They were able to maintain the amount of support they received in the special election, where turnout factors assisted Bill Redmond. This demonstrates the potential effectiveness of an aggressive party and interest-group strategy.

Overall, the congressional race in New Mexico's Third District was, for Democrats, about bringing home the base. Given the near 2-to-1 ratio of Democratic to Republican registered voters in the district, this was a sound strategy. The unknown in the race was Green Party candidate Carol Miller, who helped defeat the Democratic candidate in the special election eighteen months earlier, thereby allowing Bill Redmond to win the seat with a plurality vote. Therefore, the Udall campaign, the Democratic party, and the pro-Udall interest groups all worked diligently to ensure that those supporters of Miller returned home to the Democratic candidate. They aggressively targeted likely Democratic voters. They also emphasized to their constituents that a Green vote was a vote for Republican Bill Redmond. Numerous letters to the editor mentioned this fact, and several prominent and key Green political activists in the community endorsed Udall over their own party candidate. This strategy ultimately gave Udall a majority of voters in the general election and reduced Miller's vote total to a mere 5 percent.

Redmond's campaign had a much harder task; it needed to persuade voters, not just get out the vote. According to the Udall campaign, this was a difficult task because its public opinion polls revealed that most voters identified firmly with one camp or another.[48] Redmond's campaign, the Republican Party, and pro-Redmond interest groups therefore ran anti-Udall ads and strong pro-Redmond ads. They also attempted to increase support for Green Party candidate Carol Miller. Ultimately, they were unsuccessful, although they did manage to maintain 43 percent of the vote, which is what Redmond received in the special election in May of 1997. In a district where the Republican candidate only received on average 31 percent of the vote, this is a large and significant increase that may have future consequences as this district continues to grow and change.

NOTES

1. Brian Sanderoff, "GOP Slips into Democrats' Turf," *Santa Fe New Mexican*, 20 April 1997, A1.

2. New Mexico secretary of state, Election Bureau data, 29 October 1998.

3. Ibid.

4. Keith Easthouse, "Greens Celebrate Miller's Strong Showing, Reject Spoiler Label," *Santa Fe New Mexican*, 14 May 1997, A1; Mark Oswald, "Redmond Stuns Serna: GOP Candidate Pulls Big Upset in Primarily Democratic District," *Santa Fe New Mexican*, 14 May 1997, A1.

5. Sean Rankin, finance director for Udall campaign, interview by author, Santa Fe, New Mexico, 5 November 1998.

6. Rankin, e-mail communication with author, 9 April 1999.

7. Matthew Taylor, New Mexico AFL-CIO field director, interview by author, telephone, 12 April 1999.

8. Rankin, interview.

9. Taylor, interview.

10. Ibid.

11. Betsy Loyless, League of Conservation Voters staff member, interview by author, telephone, 16 March 1999.

12. "The Environment in the 1998 Elections," internal memo from Green and Associates to the League of Conservation Voters, 4 November 1998.

13. Gregory Green, LCV Independent Expenditure campaign director, interview by author, telephone, 23 November 1998.

14. Ibid. This was a conscious effort by the LCV, according to the independent campaign director.

15. Green, interview.

16. Loyless, interview. This is the total the organization spent on this campaign, including early polls and administrative expenses. The FEC report indicated the organization spent $239,051.

17. Linda Taylor, local LCV director, interview by author, telephone, 10 November 1998.

18. Ibid.

19. Ibid.

20. We covered eight radio stations in the Albuquerque/Santa Fe market. These included KPEK (contemporary-rock), KTBL (country), KBUL (country), KKOB (AM talk radio), KKOB FM (adult contemporary-rock, 70s and 80s), KRST (country), KNML (AM sports), KHTL (AM hot-talk), and KMGA (adult contemporary-rock, 70s and 80s).

21. Kathy Crist, Sierra Club representative, interview by author, telephone, 15 December 1998.

22. This includes $3,000 for the general election and $500 for the preceding primary.

23. Shelly Moskowitz, Neighbor to Neighbor representative, interview by author, telephone, 12 April 1999.

24. Ibid.

25. Ibid.

26. Linda Berg, NOW political director, interview by author, telephone, 12 April 1999.

27. New Mexico National Organization for Women leaflet.

28. Michelle Featheringill, president and CEO of PPNM, interview by author, telephone, 13 April 1999.

29. Ibid.

30. Ibid.

31. Terry Brunner, New Mexico Democratic Party campaign coordinator, interview by author, telephone, 9 November 1998.

32. John Dendahl, New Mexico Republican Party chair, interview by author, Santa Fe, New Mexico, 2 April 1999; Fred Harris, New Mexico Democratic Party chair, interview by author, Albuquerque, New Mexico, 1 April 1999; Brunner, interview.

33. Ibid.

34. Dendahl, interview.

35. Ibid.

36. Kevin Moomaw, New Mexico Republican Party executive director, interview by author, telephone, 6 April 1999.

37. Ibid.

38. Ibid.

39. Brunner, interview.

40. Harris, interview.

41. Brunner, interview.

42. Harris, interview.

43. Moomaw, interview.

44. Brunner, interview.

45. Dendahl, interview; Moomaw, interview.

46. Moomaw, interview.

47. Rankin, e-mail communication with author, 9 April 1999. The increase in absentee ballots was based on a comparison with the 1996 general election. The comparison consisted of a close examination of targeted counties and voting patterns of those with an inconsistent voting history.

48. Rankin, interview.

9

The 1998 Connecticut Fifth Congressional District Race

Sandra Anglund and Clyde McKee

The 1998 House election in Connecticut's Fifth Congressional District was one of the closest in the nation. Republican challenger Mark Nielsen failed to unseat one-term Democratic incumbent James (Jim) Maloney by only 1.5 percent of the vote.[1] Maloney outspent Nielsen, but this was offset by Republican Party advertising. The party spending on both sides was fueled with soft money and relied heavily on candidate attack advertising. Interest groups, particularly labor unions, were most important on the Democrat's side.

The Fifth District, in western, inland Connecticut, is anchored by the cities of Danbury, Meriden, and Waterbury. It stretches from culturally conservative manufacturing and former manufacturing areas, including one-time mill towns in the Naugatuck Valley, to well-to-do New York City commuter towns in Fairfield County on the New York state border. The black and Hispanic populations are small. In terms of party identification the Fifth District is competitive, with a whopping 43 percent unaffiliated, 30 percent Democrat, and 27 percent Republican.[2] Although Connecticut is a left-leaning state, the district sent Republicans to the House in six of the prior seven elections.

The district is particularly challenging for political campaigns because it is a very fragmented television market. The eastern portion of the district is dominated by television stations based in the Hartford and New Haven areas, while the western portion, including towns in Fairfield County, is dominated by New York City stations. Advertising rates at the New York stations are among the highest in the nation, and for an advertiser interested in reaching Connecticut voters, the stations involve a huge amount of waste. Consequently, direct mail and other ground-war efforts are attractive options for reaching voters. Both parties and labor unions used these ground-war tactics extensively in the Fifth District.

153

THE CANDIDATES AND THEIR CAMPAIGNS

The 1998 House race pitted a self-styled moderate Democrat with liberal leanings against a Republican with strong conservative credentials who positioned himself as a pragmatic Republican during the general election campaign. However, it is most appropriate to consider the election as one between an incumbent and challenger. Maloney emphasized his service to the district, and Nielsen, who centered his campaign around attacking Maloney's character, employed a challenger strategy.[3]

Maloney and Nielsen are both Harvard-educated lawyers from Danbury, Connecticut, with state legislative experience. At the time of the election, Nielsen, 34, was a second-term state senator holding the seat that Maloney, 50, occupied for eight years. Nielsen served one term in the state House prior to his election to the state Senate.

Maloney mounted an unsuccessful bid for the Connecticut Fifth District seat in 1994. Two years later, and with a lot of help from labor unions, Maloney took the seat from three-term conservative Republican Gary Franks, then the only black Republican in the House. As discussed in chapter 3, organized labor, relying heavily on television advertising, worked to defeat a number of members of Congress in 1996, and Franks was one of the targets. Given the district's profile and Maloney's narrow margin of victory—6 percent—he was immediately put on the Republican's list of targets for 1998.

Nielsen launched his challenge in September 1997. The early start was designed to stave off others in the Republican field. Although one contender for the nomination did receive enough votes at the Republican convention to force a primary, he withdrew. Thus neither of the candidates faced a primary.

In announcing his candidacy, Nielsen positioned himself as a conservative and emphasized tax cutting. His credentials as a fiscal conservative included, most notably, a suit to force the state legislature to implement a constitutional spending cap approved by voters in 1992. (The state Supreme Court rejected the suit in 1996.) At the time of the announcement Nielsen charged that the incumbent was "faking" a conservative record in Congress. He was "hedging to his right" in order to "align himself with the polls" in his district.[4]

Maloney had directed a Danbury poverty agency in the 1970s and may be a closet liberal as Nielsen charged. In 1998, Maloney was a sponsor of the labor-backed proposal to reform health maintenance organizations (HMOs), the patient's bill of rights. However, Maloney did compile a moderate voting record in Congress. A member of the House Banking and the National Security committees, Maloney sided with Republicans on key budget and tax bills, championed police issues, and in October 1998, was one of only thirty-one House Democrats to vote in favor of the Republican impeachment investigation resolution. (He did side with the Democrats on the impeachment vote that took place after the election.) Indeed, the Republicans in 1998 ended up attacking Maloney's tax votes in the state legislature rather than in Congress.

During the campaign, Maloney articulated Democratic positions on such issues as education and Social Security as well as health care emphasizing his moderate approach. And with the general election campaign, so did Nielsen. He campaigned as a "Rowland Republican" rather than as a conservative. John Rowland is the popular pragmatic Republican governor from Waterbury who was reelected in 1998 by a landslide. Rowland represented the Fifth District in the House in the 1980s.

While there certainly were issue differences between the candidates and each tried to paint the other as extreme, in the eyes of some, including a *Wall Street Journal* writer, it was a "small-bore" election when it came to national issues.[5] The Christian Coalition's candidate evaluations provide an example. Although not a major factor in Connecticut politics, this group did distribute a Fifth-District voter's guide. It reported that the candidates were at odds on only one of four of the group's issues. The religious freedom amendment was opposed by Maloney and supported by Nielsen. Both were pro-choice on the abortion issue.

Although neither candidate ignored policy issues during the campaign, the central theme of Maloney's effort was his attention to the district, and Nielsen's central theme was Maloney's character. While highlighting accessibility, constituency service, and claiming credit for federal projects for the district is a frequently used incumbent strategy,[6] this focus may have been particularly potent for Maloney because former Representative Franks had been accurately charged with ignoring the district.[7] Representative Maloney made good use of his incumbency and ties to the Democratic administration. During the campaign, he hosted Vice President Al Gore and, in conjunction with local projects, the EPA director and the secretary of Transportation. An express advocacy piece, paid for by the Democratic State Central Committee and titled "Getting the Job Done for You," featured a map of the district, keyed to a town-by-town roster of programs Maloney ostensibly helped deliver. Such projects, related events, and the representative's official activities won Maloney far more newspaper coverage than Nielsen received.[8]

As for Nielsen, his attacks on Maloney's character focused on three issues: financial irregularities in the 1998 Maloney campaign; finance problems in the Democrat's unsuccessful 1994 campaign; and the failure of Representative Maloney's former law firm, in the early 1990s, to pay certain federal taxes (since paid), which resulted in an Internal Revenue Service lien on the firm. The 1998 campaign issue evolved in late September when the Connecticut Republicans filed a federal complaint accusing Maloney of accepting $132,000 in improper donations. Although the Maloney campaign spokesperson at first insisted, "We have followed the law every step of the way," the campaign returned $5,000 in contributions and redesignated more than $29,000 in contributions.[9] The 1994 campaign finance issue dealt with Representative Maloney's brother, who pleaded guilty to charges of illegal fund-raising. The U.S. Attorney said there was no evidence that the candidate was aware of his brother's actions; however, the case provided a basis on which to question Maloney's character.

Because political party campaign communications often take a negative turn, allowing candidates to stay positive, it is important to stress that the Nielsen campaign itself advanced the Maloney character theme both in television advertising and candidate public appearances. As discussed in the next section, the attacks were reinforced and amplified by the National Republican Congressional Committee (NRCC) both in the air and on the ground. In this case, candidate and party themes were consistent.

The implicit division of labor between Maloney and the Democratic Party more closely approximated the candidate positive/party negative model found in other competitive 1998 races. The Democrats put out scalding ads on Nielsen's issue positions, while Maloney's ads emphasized his achievements. However, the Maloney campaign also ran comparison attack ads and ads rebutting attacks on the candidate's record. In addition to television, it should also be noted that the Maloney campaign bought time for comparison attack ads on New York City radio stations to counter NRCC anti-Maloney issue ads also on these stations.

On election night, Representative Maloney told the media that the Nielsen attack ads "backfired."[10] Indeed, earlier in the campaign, the media reported that the audience at an American Association of Retired Persons (AARP) forum featuring both candidates booed when state Senator Nielsen reiterated the attack theme. But Representative Maloney's narrow victory margin suggests that the attacks likely hit the mark with some voters. A University of Connecticut poll of 420 people in the district, conducted October 6–11, before the full force of the Nielsen and Republican ads hit, found Representative Maloney leading 46 to 16 percent, with the balance undecided.[11] A poll for Nielsen, conducted about a week later, screened for likely voters and found 45.7 percent for Maloney, 33.3 percent for Nielsen, and 21 percent undecided.[12]

The Maloney campaign out-fund-raised and outspent the Nielsen campaign. Federal Election Commission (FEC) filings report that Maloney raised $1,358,053 while Nielsen took in $940,008, which included a $121,000 loan from the candidate (see fig. 9.1). More than 57 percent of the incumbent's coffer came from political action committees (PACs). This included almost $300,000 from labor unions, with most of the balance from business PACs, reflecting, in part, Maloney's seat on the lucrative House Banking Committee.[13] Political organization and business PACs provided 30 percent of Nielsen's receipts.[14]

In a move to husband limited resources, the Nielsen campaign did not run ads on at least some important television stations for as much as a week in early October. Contracts on file at WFSB-TV, Hartford, a CBS affiliate, show that on October 6, the Nielsen campaign canceled a $39,200 buy that was scheduled to run October 9–15. A smaller buy on another station was cancelled October 9, and notes in the file at a third station suggest a similar action.

Figure 9.1 Connecticut Fifth Congressional District Candidate Financial Activity in the 1998 Election Cycle

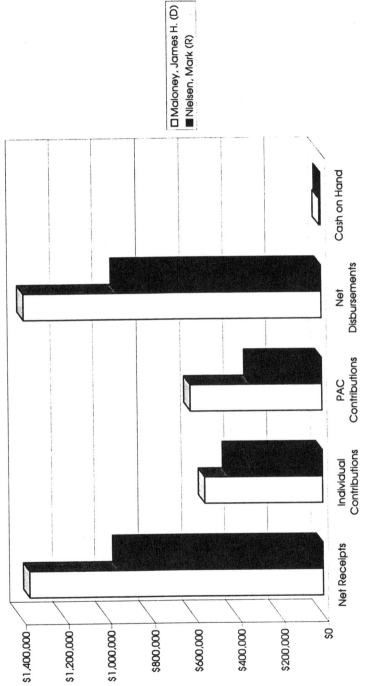

Source: Data from FEC press release, *FEC Reports on Congressional Fundraising for 1997–98*, 28 April 1999.
Note: Candidate self-support data omitted.

Because the cancellations came at the time that the national Republican's Operation Breakout advertising was expected to debut in Connecticut, they raise a question about inappropriate coordination between party and candidate campaigns. Republican television advertising, October 9–15, greatly exceeded the canceled Nielsen spots. However, the case of inappropriate coordination is impossible to make because the party plans were public information. The RNC/NRCC announced their plans in an October 6 news release. An RNC contract in the public files at WFSB-TV was dated September 29; we observed it on September 30. And, as Mark Nielsen points out, "I did not have the luxury of knowing they [party ads] would help me."[15] Indeed, even though the national Republicans did not run their Clinton scandal ads in Connecticut, Nielsen suspects that the national publicity on the ads hurt him. In the candidate's view, the ads contributed to general negativism, or what he terms "atmospherics," about Republicans.[16]

POLITICAL PARTY CONTRIBUTIONS

The national Republican campaign committees were the most visible of party organizations in the Fifth District election, but the Connecticut Republicans and Democratic State Central Committee were also heavily involved. Indicative of the importance the Republicans placed on this election, the district saw a legion of party notables during the campaign. They included Richard K. Armey, Tom DeLay, Bob Dole, John Kasich, Jack Kemp, John Linder, and John McCain. More important, we estimate that the RNC and NRCC spent a combined total of $800,000 to $1 million on advertising and direct mail, and most of it was soft money–fueled issue advocacy.[17] The RNC spent an estimated $200,000 to $250,00 to air a positive ad on the party's record, which was used nationally but localized at the end with a picture of Nielsen and a suggestion to phone him.[18] The RNC also paid for two mailings attacking Representative Maloney for voting "to give needles to illegal drug users" and Democrats in general for using "scare tactics" on Social Security.

The NRCC, to which the Connecticut Republicans had assigned most of their coordinated expenditure quota, was the bigger spender and its mode was attack. In congruence with and amplifying Nielsen's theme, the NRCC spent an estimated $200,000 to $250,000 to run three television advertisements on Maloney's campaign finance troubles. This committee also bought time for election ads on New York City radio stations, which prompted the Maloney campaign to respond on these stations, and pursued the attack via direct mail election ads. Three of six NRCC direct mailers attacked Maloney. The two most biting used the campaign finance theme. They called Maloney a "hypocrite" and, reinforcing a line used on television, asked him to "obey the law." The other attack flyer, designed to suggest a comic book, labeled Maloney "The Tax Man" and claimed to tell "a true story about one politician's efforts to raise taxes, double his own pay, and use illegal campaign money." The balance of the mailers positioned Nielsen as a "Rowland Republican," "A Congressman We Can Trust," and a tax cutter who will "never raise taxes as our Congressman."

In conjunction with the Republican Party television ads, it should be noted that Maloney's campaign staff wrote and phoned Connecticut television broadcast stations to advise them of their rights and remind them that the stations need not accept the ads. Although the campaign claimed success with one station, WVIT-TV, an NBC affiliate, a sales manager told us, "They (the NRCC) decided not to buy us."[19] Maloney's general consultant, Jason Linde, acknowledges that the NRCC's absence from this station—for whatever reason—probably had little impact.[20] He explains that the strategy was to signal the Republicans that "they could not roll us. We wanted to draw the line."

As for the state parties, both benefited from soft-money contributions from their national counterparts. During the 1997 to 1998 cycle, the RNC transferred about $400,000 to the Connecticut Republicans, and national Democratic committees provided almost twice as much soft money for the Democratic Connecticut party (see fig. 9.2). This marked the swan song for soft money in Connecticut, as in future elections state parties would be prohibited from accepting soft money from national parties.

The loss of soft-money transfers may take a bigger toll on the Connecticut Democrats than on the Republicans. The state Republican Party, which did not accept soft-money transfers in the 1996 cycle, has a much stronger individual donor base than does the Democratic Party. Robert Ives, executive director of the Connecticut Democrats, acknowledges that the demise of soft money "will hurt."[21] In his view, soft money applied to field operations, get-out-the-vote (GOTV) efforts, and related services for multiple candidates in 1998 helped the party win four statewide constitutional offices and maintain majorities in both houses of the state legislature in spite of the Republican governor's landslide victory. Further, soft money has helped the state Democrats update their computer capability and start a voter file for use by all candidates, which will improve the party's present lack of voter history. Still, Ives said, it costs $60,000 to $90,000 to provide candidates access to the file in state and federal election years.

Noteworthy among 1998 soft-money transfers to state Democrats was a $161,825 contribution received on October 15, according to reports filed with the Connecticut secretary of state. Television station public files show that on the same day the state party contracted to air an issue ad attacking Nielsen's positions. The television campaign cost about $200,000.[22]

We estimate that the state Democrats spent a total of $325,000 to $335,000 on advertising, including the television ad supporting Maloney. This includes about $95,000 on three issue ads mailed to the unaffiliated voters in the district. Taking a harder line than the candidate, the mailings as well as the television ad painted Nielsen as an extremist on budget cutting, a threat to Social Security and Medicare, and a threat to school funding. The total also includes an estimated $30,000

**Figure 9.2   Connecticut: Soft-Money Transfers from National to State Party Committees,
1 January 1997 to Year End 1998**

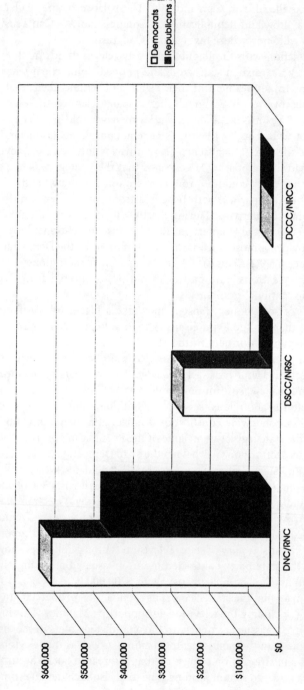

Source: Data from FEC press release, *FEC Reports on Political Party Activity for 1997–98,* 9 April 1999.

to $40,000 for the express advocacy walk piece discussed above, which, because it was distributed by volunteers, was likely a nonallocable expenditure or hard money not charged to the coordinated expenditure budget because of the party-building volunteer component. (The state party assigned its coordinated expenditure quota to the Democratic Congressional Campaign Committee.) Meanwhile, the party's campaign arm, the Campaign for Connecticut Families, led a highly publicized attack on state Senator Nielsen, charging that he had used his Danbury legislative office for campaign purposes and filing a request to obtain relevant paperwork at the state Freedom of Information Commission.

The state Democratic Party's GOTV program in the Fifth District included an early campaign poll of registered Democrats and unaffiliated voters to assess preferences in a series of races and immediate preelection telephone calls to registered Democrats and to those who had indicated a preference or a likely preference for the popular U.S. Senator Chris Dodd, who was also on the 1998 ballot. Just as the Republicans hoped Governor Rowland would have coattails (he did not), so the Democrats hoped that Senator Dodd would have coattails or at least get voters on the Democratic line (perhaps he did).

The Republican Party's GOTV activities were more extensive than those of the Democrats.[23] The Connecticut Republicans initiated the season by mailing absentee ballot applications, preceded by a postcard, to Republicans who had not voted in certain prior elections. They also conducted an early campaign poll, used preelection phone banks, mailed slate postcards, and provided slate palm cards at polling places. The Republicans added a twist to their GOTV calls. When live callers reached an answering machine, they left a message taped by Governor Rowland.

The lesser scale of the Democratic GOTV effort may reflect the fact that, as discussed in the next section, the party's labor union allies were heavily involved on the GOTV front, but it also may reflect troubles at party headquarters. After the election, calls for the ouster of the chairman surfaced, and the campaign manager for the unsuccessful Democratic gubernatorial nominee made headlines with charges that the party let down its candidates during the campaign. Indeed, the Maloney forces mounted their own volunteer-based GOTV program in selected precincts.

District turnout was 56.23 percent of registered voters, close to the statewide average of 56.59 percent.[24] There were rumblings that Republican turnout in Fairfield County was down, and labor unions supporting Maloney claimed great success. As noted in chapter 1, turnout was low among self-declared conservatives across the country. This may be the gist of the turnout story, but no exit polls were conducted in the Fifth District, so we do not know which efforts were effective and which efforts were not.

While the Connecticut Republicans focused on GOTV activities and a sophisticated voter file project, they did add to the national Republican committees' direct mail attacks on Maloney. They mailed about 96,000 flyers in Fairfield

County, and other selected areas, which reiterated the character theme. By having volunteers affix labels and stamp, sort, and mail the piece, the party was able to treat the $41,000 cost of the project as a nonallocable expenditure.

INTEREST-GROUP CONTRIBUTIONS

Interest-group campaigning in the Fifth District was one sided, working to help Maloney or attack Nielsen. The most active groups for Maloney were labor unions and, to a lesser extent, environmental groups, primarily the Sierra Club.

The notable absence of interest-group election advocacy benefiting Nielsen necessitates consideration of the groups that were not involved before considering those who were. Among those missing were The Citizens Flag Alliance, which works for a flag protection amendment to the constitution; Americans for Tax Reform, which opposes increased corporate and individual income taxes; and U.S. Term Limits. Maloney signed the pledges for all three. The groups essentially threatened that if Representative Maloney did not sign their pledges, they would advertise against him. Maloney therefore took the pledges, even though we suspect that he does not really believe in the merits of these causes. With the exception of an announcement of the tax pledge in late August, the Maloney campaign did not showcase the pledges. Nevertheless, the signed pledges removed these groups from the campaign.

Also missing from the Nielsen camp were business groups.[25] Nielsen cited the backing of some such organizations, but the only pro-Nielsen business advocacy detected was by the National Federation of Independent Business (NFIB). This group claims volunteer recruitment and GOTV efforts.[26] It also conducted a well-publicized endorsement press conference in the Naugatuck Valley and mailed a flyer to some 1,600 members in the district positioning Nielsen as "Working for Small Business in Connecticut." In July, the *Hartford Courant* reported that the Health Benefits Coalition, a business group that includes health insurers, was planning to run television ads opposing the patient's bill of rights in Hartford.[27] The ads were to counter AFL-CIO spots thanking Maloney for supporting the proposal, addressed below. However, we did not find evidence of a coalition campaign. Maloney's staff members report that they were on the watch for the coalition, but the group did not show.

Where was business? State Republican Party staff members speculate that forecasts of a very close race likely deterred pragmatic business groups that pursue access strategies. Representative Maloney's moderate voting record may also be part of the story. In the nearby Sixth District, the Business Roundtable did advertise in support of Republican incumbent Nancy Johnson, who faced and beat a liberal challenger.

THE CONNECTICUT AIR AND GROUND WARS

Interest groups supporting Maloney waged a limited, but important, air war and extensive ground war that received no media coverage.[28] One of the reasons interest groups engage in election advocacy is to influence candidate campaign and ultimately government agendas.[29] If shaping the Maloney campaign agenda was the objective of the Sierra Club, it had mixed results. Labor unions were more successful.

The Sierra Club launched its effort in late August/early September with a radio campaign praising Maloney's clean-air voting record. The club had announced its plans earlier in 1998, and, in response to the news, Maloney's campaign manager told *CQ Weekly* that he was not pleased: "You have a message you're working on and an independent group comes in and their message is the message."[30] The fact is that the environmentalist theme could have hurt Maloney in some parts of the district. Although Maloney hosted the EPA director during the campaign, the message of the major event did not deal with clean air or clean water, but cleaning up the abandoned factories or "brownfields" that dot the Naugatuck Valley.

Indeed, when the Sierra Club moved its campaign to the ground, with the exception of a half-page voter's guide issue ad in the *Waterbury Republican-American*, it switched to a niche strategy. An express advocacy flyer claiming that Maloney was protecting forests, water, and children's health, whereas Nielsen would threaten them, was mailed to 25,000 people interested in environmental issues.[31] An endorsement press conference attended by the club's national president was staged in one of Fairfield County's most environmentally oriented towns. Volunteers distributed leaflets but to only about 2,500 homes in northern Fairfield County. In addition, the Connecticut chapter of the Sierra Club, with the help of a grant from the national group, retained a field operative who, towards the end of the campaign, worked directly with the Maloney camp. This, it should be noted, was also the approach taken by the League of Conservation Voters.[32] The league urged a vote for Maloney via a postcard to members, but its major contribution was an in-kind staff member for the Maloney campaign.

While environmental groups were not major agenda setters in the Fifth District race, labor union issue advocacy may have influenced the Maloney agenda.[33] Labor emphasized the patient's bill of rights, Social Security, and education, and so did Maloney. While the candidate would probably have highlighted the latter two issues even without labor's advocacy, the patient's bill of rights is another matter. This is the only issue that labor addressed in its air war, and patient's rights did make it into one of Maloney's television ads. It is thus possible that labor's public advocacy of the patient's bill of rights did influence the Maloney campaign agenda in 1998.

The union air war on the patient's rights issue started in July when the AFL-CIO spent at least $75,690 on pro-Maloney television issue ads. The ads thanked

Representative Maloney for supporting the proposal. Stage two of the air war was a radio stealth campaign. A labor front organization, the Coalition to Make Our Voices Heard, headed by AFL-CIO Executive Director Linda Chavez-Thompson and Rev. Jesse Jackson, aired radio issue ads attacking Republicans in general for blocking HMO reforms. The coalition bought about $6,700 in radio time on a Hartford-based station that is the strongest in Connecticut and considered important for reaching voters in the Fifth District as well as other districts. This ad may have also been on a Bridgeport station that reaches portions of the district. In defense of their innocuous name, AFL-CIO Political Director Steve Rosenthal explained, "In some places it's much more effective to run an ad by the 'Coalition to Make Our Voices Heard' and to get a broader group of supporters than it is to say men and women of the AFL-CIO."[34]

On the ground, the Connecticut AFL-CIO, which has about 40,000 members in the Fifth District, sought to "educate" members about the issues, including the HMO issue, and to recruit volunteers for the Maloney campaign.[35] The group claims that about 1,000 members volunteered for Maloney on their own time at some point during the campaign. The member-education effort included work-site leaflet and person-to-person communications as well as telephone and direct mail programs. The mail campaign involved sending members literature that was keyed to their interests and preferences, which were identified in member-to-member telephone calls. The two member mailings we obtained employed the issue approach. They asked, "Which candidate has the backbone to stand up to HMO's?" and "Who will protect Social Security?" The flyers used loaded language to compare the candidates' positions and asked readers to "Decide. Then Vote." Nielsen, according to one flyer, could be expected to vote with Newt Gingrich, then speaker of the House and a favorite target of liberal groups.

In addition, about three-quarters of the AFL-CIO's member unions reportedly waged their own campaigns. Among these was the Service Employees International Union, which did four issue ad mailings—about 10,000 each—to members, other licensed health care workers, and, in one case, to members of two other liberal organizations.[36] The two flyers that we observed highlighted Maloney as an advocate of the patient's bill of rights—in opposition to "Newt Gingrich and the insurance industry lobbyists."[37]

Teacher's unions were also heavily involved. The National Education Association PAC (NEAPAC), which reported $116,103 in independent expenditures on behalf of Maloney, targeted Fairfield County and perhaps other areas with two or three full-color direct mail flyers and radio ads that recommended voting for the Democrat.[38] The NEA strategy was based on a district poll conducted to help decide who to target and what message to use, also paid for by the PAC. The NEA's express advocacy approach reflects its policy of not using dues dollars for political involvement and the finding that NEA support of a candidate is "viewed favorably by the public."[39]

While the NEA waged a public campaign, its state affiliate, the Connecticut

Education Association, recruited some 100 volunteers for the Maloney campaign and focused on its 6,000 members in the district. This group explicitly advocated voting for Maloney in a direct mail piece, a letter signed by its president, and volunteer-staffed phonebanks.[40] The Association of Retired Teachers of Connecticut also wrote to members, endorsing Maloney, as did the Connecticut State Employees Association.

The labor union campaign was intense. But, with the exception of endorsement press conferences by two police unions and a short item on the AFL-CIO's July television buys, newspapers simply did not cover labor's campaign. Yet the union campaign appears to have been effective. A national exit poll found that 22 percent of all voters in the 1998 election were from union households, and, of these, 70 percent voted Democratic.[41] The director of political education at the Connecticut AFL-CIO, which did not conduct research on turnout, believes that the state came close to the national numbers.[42]

Why did the news media fail to report on the full scope of the labor effort? Part of the explanation is that neither the Maloney campaign nor, we suspect, the unions sought coverage. As noted, part of the AFL-CIO air war was mounted through a front organization, and it appears that Maloney did not want to be pegged as a labor candidate. A campaign news release announcing the endorsement of a police union referred to the group as an "organization" rather than a union. Another news release listed endorsements and did include several unions but placed them in such categories as "teachers," "employees" and "police officers." When labor unions and The Rainbow Coalition had a preelection rally featuring Rev. Jackson, in a city near the district, Maloney did not attend.

Another part of the explanation is labor's emphasis on ground strategies. They "fell below the radar" of journalists, according to Matthew Daly, the political reporter who covered the Maloney/Nielsen race for the *Hartford Courant*.[43] "We feel we have to explain what people are seeing," he said. In short, no air war, no news coverage. The RNC, NRCC, and Connecticut Democrats, of course, were on television, and news reports did mention these campaigns; however, it was sometimes in passing. The scale of the Republican campaign assumedly would have made it big news, but journalists did not know the scale. Reporters, including the *Hartford Courant's* Daly, phoned the national committees and asked about Fifth District expenditures but did not get straight answers. As a *Waterbury Republican-American* reporter wrote, "A spokesman for NRCC would not disclose how much money the Republican Party plans spending for television ads in the Fifth District. The money political parties spend on these independent ads is unregulated."[44]

CONCLUSION

The Connecticut Fifth District race challenges the conventional wisdom that congressional elections are candidate centered. If our estimate of RNC and

NRCC Fifth District advertising expenditures is accurate, the Republican Party spent as much as or more than the Republican candidate's campaign, and Republican Party expenditures on issue advertising helped to offset the advantages of incumbency that the Democrat enjoyed. Maloney's narrow victory margin made him one of the ten most vulnerable Democrats in the House.[45] Maloney also received significant outside help. He benefited from state party-funded advertising and interest-group advocacy, primarily that of labor unions. The AFL-CIO's patient's rights advertising may have influenced the Maloney campaign agenda. By signing the pledges of the three national interest groups that threatened to advertise against him, Maloney denied his opponent these sources of assistance.

The Maloney/Nielsen contest, like many of the competitive races in 1998, also highlights the importance of the ground war, particularly direct mail. One resident of Fairfield County received eleven pieces of mail from parties and interest groups on this race alone. The direct mail strategies allowed the avoidance of high New York City advertising rates and the tailoring of messages for specific audiences. Both state parties and the NEAPAC used precampaign polls to help pinpoint target audiences and messages. The AFL-CIO also conducted a precampaign poll of its members.

Although party and interest-group campaigns were extremely consequential in this election, they received little media attention. Party and labor union ground wars fell under journalists' radar. Although reporters and their editors might be faulted, the fact is that even the most enterprising reporters would have had difficulty getting a full picture of the noncandidate campaigns. Neither party released information about the scale of issue advertising expenditures in the Fifth District. The law does not require disclosure. Only one interest group involved in the election, the NEA, filed independent expenditure reports, and finding them required patience with the FEC's website. The Coalition to Make Our Voices Heard could have been anybody. Reporters with an investigative bent and a lot of time could have found the story of the Voices Heard Coalition and gained insights into other aspects of the campaigns if they had monitored television and radio station public files. However, some major stations did not put contracts for party and interest-group issue ads in their public files. In short, the noncandidate campaigns escaped media scrutiny, in part, because of weak disclosure laws. Full public information about the noncandidate campaigns might have had no impact on the outcome of the Fifth District race, but in the interest of democratic elections, it should have been available.

NOTES

1. Connecticut secretary of state, *Statement of the Vote*, 3 November 1998, 76. A third-party candidate, Robert V. Strasdauskas, received 2,712 votes.

2. Connecticut secretary of state, "Registration and Party Enrollment Statistics," 20 October 1998.

3. On incumbent and challenger strategies, see, for example, Paul S. Herrnson, *Congressional Elections*, 2nd ed. (Washington, D.C.: Congressional Quarterly, 1998), 170–71 and 178–79; Gary C. Jacobson, *The Politics of Congressional Elections*, 4th ed. (New York: Longman, 1997), 70, 74.

4. Matthew Daly, "Nielsen Seeks Seat in Congress," *Hartford Courant*, 3 September 1997, A3.

5. Albert R. Hunt, "A Small-Bore Election," *Wall Street Journal*, 29 October 1998, A23.

6. On credit claiming, the classic is David R. Mayhew, *Congress: The Electoral Connection* (New Haven: Yale University Press, 1974), 52–61.

7. See, for example, Michael Barone and Grant Ujifusa with Richard Cohen, *Almanac of American Politics 1998* (Washington, D.C.: National Journal, 1998), 317. On ignoring problems in Meriden, see James H. Smith, "Maloney Did His Homework," *Record-Journal*, 4 October 1998, B1. On Maloney attentiveness to district, Terry Corcoran, "Maloney Offers Substance over Style," *Waterbury Republican-American*, 19 October 1998, B1–B2.

8. Newspapers monitored were the *Hartford Courant*, *News Times* (Danbury), *Record-Journal* (Meriden), and *Waterbury Republican-American*.

9. Gregory B. Hladky and Michelle Tuccito, "GOP Complaint Targets Maloney," *New Haven Register*, 24 September 1998, A3.

10. Terry Corcoran, "Maloney Fends Off Challenger," *Waterbury Republican-American*, 4 November 1998, A4.

11. Matthew Daly, "Poll Shows Maloney with a Wide Lead," *Hartford Courant*, 18 October 1998, A1.

12. Terry Corcoran, "Nielsen Poll Says Contest Is Tighter," *Waterbury Republican-American*, 17 October 1998, B1. This poll was actually released before the Courant poll and was announced to counter a Maloney poll. Each candidate questioned the findings of the other's polling consultants on this and other occasions during the campaign.

13. "Committee Contributions, James H. Maloney," *FECInfo*, 1998, at <www.tray.com/fecinfo>, 15 December 1998.

14. The proportion of PAC receipts for both candidates was higher than the 1996 averages for incumbents and challengers. That year PAC contributions made up 39 percent of the average incumbent proceeds and 19 percent of the average challenger proceeds. See Paul S. Herrnson, *Congressional Elections*, 2nd ed. (Washington, D.C.: Congressional Quarterly, 1998), 133 and 242.

15. Mark Nielsen, interview by authors, Watertown, Connecticut, 19 March 1999.

16. Ibid.

17. This is a rough estimate based on contracts in television station public files, copies of eight direct mail pieces, most in full color and professionally designed, interviews, and media reports. Estimates for television advertising—$400,000 to $500,000—are discussed below. The total expenditure estimate also includes an estimated $350,000 for seven direct mail flyers and $30,000 for an oversized postcard, all printed in color. We added $100,000 for the NRCC's New York City radio buy, an absolute guesstimate. Jane Gross, "No G.O.P. Sweep, Despite Rowland Broom," *New York Times*, 4 November 1998, B15, reports, "Mr. Nielsen . . . was enriched with $600,000 from the national party, which en-

abled him to run a vigorous television campaign." We suspect that this estimate ignores direct mail and radio ads. If the television total reported is correct, that would add $100,000–$200,000 to our estimate for television and to total RNC and NRCC expenditures.

18. Estimates of RNC and NRCC television advertising expenditures are based on contracts observed at those stations that place issue advertising in their public files, a market share breakdown (estimated) obtained at one station, and interviews with state Republican Party staff, who, in a postelection interview, 5 November 1999, said they thought our initial contract-based estimate of $250,000 for the RNC and $250,000 for the NRCC was too high. Thus, the range. Public files at all Connecticut-based broadcast television stations and most of the cable channels serving the district were monitored.

19. Mark Beckwith, sales manager, WVIT-TV, interview by authors, telephone, 4 November 1998.

20. Jason Linde, Maloney campaign general consultant, interview by authors, telephone, 26 March 1999.

21. Robert Ives, Connecticut Democratic State Central Committee executive director, interview by authors, telephone, 22 March 1999.

22. State Democratic Party expenditures on television and direct mail and the discussion of GOTV activities based on interview by authors with Matt Miller, staff member, Campaign for Connecticut's Families, the Connecticut Democrat's campaign arm, Hartford, Connecticut, 6 November 1998.

23. Discussion of state Republican Party activities based on interview by authors with Mike Broder, communications director, and George Gallo, executive director, Connecticut State Republican Central Committee, Hartford, Connecticut, 5 November 1998.

24. Connecticut secretary of state, *Statement of the Vote*, 3 November 1998, 169.

25. It should be noted that the National Rifle Association voter's guide, which was distributed in its magazine, had a pro-Nielsen tone, as did the Christian Coalition voter's guide. Connecticut Republicans for Choice recommended a vote for Nielsen in a membership mailing.

26. Brent Littlefield, National Federation of Independent Business northeast director, interview by authors, telephone, 11 November 1998.

27. John A. MacDonald, "Health Ads to Fight It Out in Hartford," *Hartford Courant*, 18 July 1998, A8. It should also be noted that the National Association of Manufacturers attempted to buy on a cable channel that reached the Fifth District in October, but the station was sold out. Whether NAM was acting for itself or the coalition and whether the intended ad was aimed at the Fifth District race was unknown. The intended buy could have been targeted at another district also served by the channel.

28. The focus is on environmental groups and labor unions. The activities of other groups either observed on the Maloney side or whose voter guides conveyed a pro-Maloney tone were minimal. These groups included the American Association of Retired Persons, Connecticut National Abortion & Reproductive Rights Action League PAC, and the Human Rights Campaign, a gay and lesbian group. In addition, the National Committee to Preserve Social Security and Medicare held an endorsement press conference in the district.

29. See, for example, Darrell M. West and Burdett A. Loomis, *The Sound of Money: How Political Interests Get What They Want* (New York: W. W. Norton, 1998), chapter 2.

30. Donna Cassata, "Independent Groups' Ads Increasingly Steer Campaigns," *CQ Weekly,* 2 May 1998, 1109–14.

31. Mark Bettinger, Sierra Club senior regional representative for the northeast, interview by authors, telephone, 5 April 1999.

32. On the in-kind contribution approach, see, for example Mark J. Rozell and Clyde Wilcox, *Interest Groups in American Campaigns* (Washington, D.C.: Congressional Quarterly, 1999), 106–08.

33. There are a number of goals that unions, as other groups, may pursue in campaigns. On various goals and strategies of labor unions, see "Labor at Work: Union Campaign Activities and Legislative Payoffs in the U.S. House of Representatives," Paul S. Herrnson, Peter L. Francia, and Peter F. Burns (paper presented at the 1998 Annual Conference of the Northeastern Political Science Association).

34. Steve Rosenthal, lunchtime discussion panel at the Pew Press Conference, "Outside Money: Soft Money & Issue Ads in Competitive 1998 Congressional Elections," National Press Club, Washington, D.C., 1 February 1999.

35. Tom Carusello, director of Committee on Political Education (COPE), Connecticut AFL-CIO, interview by authors, telephone, 29 December 1998 and 26 August 1999.

36. Jill Hurst, interview by authors, telephone, 19 November 1998.

37. HMO-bashing by labor unions and politicians in the fall of 1998 ultimately triggered a response by Aetna U.S. Healthcare, which is headquartered in Hartford. In a two-page *Hartford Courant* ad, the health insurance giant pointed out that its employees were also voters. It listed the names of about 2,000 employees who "call on politicians and others who criticized managed care to adopt a 'truth in campaigning' policy."

38. Jack Pacheo, National Education Association, interview by the authors, telephone, 9 June 1999.

39. Ibid.

40. Don Ciosek, Connecticut Education Association, interview by the authors, telephone, 9 June 1999.

41. For one report on the poll, see Karen Foerstel, "Interest Groups Seek Best Value for Copious Campaign Dollars," *CQ Weekly,* 12 December 1998, 3295.

42. Carusello, interview.

43. Matthew Daly, reporter, *Hartford Courant,* interview by authors, telephone, 30 March 1999.

44. Laura Magi, "Maloney Trails Race at the Bank," *Waterbury Republican-American,* 16 October 1998, 1.

45. "Target," *Hartford Courant,* 4 June 1998, A6.

10

The 1998 Utah Second Congressional District Race

Jay Goodliffe

In 1998, Merrill Cook beat the jinx of the Utah Second Congressional District: according to one political reporter, incumbents in the Second District "have a political life span roughly equivalent to that of a minnow in a shark tank."[1] Before Cook's reelection in 1998, the last incumbent to win a second term did so in 1990. Although Utah is a very Republican state, the Second District is less Republican than the state's other two districts. In 1996, Clinton received 41 percent of the vote of the Utah Second District, Dole received 47 percent, and Perot 9 percent; statewide, Clinton received 33 percent. Since redistricting in 1991, the Democrats had only won the seat in 1992.

The Second District attracted party and interest-group money because it is a swing district and because the Republican incumbent Merrill Cook started raising money late and was seen as vulnerable. Indeed, one conservative commentator stated that Cook was one of "the nine most endangered Republican incumbents" and that Republicans had "sent out an SOS for their big-money people to send more campaign funds" to those nine House members.[2] The Republican Party included Cook in its "Operation Breakout" campaign, spending about $200,000 on television advertisements in his behalf. The Democratic Party countered with $270,000 spent on radio advertisements, mailers, and a get-out-the-vote campaign in behalf of Lily Eskelsen. At the same time, Americans for Limited Terms spent $380,000 on television advertisements, mailers, and phone banks in an effort to defeat Representative Cook or encourage him to sign a term-limits pledge. While the efforts of the parties largely neutralized each other, the term-limits campaign significantly increased the negativity of the campaign, which ultimately reflected poorly on Lily Eskelsen, whom they were supporting.

THE CANDIDATES

Merrill Cook is a well-known entity in Utah politics: prior to 1996, he had run for office six times unsuccessfully, spending about $3 million of his own money.[3] He has also led and financed five unsuccessful state ballot initiatives, four on taxes and a term limits/runoff election measure. In this process, he has angered many Utah Republicans by founding the Utah Independent Party, running as an independent for governor in 1988 and 1992 and for Congress in the Second District in 1994. Through his early political activities, Cook established a reputation as a political jester—never seeming to be able to win a race. His 1998 campaign manager—Caroline Roemer—echoed this sentiment when she said, "Many people expected Cook to be a bit of a buffoon."[4]

In 1996 Cook ran as a "rehabilitated" Republican against an opponent with even more negative associations than Cook. Cook's opponent, Ross Anderson, was noted for his support of same-sex marriages and abortion rights, opposition to the death penalty, and for serving as president of the Utah chapter of the American Civil Liberties Union. Cook won in 1996, outspending his opponent 2 to 1, mostly from his own pocket.[5] In 1998, running as an incumbent, Cook used all the benefits of office. As a member of the Transportation and Infrastructure Committee, he helped secure transportation funds for the state. He used the power of the frank, the privilege of congressmen to send mail free of postage, spending more than four times as much as other House representatives from Utah.[6] As a member of the Banking and Financial Services Committee, he raised campaign funds from banks, credit unions, and financial service companies.[7]

Lily Eskelsen, Cook's Democratic opponent, entered politics when, as she accepted a Utah Teacher of the Year award from the Utah Education Association (UEA), she gave a speech decrying a proposed reduction of taxes that, ironically, was a 1988 Cook initiative. She became active in the UEA, served as president from 1990 to 1996, and is currently on the executive committee of the National Education Association. In previous years, she was approached by prominent Utah Democrats several times to run for office but declined—until she was approached to run against Cook.[8]

Campaigns and Platforms

Cook's primary campaign theme was his congressional record: bringing home money for transportation infrastructure and supporting education and Social Security.[9] Federal transportation dollars were a major issue, as both of the interstate highways that cut through Cook's district were under reconstruction with the hope of federal support. Had he not secured the funding it would have been a major issue against him. The Cook campaign assumed that Social Security and education would be issues emphasized by Eskelsen; Cook sought to define himself on these issues. The Cook campaign also attempted to heal his rift with the

Republican Party by having Governor Michael Leavitt endorse him. In 1992, Cook had said some unflattering things about Leavitt when running against him for governor as an independent; Leavitt had also been cochair of the bipartisan campaign against Cook's 1988 tax-cutting initiatives.[10] According to Dan Jones, Cook's pollster, the Leavitt ads "definitely had a positive effect." Voters were not sure if Cook was a true Republican, and the Leavitt ads showed he had been "redeemed" or "sanitized by the Republican Party."[11] In the last two weeks of the race, the Cook campaign ran negative ads against Eskelsen criticizing her stances on various issues. At the same time, in mailers, the Cook campaign emphasized that Eskelsen was the usual tax-and-spend liberal, out of touch with Utah voters.

The Eskelsen campaign ran against Cook's record—his record in office and his record before he took office. The general theme was "Merrill Cook—Doing, Saying, and Spending Anything to Get Elected." This message appeared in TV commercials and mailers sent to women and seniors. The campaign specifically mentioned issues such as education, Social Security, and the environment. In these ads, Cook is shown in an unflattering manner, with what he called a "bad hair day."[12] The Eskelsen campaign was criticized for running negative ads.[13] In the last week of the race, the Eskelsen campaign also ran a limited radio ad featuring an endorsement from the League of Conservation Voters, using Robert Redford as the voice-over.

Money in the Candidate Campaigns

Cook, who called himself a "mediocre" fund-raiser,[14] raised $656,985, nearly two-thirds of which came from political action committees (PACs), primarily business PACs (see fig. 10.1). He did not use any of his own money and started fund-raising late, which he called an "error," stating that this was because he was "a little shy about asking people for money."[15] Later, Cook was less shy about asking for money. Cook was able to use the prospect of outside groups for fund-raising. For example, he warned potential contributors that organized labor would come in just before election day and try to buy the election.[16] In the end, since labor did not come in, Cook stated that he got the "best of both worlds." He used labor as fund-raising foil, but labor spent no money outside of its membership.

Eskelsen started raising money early, and by the end of March 1998, she had almost twice as much money in the bank as Cook, an unusual circumstance against an incumbent, much less a first-term incumbent. In all, she raised $712,473, almost two-thirds of which came from individual contributors and one-third from PACs (primarily labor). According to her campaign manager, Eskelsen raised money from individuals through a concerted grassroots effort. For example, supporters of Eskelsen would host a "house party," in which the supporter would invite others over to his or her house and encourage them to

Figure 10.1 Utah Second Congressional District Candidate Financial Activity in the 1998 Election Cycle

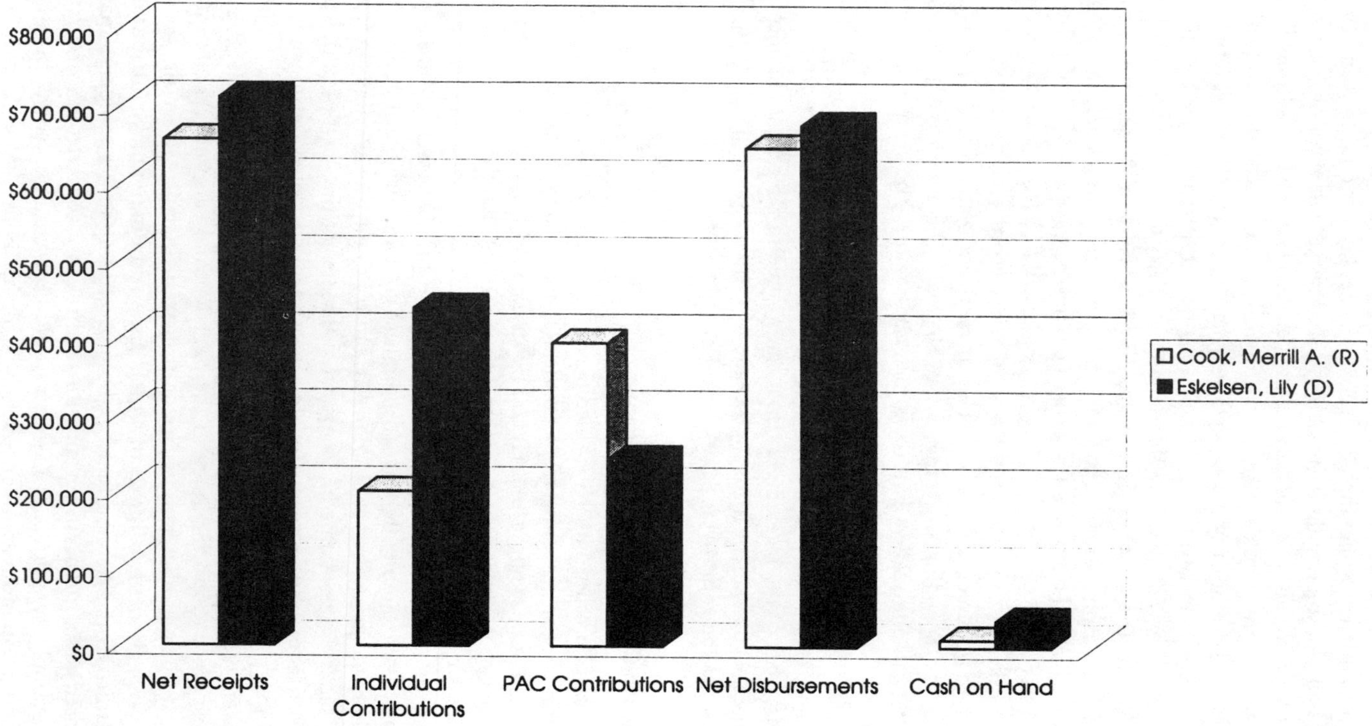

Source: Data from FEC press release, *FEC Reports on Congressional Fundraising for 1997–98*, 28 April 1999.
Note: Candidate self-support data omitted.

make donations. Eskelsen also sent out fund-raising letters to everyone she knew. At the end of the campaign, the Eskelsen campaign appealed to potential donors to contribute to combat the Republican Party's Operation Breakout ads.[17]

POLITICAL PARTIES

Republicans

The national parties were heavily involved in the Cook-Eskelsen campaign. Cook was one of the thirteen incumbents who received Operation Breakout ads from the National Republican Congressional Committee (NRCC).[18] The NRCC spent about $200,000 in TV advertisements on Salt Lake City stations, which began airing at the beginning of October, the same time the candidates began airing ads. The money was funneled through the Utah Republican Party, which was also listed as the sponsor. The first ad emphasized all the good things the Republican Congress had done. Part of the script read:

> So what has the Republican Congress done? How about a $500 per child tax credit? . . . Or health insurance that goes with you when you get a better job. . . . Even a budget surplus that's helping save Social Security. . . . Republicans like Merrill Cook are reaching out to find solutions to the problems families face.

A later ad proclaimed how the Republican Congress had balanced the budget in four years, whereas Clinton had said it would take longer, with oblique references to the Lewinsky scandal and Clinton's equivocations and prevarications. Part of the script read:

> It took this Republican Congress just four years to balance the budget. Now there's a surplus and a Republican plan to save Social Security for the future. . . . And provide tax relief to working families by ending the marriage tax penalty. Republicans like Merrill Cook support this balanced plan to protect seniors and strengthen families.

Thus, the theme of these ads correlated well with Cook's general message of competence and specific message about protecting Social Security. Furthermore, it reinforced the positive parts of Cook's campaign. The correlation, though, was fortuitous, not intentional—the same ads were used for all Republican candidates in the Operation Breakout campaign.

Spencer Stokes, who was executive director of the Utah Republican Party, thought that the national party soft money could have been put to better uses. He stated that if he had controlled the NRCC's efforts, he would have used some of the money for get-out-the-vote (GOTV) efforts. And he was also irked that the national party had not consulted with the state party on its ad buy concerning what times and age groups to target. Finally, Stokes thought that the ads began running too early. This is an interesting twist of soft money: the state parties would like to use it for party building, while the national party would like to use it for campaigning.

In the last two weeks of the campaign, the NRCC used their coordinated expenditure money ($64,000) to send out five different mailers to identified Republicans who supported Bob Bennett, the incumbent Republican U.S. senator up for reelection, and Lily Eskelsen. The issues of the mailers included taxes, abortion, Social Security, and the environment, specifically the possible draining of Lake Powell. The mailers praised Cook and derided Eskelsen, saying, "Lily Eskelson [sic] wants you to keep less of your hard-earned money." One mailer had an unflattering picture of Eskelsen. Some mailers were regarded as misleading. For example, the last mailer sent reads, "Merrill Cook will not allow Lake Powell to be drained!" However, Eskelsen was also opposed to the draining. These mailers reinforced the messages of Cook's television advertisements. This is not surprising, since the Cook campaign designed them; the NRCC merely paid for them. The mailers were more negative than the television ads and were created to counter what Cook's campaign manager called Eskelsen's "Lily seems nice and pretty" campaign.

The Republican National Committee and NRCC also contributed about $90,000 to the Utah Republican Party for general party building across the state. The funds were used for voter identification, GOTV, and helping Republican candidates get elected, specifically, the Salt Lake County commissioners: the whole Second District is in Salt Lake County. According to Stokes, those who came out to vote for the Republican county commissioner candidates would also vote for Cook. Thus, the funds may have helped Cook indirectly. This strategy seems to be the reverse of the usual strategy of getting voters excited about the top of the ticket and assuming they will vote for the party candidates in lower races. Perhaps this was because the Senate race was not close, and Republicans still had reservations about Cook. Cook was not particularly pleased by this strategy. In the last week of the campaign, Cook was upset when he learned that his name was not mentioned on a GOTV phone call placed by the state party. His profane outburst caused him to be banned from party headquarters for a week, an occurrence not known to the public until after the election.[19] The irony here was that both Republican candidates for county commissioner won by narrow margins, while Cook won comfortably. An interest group, Americans for Limited Terms, campaigned aggressively against Cook after he refused to sign its term-limits pledge. The Republican Party took steps to neutralize the term-limits ads against Cook. Jake Garn, a popular former Utah senator who opposes term limits, recorded a phone message to be sent to 80,000 Republicans, saying that an out-of-state group was spreading misinformation about Cook's term-limits record. The Utah Republican Party mounted an unprecedented absentee ballot drive in the Second District, sending about 60,000 applications, which included only the Republican slate of candidates, to likely Republican voters.[20] The Democrats responded in kind by sending out about 50,000 applications, but without any candidate names. About 2,000 voters sent in the preprinted Republican absentee ballot request; about 1,200 voters sent in the Democratic version. According to the Salt Lake County clerk, absentee ballots increased 67 percent, compared to the previous midterm election.

Democrats

The Democratic Congressional Campaign Committee (DCCC) spent $60,000 less than the NRCC in the race, most of which was spent on radio and mailers. The money was funneled through the Utah Democratic Party, which was also listed as the sponsor. Two radio ads were broadcast in the last two weeks of the campaign and criticized Cook's votes on education and Social Security and were somewhat negative. The script for one ad read, in part:

> You know, there's nothing more important in Utah than educating our children . . . ensuring that they get the best possible education. Preparing them for their future. Our pioneer ancestors often built their school houses before their own houses. They knew how important education was. But, now, not everyone agrees. You see, Congressman Merrill Cook voted against smaller class sizes and increased funding for proven programs like Head Start.

The Democratic Party chose to broadcast radio ads because they were cheaper and because the Eskelsen campaign had done no radio advertising. Unlike the national Republican Party's use of television ads, the national Democratic Party gave the state party some choice as to what issues to emphasize in the script and what radio stations to broadcast its ads on.[21] Thus, the Democratic radio ads correlated more strongly with Eskelsen's message than the Republican television ads did with Cook's message. At the same time, the Democratic Party radio ads also reinforced the strong negative nature of some of Eskelsen's television advertisements.

Through the Utah Democratic Party, the DCCC also paid for three mailers sent in the last two weeks of the campaign: an absentee ballot application and issues mailer that echoed Eskelsen's issues; a generic "Vote Democratic" mailer sent to Democrats; and one mailer sent to seniors that echoed the Eskelsen campaign against Cook's stands on Social Security with a picture of crossed fingers that reads, "Saying one thing . . . then doing another." Besides emphasizing the issues of Eskelsen's campaign, the party Social Security mailer echoes the exact language used in Eskelsen's own campaign: "Merrill Cook—Doing, Saying, and Spending Anything to Get Elected." The Social Security mailer even included the same "bad hair day" photograph of Cook that Eskelsen used in her television ads and mailers, thus tying the party and the candidate campaigns closer (and reinforcing the negative aspects).

The DCCC and other party sources contributed money for the Utah Democratic Party's GOTV campaign. The Utah Democratic Party did three sets of GOTV telephone calls to likely Democratic voters in the Second District, one of which was a recorded message in Eskelsen's voice using election advocacy language that did not explicitly call for her election. The first telephone call was a live call on the Thursday or Friday before the election to identify Democrats who had failed to vote in a recent election. The second telephone call was also a live call that asked if the prospective voter would like to hear the message from Eskelsen, and was made on the Saturday and Monday before the election, again targeting Democrats who had failed to vote recently. The third call was a live call made on election day to all identified Democrats and heavy Democratic precincts. In addition, the party had an extensive poll-watching effort in the Second District. The Democratic Party put about 400 persons at district polling places to check who had voted, and telephoned likely Democratic voters who had not yet voted. Some of the money spent in these efforts came from Eskelsen supporters who had maxed out their contributions directly to the campaign. The executive director of the Utah Democratic Party considered this GOTV effort to be very effective. Although Eskelsen lost the race, Democrats picked up two Senate seats and one House seat in the state legislature. In all, the Utah Democratic Party received about $270,000 from outside sources to be used for the Eskelsen campaign. Although the Utah Democratic Party was under no obligation to use the money for Eskelsen, this was the understanding.

INTEREST GROUPS

Term-Limits Groups

One group had a significant presence in the Utah Second District: Americans for Limited Terms (ALT). ALT followed all of the competitive House races in 1998, inviting each candidate to sign a pledge from its allied group, U.S. Term Limits, agreeing to limit his or her future terms to three. If one candidate signed and the other did not, ALT spent money denouncing the unsigned candidate.

In the Utah Second race, the story began in August, when Howard Rich, president of U.S. Term Limits, telephoned Cook, asking him to sign the pledge. According to Cook, Rich threatened to put $100,000 into the Eskelsen campaign if Cook refused to sign the pledge. Cook's reasons for not signing even though he supports term limits are long and labored, involving the number of terms to be limited and his distrust of U.S. Term Limits, which he dealt with in the 1994 initiative. Paul Jacobs, national director of U.S. Term Limits, stated that Rich never issued such threats and that Cook's version was "categorically false."[22]

Eskelsen stated that she signed the pledge to limit her terms because she was not planning to serve a long time anyway and that it would demonstrate her credibility as a "real person, with a real paycheck, not a millionaire." Before she was approached by U.S. Term Limits, Eskelsen had not considered term limits as an issue.

U.S. Term Limits did not spend any money for Eskelsen or against Cook, but they did hold a press conference with Eskelsen in mid-October, where she ceremonially signed the term-limits pledge. Americans for Limited Terms spent $380,000 in the race: $250,000 on TV ads in the last three weeks, $100,000 on three mailers, and $30,000 on phone banks.[23] All of these activities were conducted as election advocacy.

The theme of the TV ads was that Washington had a corrupting influence, and because Cook refused to limit his terms, he would also become corrupt. One advertisement specifically tailored to the Second District had ordinary citizens asserting that if Cook supported term limits, he should sign the pledge: "What's good for the goose is good for the gander," the ad said.

The mailers were sent to registered Republicans and independents because they were the most likely to influence Cook to sign or change their votes, respectively. In case Cook decided to sign the U.S. Term Limits pledge, ALT taped another advertisement thanking Cook and Eskelsen for signing the pledge. This advertisement would have run in place of the ads criticizing Cook for not signing, since the time was already bought. The tone of the mailers was more harsh than the television ads: One mailer showed cash changing hands with the caption, "Can You Be Tempted?" Another mailer began outside with the words, "Abuse . . . Corruption . . . Neglect . . ." and continued inside, "We Deserve Better. We Can Have Better." The mailers specifically denounced Cook and thanked Eskelsen. For example, one mailer reads:

> Lily Eskelsen has signed the U.S. Term Limits Declaration pledging to serve no more than three terms in Congress. Mrs. Eskelsen has openly stated her position that being a representative of the People is more important to her than becoming a career politician.
>
> Merrill Cook has *refused* to limit his own terms. While Cook likes to say he supports term limits, his actions don't follow his words. He has only supported sham term limits proposals in Congress, and then only when it was certain they wouldn't pass. And he has been so desperate to hold office that he first ran as an Independent and then as a Republican before securing a seat in Congress.

The phone banks asked if term limits mattered to the voter and then informed the voter of the candidates' stands. The phone banks were generally regarded as push polls.[24] Although the callers did not identify themselves, it was understood by the campaigns and the press that the telephone calls were not done by the campaigns themselves, as some of the phone calls were made on Sunday, a Utah-specific error that neither campaign would have made. The last question in the four-question poll reads: "Lily Eskelsen supports term limits and has signed the term-limits declaration limiting herself to no more than three terms. Merrill Cook refuses to take this stand and wants to stay in Washington for as long as possible. Which candidate reflects your views?"

The tone of the ALT messages was quite negative. Interestingly, ALT's derision of Cook for saying he supports term limits while not limiting himself appears quite similar to the Eskelsen and Utah Democratic Party theme that Cook would do anything to get elected. But beyond the general similarity, the issue of term limits was not one that would have been discussed without the term-limits groups' involvement. Seen this way, U.S. Term Limits and ALT helped push term limits on the agenda, at least as a subject of discussion. Once it became a subject of discussion, however, it took on a life of its own. Instead of focusing discussion on term limits and their potential normative value, Cook made the term-limits groups' tactics and motives the issue. Cook asserted that the term-limits ads were a personal attack conducted in complicity—if not in complete collaboration—with Eskelsen.[25] He made this case even though similar television ads, mailers, and phone banks were run by ALT in every close race in which only one candidate had signed the pledge. However, ALT spent more in the Cook-Eskelsen race than in most other contests. According to ALT's president, this was because the race was "rated higher," and the media market was more efficient. ALT was also worried about partisan implications: more Republicans than Democrats signed the pledge by a margin of three to one, so they placed extra emphasis on supporting the Democrats that had signed. It was important to ALT to appear nonpartisan and try to equalize spending.

While the Eskelsen campaign attempted to keep its distance, Cook connected Eskelsen and the term-limits groups together as often as he could. In a KBYU television debate, Cook claimed that the candidates should be judged by "the company they keep" and that he was proud of the company he kept. The implicit assertion was that Eskelsen should be held responsible for the actions of the term-limits groups and their negative campaigns.

The reaction to the ALT efforts was not positive. In fact, even the *Salt Lake Tribune,* not known as a Cook supporter, ran an editorial decrying the misleading nature of the ads.[26] The Republican Party came to Cook's defense, as mentioned above, through its own phone banks. The ALT advertisements may even have hurt Eskelsen's campaign. Before ALT decided to enter the race, the Eskelsen campaign had already decided on the mixture of positive about Eskelsen and negative about Cook messages that they would use during the race. Eskelsen noted that if she had to do the race over again, she would "use no pictures whatsoever." The ALT advertisements shifted the perceived balance decidedly toward negative messages that voters would hear about Cook. Thus, Eskelsen called outside money "a double-edged sword." It was nice to have a group thank her and attack her opponent, but that group was "out of control of the candidates." She further stated that "people who did not like the [term-limits] ads assumed we put them on." In fact, voters may have blamed the Eskelsen campaign for the negativity of the ALT ads. According to the KBYU-Utah Colleges Exit Poll, 47 percent thought that the Cook-Eskelsen race was more negative than recent House races, 36 percent thought it was about the same, and 11 percent thought it was less negative (see table 10.1). Of those who thought the race was more negative, 74 percent blamed the candidates, 15 percent blamed the parties, and 8 percent blamed interest groups. Thus, Americans for Limited Terms received little blame for the negativity of the race, although they did a lot to contribute to it.

Without ALT's foray into the Second District, the race would have been less negative and given one less issue for Cook to attack Eskelsen with. Although Eskelsen was already using unflattering pictures of Cook and "scrappy" strategies of attack, ALT's tactics exacerbated the perception that Eskelsen was being unfair to Cook.

NRA and Proposition 5

Another group to spend money getting its message out to the general public was the National Rifle Association (NRA). The NRA endorsed Cook through its publications sent to members. Over the last weekend of the campaign, the NRA spent $51,370 on independent expenditure radio advertisements directly endorsing Merrill Cook's election, using Charlton Heston as the voice-over.[27] The NRA also made $10,900 in direct contributions to Cook's campaign through its PAC (NRA Political Victory Fund): $5,950 for the 1998 campaign and $4,950 for debt retirement in the 1996 campaign, thus "double-dipping" contributions to Cook. While this was not a lot of money, it interacted with a related issue in Utah politics—Proposition 5. Proposition 5 was a ballot measure to amend the Utah Constitution, raising the initiative requirement to change wildlife/hunting laws from a majority to two-thirds. Proposition 5 most likely increased turnout at the ballot box, with over $610,000 spent in a major media campaign by groups supporting Proposition 5.[28] Those who voted for Proposition 5 were more likely to vote for Cook, especially since Charlton Heston had endorsed him (see fig. 10.2). Cook

Table 10.1   Comparison of 1998 House Campaign to Recent Contests

Voted for	More Negative	Same	Less Negative	Don't Know
Cook	57%	30%	8%	5%
Eskelsen	34%	43%	15%	7%
Other	65%	26%	—	9%
Totals	**47%**	**35%**	**11%**	**7%**

Source: Data from 1998 KBYU–Utah colleges exit poll.

Figure 10.2 1998 Proposition 5 Vote and House Vote

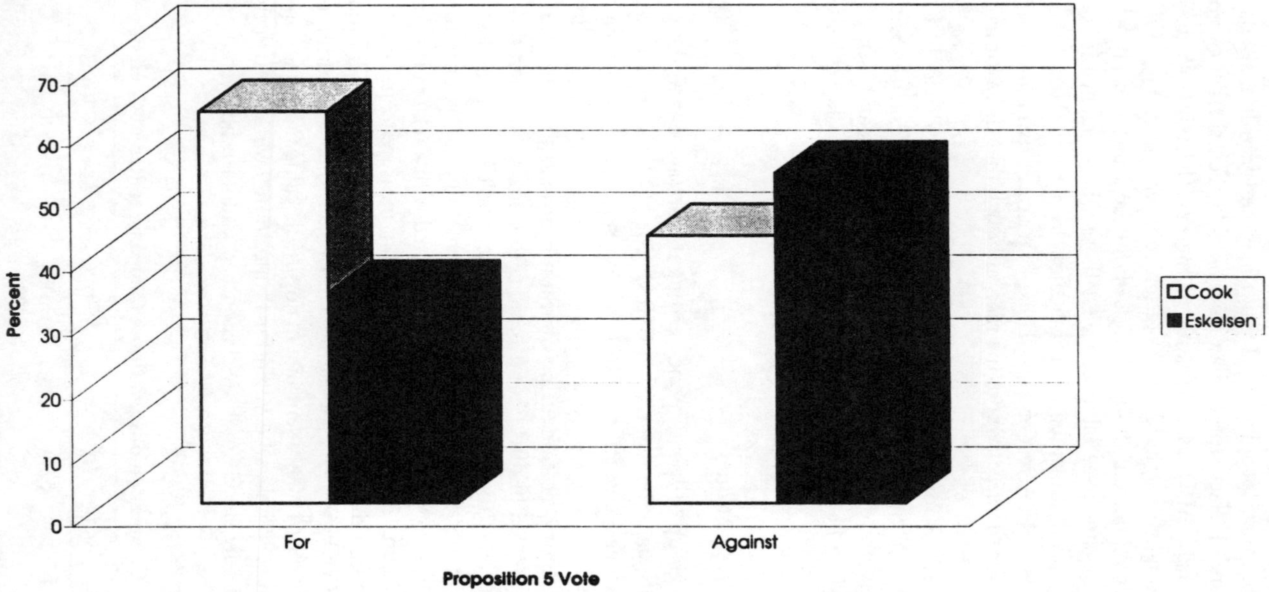

Source: Data from 1998 KBYU–Utah colleges exit poll.

and Eskelsen officially opposed Proposition 5 in the *Utah Voter Information Pamphlet* but did not publicize it. In fact, according to the KBYU–Utah Colleges Exit Poll, in the Second District, Proposition 5 supporters voted for Cook by a margin of 2 to 1.

Other Groups

Other interest groups ran newspaper ads expressing their thanks to Merrill Cook for his good work. The Utah credit unions ran full-page ads thanking Merrill Cook in both of the Salt Lake City newspapers the Sunday before the election. In addition, the credit unions assisted Cook by holding fund-raisers and sending volunteers to work on his campaign.[29] Associated Builders and Contractors ran some small newspaper ads as well, saying: "Merrill Cook. Call and thank him for supporting H.R. 4579, the Taxpayer Relief Act of 1998." These business groups helped reinforce Cook's campaign theme by praising Cook for the work he had done in their behalf. For example, the Credit Union newspaper ad read, "Thank You Congressman Merrill Cook for voting to preserve credit unions for all Utahns."

All other groups that supported either candidate did so by targeting their membership. The AFL-CIO first targeted its 29,485 union members in the Second District by sending out a mailer announcing its support of Eskelsen.[30] Then, through phone banks, the AFL-CIO canvassed its members who were registered voters about their voting intentions. Earlier in the year, the AFL-CIO encouraged its members to register to vote. If a union member was unsure, the union sent a follow-up persuasion mailer supporting Eskelsen and made a follow-up phone call. The AFL-CIO also organized a GOTV effort the week before the election.[31] The Sierra Club also endorsed Eskelsen, who was on the cover of the Utah chapter's fall newsletter. About two weeks before the election, the Sierra Club sent out a mailer to its roughly 2,000 members. One week before the election, the club did a follow-up GOTV telephone call.[32] The Utah Education Association (teachers union) also did GOTV and persuasion calls to its members, along with mail, while the National Education Association donated $19,000 to the Eskelsen campaign and the Utah Democratic Party (to be used to support Eskelsen). Other groups that sent mailers to their members in support of Eskelsen include Utahns for Choice, Handgun Control, Human Rights Campaign, and Peace Action. The National Federation of Independent Businesses (NFIB) sent out a poster/mailer to its members (about 1,500 businesses) supporting Cook.[33]

CONCLUSION

The Republican Party and interest-group support for Cook totaled about $936,000 (not including the resources expended by groups lobbying their own members). Of this amount, the Cook campaign spent 70 percent ($655,000), the Republican Party spent 25 percent in soft money ($230,000, including one third of party-building money), and the NRA spent 5 percent in independent expenditures ($51,000).

Those in favor of Eskelsen spent about $1,353,000 (not including the resources expended by groups lobbying their own members). The Eskelsen campaign spent 52 percent ($703,000), the Democratic Party spent 20 percent ($270,000), and Americans for Limited Terms spent 28 percent on election advocacy ($380,000).

Seven months before the election, Cook held a ten percentage-point lead over Eskelsen.[34] In the election, Cook also won by ten percentage points (53–43 percent). Cook concluded that "unanswered money" by outside groups is effective but, since the Republican Party answered the spending by ALT, that the two sides "canceled out." Speaking not only about the Cook-Eskelsen race, the president of Americans for Limited Terms noted that since there are now many other issue ads and partisan ads, it "reduced the effectiveness in the general election" of ALT's ads. Given that the groups canceled out, Eskelsen's campaign manager declared that the "voters chose the devil they knew."

A political campaign is like a military battle. It is difficult enough to win the battle with one opponent, but when outside groups and parties enter the battle, things get messier. Parties are more concerned about the general war than a particular battle and may not use their resources effectively in the local battle, and outside groups may launch a campaign on a completely different front and confuse both sides. Another difficulty is that the candidates do not know which outside groups may enter the battle. Six weeks before the election, Eskelsen expected conservative groups to run an "outside attack ad campaign" against her. Cook expected outside help from the National Association of Independent Businesses, Republicans for Environmental Protection, and the U.S. Chamber of Commerce, and perhaps a flat-tax group. Only the NFIB became involved, and then only with its members.[35] Since groups and candidates cannot coordinate, such groups may harm those they are trying to help. Oftentimes, as was the case with Eskelsen and ALT, voters blame candidates for the negative attack ads run by interest groups or political parties. Voters are bombarded on all sides and cannot distinguish between the munitions of the candidates, parties, and outside groups. They can only express their opinions through their vote (or refusal to vote), and thus candidates may feel the effects of other groups' strategies.

In the Cook-Eskelsen race, each side had about the same number of forces, so they largely canceled out. If one side had possessed superior forces, however, it could have made a difference. In this race, the primary effect that outside money had was on the negativity of the campaign, which hurt both the candidates and the voters.

NOTES

The author would like to thank those who assisted with this paper, including those interviewed (at times anonymously), for their patience; members of Common Cause and

League of Women Voters, who provided information on the ground war; David Magleby and Marianne Holt and their team of research assistants for guidance and coordination of the research project; Natalie Capps and Damon Cann for research assistance; Dick Fenno for helpful suggestions and comments; and the Pew Charitable Trusts and the Brigham Young University College of Family, Home, and Social Sciences for providing the resources that made this research possible.

1. Lee Davidson, "Cook Testing His Luck in Jinxed 2nd District Race," *Deseret News,* 21 October 1998, A11.

2. Robert Novak, on CNN's "Inside Politics," 13 August 1998 (located through Lexis:Nexis).

3. John Heilprin, "Fickle 2nd District Draws U.S. Attention," *Salt Lake Tribune,* 12 October 1998, A1.

4. Caroline Roemer, campaign manager for Merrill Cook, interview by author, telephone, 24 November 1998.

5. "Financial Activities of House Candidates through December 31, 1996," *FEC,* 1996, at <http://www.fec.gov/1996/states/ut_01.htm>, 19 November 1998. Cook spent $1,061,793, of which $865,624 was his own money.

6. Dan Harrie, "Congressional Mail: Cook Is a Big Sender—Rival Says He's a Big Spender," *Salt Lake Tribune,* 6 August 1998, A1. Cook spent about $168,000, four times more than Chris Cannon (R, UT-3) and fifteen times more than Jim Hansen (R, UT-1).

7. Cook raised over one-third of his political action committee (PAC) contributions ($150,537 of $437,460) from finance, insurance, and real estate and services PACs (companies according to Standard Industry Codes). "Categorized Committee Contributions, Merrill A. Cook," *FECInfo,* 1998, At <http://www.tray.com/cgi-win/_catptoc.exe?H4UT-02106COOK,$MERRILL$A98>, 15 January 1999.

8. Lily Eskelsen, interview by author, telephone, 24 November 1998.

9. In an article about a week before the election, reporter Lee Davidson noted that Cook's "legislative batting average" was 0.000—he "didn't pass any bills at all" ("Hatch Tops Utah Hitters; Cook Whiffs," *Deseret News,* 24 October 1998, A1) Cook's campaign manager stated that she was glad that the article came out so late in the race (Roemer interview).

10. Spencer Stokes, executive director of the Utah Republican Party, asserted that Eskelsen was "despised by Republican opinion leaders and office holders" such as Leavitt, which led to their reluctant support of Cook. Interview by author, telephone, 17 November 1998.

11. Dan Jones, pollster for Merrill Cook, interview by author, telephone, 13 April 1999.

12. Merrill Cook, quoted by Bob Bernick Jr., "End Game Begins in Eskelsen, Cook Race," *Deseret News,* 27 October 1998, B1.

13. Lee Davidson, "Mudslinging May Work Elsewhere—Not in Utah," *Deseret News,* 5 November 1998, A1; Megan Sather, campaign manager for Eskelsen, characterized the strategy as being "scrappy," in an interview by author, Salt Lake City, 23 November 1998.

14. Cook, interview by author, Salt Lake City, 10 December 1998.

15. Quoted by John Heilprin, "Cook, Eskelsen Differ in Fund-Raising Style," *Salt Lake Tribune,* 28 April 1998, B1.

16. John Heilprin, reporter for the *Salt Lake Tribune,* interview with the author, 1 December 1998. Heilprin attended the fund-raiser Dick Armey had for Cook.

17. Megan Sather, interview by author, telephone, 13 April 1999.

18. NRCC press release, " 'Operation Breakout' Goes Nationwide," 6 October 1998,

<http://www.nrcc.org/html/pr_100698opbrk.htm>, 20 October 1998. The television ad scripts that follow are also found on the NRCC's website.

19. Dan Harrie, "Cook Blows Stack," *Salt Lake Tribune*, 12 November 1998, B1.

20. Judy Fahys, "County Clerk Bends on Absentee Ballots," *Salt Lake Tribune*, 22 October 1998, C2.

21. Todd Taylor, interview by author, telephone, 18 November 1998. Taylor also provided the preceding radio script criticizing Cook's stand on education.

22. Paul Jacobs, interview by author, telephone, 13 April 1999.

23. Eric O'Keefe, president of Americans for Limited Terms, interview by author, telephone, 1 December 1998. O'Keefe also provided the calling script that identifies Eskelsen as a term limits supporter. ALT's media company (Thompson Communications) provided a copy of ALT's advertisements on videotape.

24. Bob Bernick Jr., "Survey Looks Like a 'Push-poll' Aimed at Cook," *Deseret News*, 22 October 1998, B2; John Heilprin, "Eskelsen Denies Camp Is Push-Polling in 2nd Congressional District Race," *Salt Lake Tribune*, 28 October 1998, B2.

25. The Cook campaign hinted that there was collusion between Eskelsen and ALT, in Bob Bernick Jr., "Term-limits Group Praises Eskelsen, Not Cook," *Deseret News*, 14 October 1998, B5; in an interview with the author, Cook stated, "I believe [Americans for Limited Terms] coordinated with Eskelsen," 10 December 1998.

26. "Cook and Term Limits," editorial, *Salt Lake Tribune*, 27 October 1998, A6.

27. Bill Powers, director of Public Relations and Communications of the NRA Institute for Legislative Action, interview by author, telephone, 1 December 1998; and "Itemized Independent Expenditures," *FEC*, 1998, <http://herndon1.sdrdc.com/cgi-bin/fecimg/ ?98034034104>, 15 January 1999.

28. "Utah Political Issue Committee 1998 Year-End Report," 1998, <http://governor. state.ut.us/It_gover/9798PIC98Yearend.htm>, 15 January 1999. See also Judy Fahys, "Special Interests Pumping Money into Prop 5 Duel," *Salt Lake Tribune*, 29 October 1998, A10.

29. Tracie Karls, vice president of Dues Supported Services, Utah League of Credit Unions, interview by author, telephone, 3 December 1998.

30. Ken Gardner, Utah state COPE director, interview by author, telephone, 13 April 1999.

31. Ed Mayne, president of Utah AFL-CIO, interview by author, telephone, 23 November 1998.

32. Lawson LeGate, southwest regional representative of the Sierra Club, interview by author, telephone, 24 November 1998.

33. Ronald Casper, NFIB Utah state director, interview by author, telephone, 15 January 1999.

34. According to a Dan Jones & Associates poll conducted April 7–9 for the *Deseret News*, 41 percent of respondents were more likely to vote for Cook, 31 percent more likely to vote for Eskelsen, and 22 percent did not know ($N = 314$; margin of error, ± 5.5 percent). The margins were closer for registered (8 percent) and likely voters (4 percent), in Bob Bernick Jr., "Cook Leads Now but Can't Afford to Rest," *Deseret News*, 12 April 1998, A1.

35. Bob Bernick Jr., "Eskelsen vs. Cook: Irony Abounds," *Deseret News*, 18 September 1998, A1.

11

The 1998 Kentucky Senate and Sixth District Races

Donald A. Gross and Penny M. Miller

The Senate race between former University of Kentucky basketball player Scotty Baesler and hall-of-fame baseball pitcher Jim Bunning, decided by only 7,000 votes, pitted experienced sportsmen on a different playing field. At the same time, a pitched battle was going on in the middle of their state: the Sixth District race between Ernesto Scorsone and Ernie Fletcher. Each race was heavily influenced by both party and interest-group money, and the congressional race deeply affected the Senate race.

With nearly four million residents and a slow population growth rate, Kentucky is primarily rural. Less than 50 percent of its population lives in metropolitan areas, and about 93 percent is Caucasian. Kentucky is well below the national average in per capita income and education. Above average percentages of its citizens live below the poverty level, receive public assistance, and face unemployment. Economic disparity forces candidates to appeal to very different audiences; unemployment, for instance, ranges from under 4 percent in some counties to over 30 percent in others. Most of the wealth and economic stability in the state exist in a triangle formed by Louisville, Lexington, and the Cincinnati satellites in northern Kentucky. Kentucky is a fairly conservative state, with pockets of liberalism in the coal fields of eastern Kentucky, the union base in Louisville, and the African American communities of Louisville and Lexington. The south and east ends of Lexington, the suburban communities around Louisville, and the northern Kentucky area across the river from Cincinnati have become bases of conservative Republicanism in the state. Traditionally Democratic western Kentucky has followed the southern shift toward Republicanism.[1]

Going into the 1998 federal elections, Republicans held five of the six congressional seats and one of the Senate seats. Before Clinton's back-to-back victories in Kentucky in the 1990s, Republicans had carried the state in seven of the previous nine presidential elections. Democrats do better in statewide and local elections, winning every gubernatorial election for the last twenty-five years. In terms of party registration, the Democratic Party still has an overall advantage of just under 2 to 1.

The Sixth Congressional District lies in east central Kentucky in the heart of the Bluegrass region. The Sixth District can be characterized as moderate to conservative overall with significant pockets of liberalism, especially around the University of Kentucky. The Sixth District is predominantly Caucasian. While Lexington contains the second largest African American community in the state, African Americans comprise only about 8 percent of the district. In addition, the African American community in Lexington has never exhibited a strong activist tradition. Other minority groups comprise less than 2 percent of the population. Voter registration figures in the Sixth District favor the Democrats by about 2 to 1. The Sixth District has a long tradition of giving only token consideration to partisanship when it comes to voting for candidates for national office. Represented by Democrat Scotty Baesler since 1992, the Sixth District was represented, for twelve previous years, by a Republican.

Just prior to the 1998 election cycle, Kentucky altered the timing of its elections, moving municipal, county, and judicial elections to the same ballots as state legislative and congressional elections. The large number of elections and referenda likely resulted in a statewide voter turnout rate (44.1 percent) higher than generally seen in Kentucky off-year elections.[2] Hotly contested races in the Fourth and Sixth Congressional District races were of particular significance.[3] The election consolidation of 1998 and a close mayoral race in Lexingron helped to boost turnout to 45 percent in the Sixth District.[4] Conversely, the crowded field of elections meant that individual races had unusual competition for media coverage and for voter attention. There was so much paid advertising that television stations in metropolitan markets had to reject some party soft-money and interest-groups advertising requests during the last weeks of the election.[5]

Running for statewide office in Kentucky, and in four of the six U.S. House districts, means advertising in surrounding states. To reach all Kentucky votes via television, candidates must buy time at stations outside the state that broadcast in Kentucky and at Kentucky stations that reach voters in five other states. Only the Lexington television market can be considered efficient, as an overwhelming majority of the Sixth District voters is reached by the four Lexington commercial television stations.

THE SENATE CANDIDATES AND THEIR CAMPAIGNS

Voters in the U.S. Senate race in Kentucky had a choice between two congressmen trying to advance to the Senate. Democrat Scotty Baesler (still remembered as the captain of an Adolph Rupp basketball team at the University of Kentucky) was a moderate conservative who established himself in recent years as one of the "Blue Dog Democrats" in Congress.[6] Baesler has a record of fiscal conservatism, support for federal tobacco subsidies, as well as health care reform and protection of Social Security; he maintained a pro-choice abortion position and developed a recent interest in campaign finance reform. Baesler, a tobacco farmer and attorney and Lexington mayor for ten years before his six years representing the Sixth Congressional District, won the Senate nomination in a competitive and expensive primary against Lieutenant Governor Steve Henry and wealthy businessman Charlie Owen.[7] Owen spent over $6.5 million, much of it his own money, while Henry and Baesler spent approximately $1.5 million each. Both primary opponents aimed negative attacks at Baesler. The primary race modestly raised Baesler's negative poll numbers but, more importantly, drained his campaign coffers for the early months of the general election race.[8]

Republican Jim Bunning entered the race best known as a Kentuckian who pitched a "perfect" baseball game. As a congressman from northern Kentucky, he had established strong conservative credentials on issues such as tax cuts, health care reform, gun control, abortion, education, and the environment. Unlike most Republicans, he voted against NAFTA, citing the loss of thousands of Kentucky garment industry jobs. Bunning's political career began in local politics and in the state Senate. He later was the unsuccessful Republican nominee for governor in 1983. Bunning sprang back in 1987 when he was elected to the U.S. House, becoming chairman of the Ways and Means Subcommittee on Social Security in 1995. With early support from Senator Mitch McConnell and other party stalwarts, Bunning avoided a serious primary contest in his 1998 U.S. Senate race, beginning the fall campaign with over $1.4 million on hand.

Senate Candidate Campaign Strategies

With a "down home" image, focusing on safer schools, pay equity, affordable health care, and tuition tax breaks,[9] Baesler began the fall race emphasizing his empathy with the working people of Kentucky. Attacks on Bunning and the Republican Party were left to ads run by interest groups and the Democratic Party. A major get-out-the-vote effort by the AFL-CIO and the African American community had helped Democrats win the 1995 governor's race and was the "ace-in-the-hole" the Democrats hoped to reuse at the end of the 1998 Senate race.

Although Baesler began the general election race with a double-digit lead in the public opinion polls, his funds had been depleted by the primary, permitting Bunning to dominate the airwaves early with a very positive image of himself. He also lay claim to the traditional Democratic issue of protecting Social Security. Bunning argued that his position as chairman of the Subcommittee on Social Security of the House Ways and Means Committee had established his sincerity on this commitment.[10] He moved early to soften his image, with ads showing him in casual clothes, in farm scenes, or with his extended family, discussing his commitment to education. He had pulled within striking distance of Baesler by the end of September.

After about a month into the fall campaign, Bunning switched to an attack mode that would help propel the race into one of the nastiest in the nation. One of the Bunning ads received nationwide attention: it used a video of Baesler apparently ranting, while Wagner's *The Ride of the Valkyries* played in the background. Bunning continued to use variations of that ad, despite critics' complaints about its Nazi overtones. Charges of race-baiting followed a set of Kentucky Republican Party ads that criticized Baesler's vote in favor of NAFTA. The first ad ended with a stereotypical Mexican saying, "Muchas gracias, Señor Baesler." A second Kentucky GOP ad used Asian and Mexican stereotypes to send the same message. The ads put Bunning on the side of jobs for Kentucky voters, a popular position since Kentucky has lost a number of jobs to foreign competition both before and after NAFTA, especially in the textile industry. The Republican national and state parties reinforced the themes discussed in those TV ads by broadcasting radio spots and distributing thousands of direct mailings projecting the same images. The attack ads put the Baesler campaign on the defensive, although the Baesler and Democratic Party campaigns began their own set of attack ads that heavily focused on Bunning's record on Social Security and health care. Attacks remained the prime focus of the advertising budgets, including an ad that challenged Baesler's credentials as the candidate of the working man: "Baesler is the only millionaire in the race," it claimed. There were some positive image-softening ads in the last days of the Bunning campaign.

Senate Candidate Spending

The candidate campaigns in the Kentucky Senate race themselves spent over $7.5 million, with Bunning spending slightly more than Baesler (see fig. 11.1). Because of the primary challenge, Bunning had about $1 million more to devote to the general election campaign.

Baesler received about 21 percent of his contributions from PACs; about 79 percent of his total money came from in-state sources. Labor PACs were the single largest group of contributors to the Baesler campaign, contributing over $300,000.[11] In addition, the campaign received funds from service industry, agricultural, transportation and communication, and financial and insurance PACs. Most of the money Baesler received from the agricultural sector came from the tobacco industry, reflecting his long support for tobacco interests (see table 11.1).

Bunning received nearly twice as much PAC money as Baesler received; about 38 percent of his receipts and about 66 percent of his total funds came from in-state sources. Bunning raised more money from business and industry, a pattern of giving elevated by Senator Mitch McConnell of Kentucky, chair of the Na-

Figure 11.1 Kentucky Senate Candidate Financial Activity in the 1998 Election Cycle

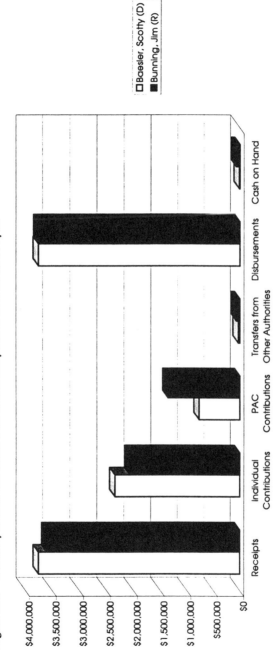

Source: Data from FEC press release, *FEC Reports on Congressional Fundraising for 1997–98,* 28 April 1999.
Note: Candidate self-support and closing debt data omitted.

Table 11.1   PAC Contributions to the 6th District and Senate Candidates*

PAC Contributors in KY 6th Race	Fletcher (R)	Scorsone (D)
Finance/Insurance/Real Estate	$28,500	$3,000
Manufacturing	$55,000	0
Political Organizations	$126,983	$32,510
Service Industry PACs	$66,378	$27,422
Transportation/Comms. PACs	$40,203	$500
Labor	0	$176,461
Agriculture/Forestry/Fishing	$14,692	$500
Retail Trade	$34,500	0
Mining	$23,200	$250
Wholesale Trade	$23,000	$300
Construction	$12,500	0
Total**	**$405,446**	**$230,425**

PAC Contributors in Senate Race	Bunning (R)	Baesler (D)
Finance/Insurance/Real Estate	$252,431	$33,250
Manufacturing	$247,098	$13,000
Political Organizations	$580,513	$174,635
Service Industry PACs	$170,567	$134,655
Transportation/Comms. PACs	$129,740	$42,250
Labor	$13,000	$300,100
Agriculture/Forestry/Fishing	$66,141	$69,050
Retail Trade	$92,599	$6,750
Mining	$84,248	$2,000
Wholesale Trade	$59,173	$2,000
Construction	$43,317	$12,500
Total**	**$1,363,896**	**$771,022**

Source: Data from "Congressional and Presidential Campaign Finance Profiles," *Center for Responsive Politics,* 1998, at <www.opensecrets.org/politicians/index.htm>, 24 September 1999.
  *PAC contributions totaled by SIC interest heading, FEC data.
  **Actual PAC contribution totals, FEC data.

tional Republican Senatorial Committee. McConnell's strong personal interest in his home state was responsible for much of the money Bunning received.

As is the case in most senatorial campaigns, television and radio advertisements were the largest budgetary expenses for both the Bunning and Baesler campaigns. Bunning's organization spent more than $2.5 million on over 10,000 television spots, over $1 million more than was spent by Baesler's campaign on 5,300 television spots.[12] More than $90,000 was spent by the Bunning campaign on radio ads, three times the amount spent by Baesler's organization.[13]

THE CONGRESSIONAL CANDIDATES AND THEIR CAMPAIGNS

The 1998 congressional race in the Sixth District provided voters with a clear choice between political philosophies. Ernesto Scorsone, the Democratic candidate and practicing attorney, is a progressive liberal. His voting record during his long tenure in the state legislature and his policy statements were liberal on health care, education, Social Security, collective bargaining, abortion, gay rights, and the environment. He spent $250,000 to win the most expensive Sixth Congressional District Democratic primary in history, a contest in which the seven candidates spent a total of over $2 million. Two issues from the primary race played a major role in the fall campaign: religious values and Scorsone's job as a criminal defense attorney.

Republican Ernie Fletcher, a Lexington physician and former Baptist minister, was a classic Christian conservative candidate. In 1996 he ran against incumbent Democratic Congressman Scotty Baesler, losing by 12 percent. During Fletcher's two-year term in the state legislature, his policy statements earned him a reputation as anti-abortion, anti-gay, a supporter of the Christian right agenda, and a conservative on issues such as reform of Social Security, education, health care, and the environment. Fletcher had only token opposition in the primary, permitting him to focus his resources on the fall campaign.

Each general election campaign tried to repackage its candidate as the moderate and convince voters that the other candidate was the extremist. For example, Scorsone ran a TV ad emphasizing the need to get tough on criminals, his support of the death penalty, and his campaign's support by the Fraternal Order of Police. In a similar vein, Fletcher ran ads emphasizing the need to save Social Security and reform the health care system.

Fletcher's campaign began with an effort to soften his image. During his unsuccessful 1996 run for Congress, Fletcher was often portrayed as overly aggressive, nasty in his attacks, and a tool of the religious right. As a campaign continued, the Fletcher campaign began to attack Scorsone's record, especially on taxes, crime, and health care, and ended with personal assaults.

The Scorsone campaign focused on his legislative experience and his positions on education, Social Security, health care, and crime. As the campaign heated up, a number of individuals in the Scorsone camp suggested the need to respond to the ever increasing personal attacks by the Fletcher camp. He did not respond directly to personal attacks, heeding the advice of his professional campaign consultants and staying on message.[14]

Both Fletcher and Scorsone were well funded, with Fletcher spending $1,286,068 and Scorsone $1,025,395. As shown in figure 11.2, Fletcher received about 32 percent of his contributions from PACs, with strong support from the business and conservative communities. Scorsone received approximately 23 percent of his contributions from PACs, primarily from labor PACs.

Figure 11.2 Kentucky Sixth Congressional District Candidate Financial Activity in the 1998 Election Cycle

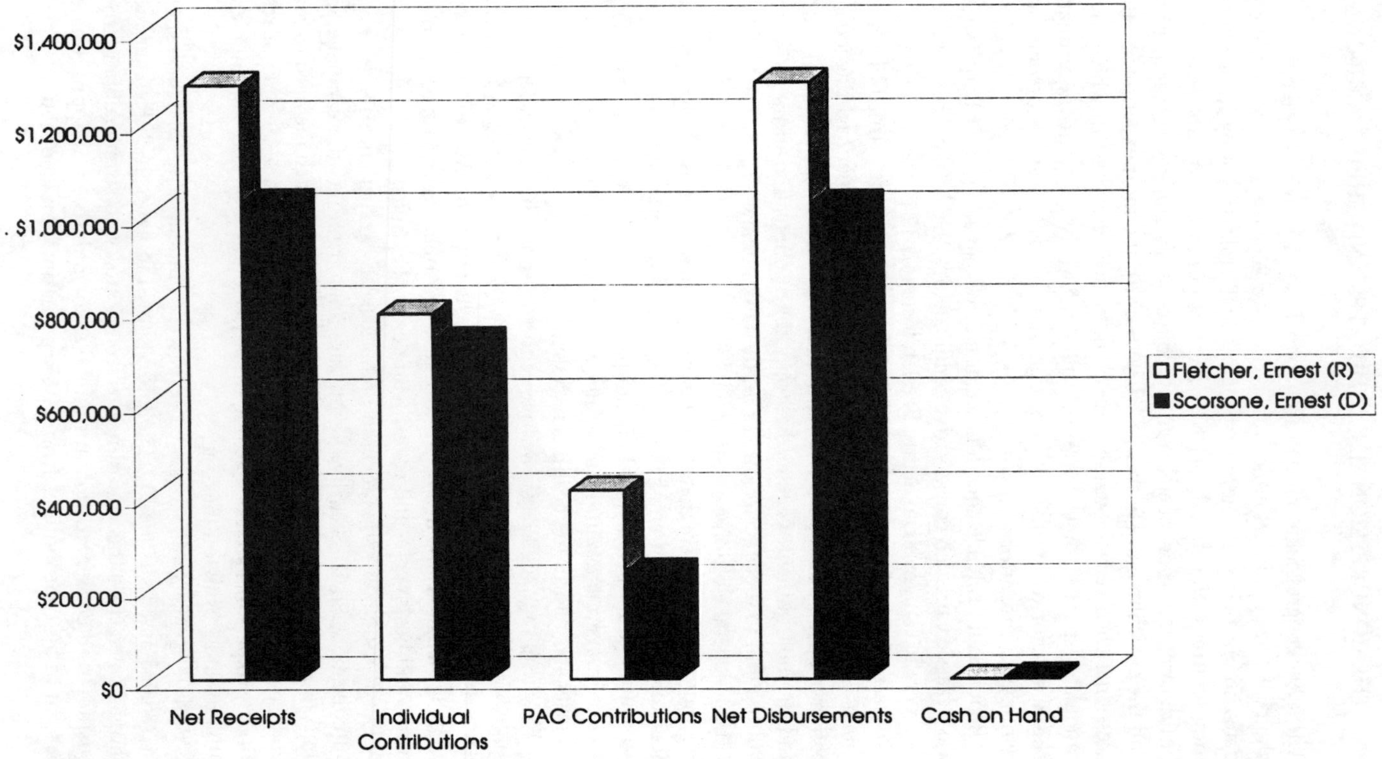

Source: Data from FEC press release, *FEC Reports on Congressional Fundraising for 1997–98*, 28 April 1999.
Note: Candidate self-support data omitted.

THE POLITICAL PARTIES IN THE SENATE AND HOUSE CAMPAIGNS

Political parties spared nothing in their fight for the Senate and Sixth Congressional District seats. The national parties transferred considerable federal and nonfederal monies to state and local party committees in Kentucky. As shown in figure 11.3, there were considerable differences between the two parties in the amount of money that was transferred to state and local party committees in Kentucky: combining federal and nonfederal accounts, the DNC transferred over $285,000 more than the RNC, and the DSCC transferred almost $1 million more than the NRSC. In the Senate race, these transfers helped the state and national Democratic parties outspend the state and national Republican parties on television ads.

The Kentucky Republican Party and Mitch McConnell

More than any other person, U.S. Senator Mitch McConnell can be credited with revitalizing the Kentucky Republican Party. McConnell's interest in electoral politics is one reason he has served as the chair of the NRSC in the 1998 election cycle. McConnell was a key ally and mastermind of the Bunning campaign, closely orchestrating the campaigns of Bunning and Fletcher. Sensing disorganization and a lack of grassroots initiatives in the Bunning primary election efforts, McConnell loaned two of his key staffers to coordinate the campaign and build a grassroots effort. McConnell and Fletcher talked frequently, and McConnell suggested Fletcher use the same advertising and polling consultants McConnell has used.[15] In addition, McConnell was instrumental in helping Bunning and Fletcher raise money and in directing national Republican Party money to Kentucky. The Bunning and Fletcher victories confirmed the ascendancy of McConnell in Kentucky. Until 1998, McConnell was the only Republican to win statewide in thirty years.

The Republicans ran a well-rounded campaign, investing resources both in the air and on the ground. An estimated $3 million was spent by various Republican committees on behalf of Bunning, while $70,000 RNC/NRCC coordinated hard money was spent on behalf of Fletcher. For example, the Republican Party of Kentucky spent over $1,525,000 on television ads throughout the state, most of which were election advocacy ads attacking Baesler. NRCC Operation Breakout television ads were run in early and late parts of the campaign. The first of these candidate ads touted congressional Republican achievements and asked that viewers call Fletcher to indicate support for Republican programs. The late commercials were impeachment ads run by the NRCC in a number of congressional districts nationwide (see table 11.2).

The state party sponsored a volunteer mail program, Victory '98, which mailed over 2.3 million pieces using nonprofit postage rates, which did not count against hard-money limits on party contributions because of the volunteer component

Figure 11.3   Kentucky: Soft-Money Transfers from National to State Party Committees, 1 January 1997 to Year End 1998

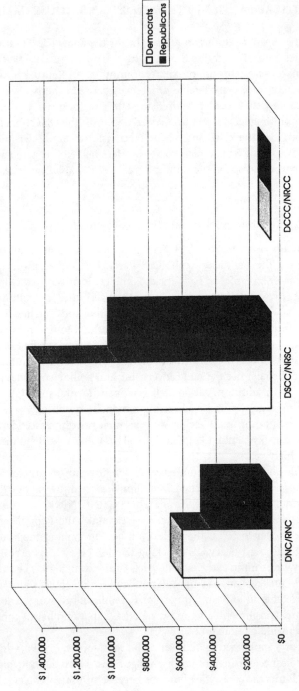

Source: Data from FEC press release, *FEC Reports on Political Party Activity for 1997–98,* 9 April 1999.

Table 11.2   Media Campaign Expenditures by Senatorial Candidates and Political Parties

Campaign Expenditures	Bunning (R)	Baesler (D)
Louisville TV Market	$702,035 (1,325 ads)	$484,095 (971 ads)
Lexington TV Market	$386,820 (1,517 ads)	$211,155 (875 ads)
Evansville TV Market	$384,960 (1,664 ads)	$247,275 (887 ads)
Cincinnati TV Market	$385,205 (608 ads)	$44,690 (66 ads)
Paducah TV Market	$290,341 (1,142 ads)	$162,898 (663 ads)
Charleston-Huntington TV Mkt	$258,673 (1,014 ads)	$227,411 (942 ads)
Hazard TV Market	$55,175 (423 ads)	$14,180 (171 ads)
Hopkinsville TV Market	$37,471 (1,532 ads)	$5,727 (272 ads)
Bowling Green TV Market	$86,560 (1,077 ads)	$43,960 (537 ads)
Total TV Expenditures	**$2,587,240 (10,302 ads)**	**$1,441,391 (5,384 ads)**
Total Radio Expenditures	**$90,000**	**$30,000**

Campaign Expenditures	KY Republican Party	KY Democratic Party
Louisville TV Market	$518,656 (1,077 ads)	$472,555 (1,031 ads)
Lexington TV Market	$367,056 (1,495 ads)	$336,985 (1,256 ads)
Evansville TV Market	$286,563 (1,375 ads)	$241,990 (788 ads)
Cincinnati TV Market	—	—
Paducah TV Market	$204,800 (852 ads)	$156,503 (439 ads)
Charleston-Huntington TV Mkt	—	$426,692 (1,256 ads)
Hazard TV Market	$29,767 (254 ads)	$8,220 (50 ads)
Hopkinsville TV Market	$4,970 (202 ads)	—
Bowling Green TV Market	$114,100 (1,099 ads)	$55,618 (488 ads)
Total TV Expenditures	**$1,525,912 (6,354 ads)**	**$1,698,563 (5,308 ads)**
Total Radio Expenditures	**—**	**$400,000 (generic ads)**

Source: Data gathered by authors from twelve different media markets; see also Robert T. Garrett and Al Cross, "Soft Money Eclipsed Candidates' Spending: Issue Ads Avoid Limits on Giving in Senate Race," Louisville *Courier-Journal*, 28 December 1998, A6.

Note: Republicans were outspent by roughly $735,893 on these TV stations, if you combine the DSCC television expenditures with the Democratic state party expenditures.

of the program.[16] The content varied: military constituents at Fort Knox and Fort Campbell were sent mail that denounced Bill Clinton and the Democrats; western Kentucky voters received mail criticizing the Clinton Democrats' antitobacco positions; eastern Kentucky voters received information attacking NAFTA and Baesler's pro-NAFTA vote; and Sixth Congressional District voters received handwritten two-page personal letters from Mary Bunning and fliers promoting Bunning's protection of Social Security. In the Fifth Congressional District, the Republican Party of Kentucky used an estimated $50,000 in soft money to mail 280,000 pieces of literature on behalf of Fletcher.

The Republican Party of Kentucky contracted multiple out-of-state vendors to make 147,000 canvassing phone calls to Democrats at the end of September, at a cost of $95,550. The state GOP spent $225,000 on out-of-state vendors who made 410,000 GOTV phone calls to Republicans, beginning the Saturday before the election. After the election, Baesler commented that Bunning had a decisive advantage in party-funded mail, phone banks, and radio; and said, "I suspect the calculations on mail will blow your mind."[17]

In western Kentucky, the state Republican Party urged fledgling county organizations to develop door-to-door campaign blitzes on behalf of Bunning. State leaders called local party chiefs to rev them up. In the First District, the state's most heavily Democratic in registration, Democratic Party operative Kim Geveden claimed that Republican mail and phone calls went to Democrats who had voted in all of the last five elections; these ground-war tactics were probably designed to discourage these loyal Democrats from voting.[18] The attacks included material on Social Security, and Democratic activist Merryman Kemp of Paducah said that when she called Democrats in efforts to get them to the polls, "I got a lot of Social Security questions. They were afraid that Baesler was going to be bad for Social Security."[19]

During the last week of October the Republican Party organized a bus tour to key areas of the commonwealth with major Republican Party figures: Bob Dole, Mitch McConnell, and others. These political personalities helped make it appear that there was widespread support for Bunning and also made appearances for Fletcher. This big push at the end helped rally the stalwart troops, and the tour received a lot of free publicity and allowed Bunning to meet the Republican voters in the Fifth Congressional District, where traditional face to face is very important.

The Republican ground war was successful. Republicans exploited Scorsone's negatives on morality and alternative lifestyle issues. Issues like abortion and lifestyle lend themselves to more intimate discussion. Ultimately, the large number of evangelical Christian activists in the Sixth Congressional District and other areas in Kentucky appeared especially responsive to these issues and the ground-war tactics.

Role of the Kentucky Democratic Party

Underestimation of the importance of early campaigning and weak coordination with Democratic county chairs resulted in a less coordinated and less effective Democratic campaign. Nevertheless, resources were not in short supply. The Kentucky Democratic Party spent about $4 million for its coordinated campaign on behalf of its state legislative and congressional candidates, with Scorsone receiving about $50,000 from national party committees. Scorsone benefited from $107,911 in candidate advocacy television paid for by the Kentucky Democratic Coordinated Campaign. The DNC and DCCC also invested $25,000 in various GOTV campaigns. In the Senate race, the Democratic Party spent more on television ads than Baesler's own campaign—$1,850,681 for Baesler on issue-advocacy television and an additional $370,000 in coordinated spending on candidate-specific Baesler ads. The DSCC's independent expenditure TV and radio ads—$563,242 on TV ad buys (989 ads) and $28,000 on radio ad buys—featured Senator Wendell Ford attacking Bunning's "shameless" attack ads. This coordinated campaign also spent more than $116,300 on issue-advocacy mail, primarily in northern Kentucky, where the Baesler campaign was not on TV.

The Kentucky Democratic Party filled statewide radio airwaves, spending $400,000 touting Democrat accomplishments for Kentucky. But Republican candidate Bunning outspent Democrat Baesler on radio ads; for most of the campaign, Bunning dominated the radio.

With a goal to boost turnout, the Democratic Coordinated Campaign utilized paid phone banks. In September, the party contracted with out-of-state vendor Landmark Strategies to make canvassing phone calls to 285,000 households statewide, beyond Democrats, at a total cost of $197,663. In the last ten days of the election, 124,372 persuasion phone calls for Baesler were made primarily to undecided voters as identified by earlier phone contact made in September and October (costing $79,958).

In a sophisticated and coordinated GOTV campaign, the state Democrats targeted phone calls, canvassed door-to-door, and sent thousands of nonallocable mass mailings, using nonprofit bulk rates. The series of GOTV phone calls, beginning Friday before the election, paid for by the Kentucky Democratic Party, crystallized their refined targeting: (1) generic Democratic GOTV phone calls to 228,271 households who had been identified as ticket supporters, at a cost of $91,548; (2) prerecorded phone calls by Hillary Clinton to 120,208 Democratic women voters in the Second and Fifth Congressional Districts, at a cost of $23,310; (3) Baesler-specific GOTV phone calls to 34,250 households in parts of eastern Kentucky and of western Kentucky, at a cost of $13,700; (4) generic GOTV phone calls to 62,255 African Americans statewide, at a cost of $24,902; and (5) prerecorded President Clinton GOTV phone calls to 13,614 African Americans in the Louisville area, at a cost of $2,640. Scorsone's campaign benefited from multiple phone campaigns: 30,000 women received prerecorded Hillary Clinton phone calls at a cost of about 45 cents each, and during the last week of the election 15,385 persuasion phone calls were made (costing $10,000).

Various GOTV volunteer phone banks supplemented the paid phone banks. The campaign field people distributed lists of likely Democratic voting households to loyal Democratic Party supporters around the state. Many lists were farmed out, some to older retired people or housewives, often getting more volunteers in areas with some competitive race overlap. The state party also spent $28,326 on African American GOTV radio in Lexington and Louisville.

Prospective Kentucky Democratic voters received party mail: 215,512 households statewide received general GOTV mail (at a cost of $155,580); 33,000 African American households statewide were sent a strong pro-Clinton, anti-Republican message the Friday before the election; and the Kentucky Democratic Party did a $27,000 GOTV bulk mailing for Scorsone. In addition, there was a GOTV ticket tabloid in Jefferson County on behalf of the entire Jefferson County delegation, with Baesler for Senate on top; it was distributed to 83,000 Democratic households (a cost of $18,885). Almost $10,000 was spent on printing costs for ticket palm cards used for door-to-door campaign canvassing. There were forty-four different combinations of ticket palm cards that were used in targeted precincts.

The Kentucky Democratic Party strongly supported Baesler's late September Victory '98 train trip around the state, tracing the route of President Harry Truman's 1948 trip. Substituting for Baesler along much of the route was his popular wife, Alice.[20] The train trip permitted Kentucky Democratic Party elites like Governor and Mrs. Patton, his primary election opponents Lt. Governor Steve Henry and Charlie Owen, as well as Louisville Mayor Jerry Abramson and U.S. Senator Wendell Ford to show support for Baesler's campaign. At one point along the campaign route, former UK Basketball coach, Joe B. Hall, gave a rousing endorsement for Baesler. For Scorsone, the DCCC paid for Tipper Gore's fundraising visit, and Jessie Jackson came to encourage Democratic turnout.

Because of limited resources, Baesler's campaign did not buy into the Kentucky Coordinated Campaign until August. This appears to have been a serious mistake, as Baesler lacked a strong field organization throughout much of the state, including his own congressional district, the Sixth District. Democratic county chairs vented about the lack of connection with the Baesler campaign, complaining that contact appeared limited to fund-raising requests. This contrasted sharply with the tradition of Kentucky Democrats heavily relying upon help from county chairs.

INTEREST GROUPS IN THE SENATE AND HOUSE CAMPAIGNS

As with other competitive federal contests in 1998, interest groups made both Kentucky races major battlegrounds. Among the major groups supporting Bunning and Fletcher were the National Rifle Association, National Right to Life, and the Christian Coalition; the Campaign for Working Families and Traid bolstered Bunning, and the American Medical Association supported Fletcher. Baesler received significant help from Campaign for America and the AFL/CIO and marginal support from the Kentucky Education Association and AFT-Kentucky. Scorsone's more diverse supporters included the AFL/CIO, Kentucky Education Association, Sierra Club, Kentucky Trial Lawyers Association, Kentucky Association of Sexual Assault Programs, and Fairness Alliance. Overall, the television and radio ads as well as targeted direct mail flyers and phone calls by interest groups reinforced the candidate and party campaign themes.

Campaign for America

Campaign for America, a nonprofit organization dedicated to an overhaul of campaign finance laws and funded almost exclusively by billionaire former corporate raider Jerome Kohlberg, spent over $325,000 on television ads attacking Jim Bunning, because Baesler had led the 1998 House effort to reform campaign finance.[21] The group's ads did not focus on campaign finance but on Bunning's conservative voting record, especially his "opposition" to HMO reform. The thirty-second spots called Baesler "a leader for campaign-finance reform," then said of Bunning: "After HMOs gave him thousands in contributions, Bunning flip-flopped and opposed HMO reform."

According to Doug Berman, president of Campaign for America, the group considered becoming involved in close Senate races in New York, North Carolina, and Wisconsin, but picked Kentucky because New York was too expensive, TV time was scarce in North Carolina, and Senator Russell Feingold, D-Wisconsin, "has made it very clear that he doesn't want this kind of advertising. We wanted a race where we saw a stark contrast between the two Senate candidates, where there had been votes cast on the record."[22] Backing Baesler had the additional benefit of possibly reducing the chief opponent of campaign finance reform, Mitch McConnell. "In a subtle dig at McConnell, Kohlberg's ads featured bloodhounds, the stars of celebrated ads that propelled McConnell to the Senate fourteen years ago."[23] The ad said that Bunning is "hunting for money" and "listening to special interests, not the people of Kentucky. Maybe that's why Bunning voted no on campaign-finanace reform. When you vote on November 3, show Jim Bunning that in Kentucky, that dog don't hunt."[24]

AFL-CIO

AFL-CIO support for Baesler and Scorsone primarily took the form of three activities: television and radio ads, phone banks, and direct mailings. Spending over $150,000 on television ads, with $75,000 in TV and radio ads in the Sixth District alone, the AFL-CIO used issue-advocacy ads that attacked Republican policies in general and urged citizens to vote. Labor also purchased radio ads in targeted areas, with more than $15,000 on issue advocacy in the Louisville area, and funded direct GOTV mailings to its membership. GOTV phone banks were used extensively during the last days of the campaign to call union members on behalf of Baesler and Scorsone. In fact, after the election, Senator McConnell claimed, without offering proof, that labor groups targeted their telephone banks at nonmembers as well.[25] Although the AFL-CIO effort was significant in 1998, it was probably somewhat diminished from its earlier gubernatorial GOTV because of recent indictments surrounding its 1995 activities.[26]

Abortion Groups

National Right to Life, the Christian Coalition, and the Campaign for Working Families supported Bunning and Fletcher by attacking Baesler's and Scorsone's position on abortion. Flyers handed out in churches (including 500,000 voter guides, 100,000 in the Sixth District alone), mailings, and phone banks were used to press Bunning's strong pro-life position. Campaign for Working Families, a conservative group led by Newport native Gary Bauer, spent approximately $40,000 on radio ads saying, among other things, that Baesler supported "using tax dollars to pay for abortions" and "government intrusion into our schools." Targeted phone banks paid for by Right to Life were used on the preelection Sunady to contact registered African Americans before they went to church. The gist of the message was that Democrats Scorsone and Baesler are pro-abortion-on-demand, and that, as good Christians, blacks should vote for pro-life candidates Fletcher and Bunning.

The National Right to Life Association claimed it spent $33,258 on radio spots that said Baesler "supports a policy of abortion on demand . . . even as a method of birth control."[27] According to Baesler, radio ads saying he supported abortion "probably . . . hurt me more than anything else."[28] J. B. Poersch, Baesler's campaign manager, said, "The spots had some effect, and he wished that he had responded with ads more accurately portraying Baesler's record, as favoring a ban on so-called "partial birth" abortions and requiring parental consent for minors' abortions."[29] Right-to-Life's PAC also paid for 150,000 telephone calls and 300,000 direct mailers that were critical of Baesler. According to Poersch, "The abortion thing kicked in during the last two or three days."[30] Douglas Johnson, National Right to Life Committee's legislative director, said that his organization "had seen Baesler's race as one of its top two priorities in the nation." The same group had also clashed with Baesler over campaign finance reform.[31]

National Rifle Association

During the last week of the election, the National Rifle Association (NRA) ran radio ads statewide on behalf of Bunning, spending more than $36,000 on radio spots in the Louisville area. The cookie cutter ads contained a spot from NRA President Charlton Heston praising Bunning and another clip attacking Baesler. It also ran radio ads spending about $18,000 supporting Fletcher and attacking Scorsone. The NRA Political Victory Fund spent an estimated $140,000 in independent expenditures on radio ads and direct mailings in support of Bunning. The NRA mounted radio and direct mail campaigns noting Baesler's votes for an assault-weapons ban and a waiting period for handgun purchases.

American Medical Association

The American Medical Association (AMPAC) spent over $43,000 on television, over $6,000 on radio ads, and additional monies on first-class direct mailings encouraging individuals to vote for Fletcher. According to FEC reports, AMPAC spent more than $286,000 in independent expenditures on behalf of

Fletcher. Very positive in tone, the ads portrayed Fletcher as a caring physician who helped the less fortunate and an individual who had personal expertise in health care issues.

Other Groups

The Sierra Club sent mailings to its members benefiting Scorsone as did the Kentucky Education Association. Both the Kentucky Trial Lawyers Association and the Kentucky Association of Sexual Assault Programs issued press releases and letters to the editor criticizing a Fletcher campaign ad that used a rape victim to criticize Scorsone's credentials on crime issues. The Fairness Alliance, a gay rights organization, was asked indirectly not to be overtly active in the campaign, and so their actions were limited to interpersonal contacts in support of Scorsone.

RUMOR POLITICS AND THE SIXTH CONGRESSIONAL DISTRICT

As in other races in 1998, the less visible ground-war components of mail, phone banks, and word-of-mouth rumors comprised a significant part of the story in the Sixth District election. During the primary season, rumors began to spread about Scorsone's lifestyle. His alleged alternative lifestyle, in association with his past efforts to have the sodomy laws in Kentucky eliminated, and his vote against a bill to outlaw homosexual marriages in Kentucky, provided the basis for a potentially explosive campaign issue. Fletcher's camp, however, seemed reluctant to address publicly the issue because of a fear that Fletcher would once again be labeled as intolerant and a tool of the religious right, as had happened in his 1996 race for Congress. Fletcher supporters became increasingly frustrated that the major broadcast and print media outlets did not address the issue. For example, no letters to the editor referring to Scorsone's alleged alternative lifestyle appeared in the *Lexington Herald-Leader*. At least some leaders of conservative Christian groups were, at the same time, frustrated with Fletcher, who would not openly and aggressively attack Scorsone's liberal record on "social issues." It is in this context that the "stealth" aspects of the campaign environment became important. Throughout the campaign, but especially in the final weeks, callers to radio talk shows, phone banks, and organized letter writers questioned Scorsone's lifestyle and portrayed him as a gay activist. Fletcher's camp denied association with these efforts. Scorsone himself would always be asked about gay rights whenever he held a public forum. Only during the last week of the election did Fletcher's campaign publicly raise the gay issue on radio.

There were also a number of anonymous organizations that operated during the election, with indications of significant monetary support. Push polls were used against Scorsone beginning about a week before the election. The call began with positive statements about Fletcher and then began to attack Scorsone on tax and health care issues. In the days just before the election, the attacks also included statements about Scorsone's support for gay marriages, his help in eliminating sodomy laws, and the accusation that he wanted homosexuality to be taught in school. When the push polls first appeared, the callers identified themselves as being from the Fletcher campaign. Near the end of the week the callers did not identify themselves as belonging to any political organization. Fletcher did not pay for these efforts, and his campaign even suggested that it was the Scorsone camp that might be making the calls in order to embarrass Fletcher.[32]

Groups of self-proclaimed Christians sent pro-Fletcher letters primarily to men in rural areas. The letters were anti-Scorsone, with a particular focus on the gay rights issue and questions about morality. First-class stamps were used in the mailings, and indications are that upward to 30,000 individuals received such letters at a total cost of about 50 cents per mailing. The Scorsone camp felt that there was an organized effort to "plant" Fletcher supporters at almost all public forums to ask embarrassing questions of Scorsone, especially questions regarding gay rights. In all these cases, whether they were phone banks, letter-writing campaigns, or efforts to disrupt the candidate, it was impossible to determine who organized the efforts or who paid for them. As outside money grows in importance, the possible use of it for rumor and stealth campaigns raises important issues of campaign accountability.

Outside support for Scorsone was neither as extensive as that for Fletcher nor was its effect clear. Operation Big Vote, a nonpartisan get-out-the-vote effort backed by the American Federation of State, County, and Municipal Employees and The Way, a Lexington Christian community development corporation, largely merged their efforts in a last-minute push for Scorsone, Baesler, and Lexington Mayor Pam Miller. According to Jacques Wigginton, political liaison for The Way, the volunteers went to each home in the First and Second Lexington Urban County Districts (predominantly African American) three times in the final days before the election.[33]

CONCLUSION

Both Kentucky races were influenced by outside money, but in different ways. While there was a great deal of party soft-money spending in the Senate race, such spending did not appear to have much of an impact in the Sixth District race. One constant across the Republican Senate and House races was the substantial involvement of Kentucky Senator Mitch McConnell. Interest groups played a larger role in the House race, especially the AMA's heavy investment in support of Fletcher and its ability to help set the agenda in ways favorable to him. Scorsone lacked the heavy party and interest-group support so prevalent in other competitive contests studied in the outside-money project.

When a U.S. Senate election is decided by less than 7,000 votes, it is impossible to specify the deciding factor in the election.[34] During the early general election season, Bunning was able to dominate the airways with a positive message of a family man who deeply cared about the future of Social Security, an issue that generally helps Democrats. Baesler mistakenly conceded northern Kentucky to Bunning. Bunning spent over $380,000 on the Cincinnati television market, compared to Baesler's $45,000. Bunning carried the Fourth Congressional District by over 38,000 votes, even though a Democrat won the congressional seat. It was a vote margin that Baesler could not overcome in the rest of the state. Baesler may have miscalculated when he failed to invite Hillary Clinton to come to Louisville to help him. Polls indicate that Mrs. Clinton is very popular in Louisville, which had provided a large enough margin to give Democratic Governor Paul Patton his victory in 1995. Mrs. Clinton's presence might have been used subtly to remind moderates and liberals that Baesler was the pro-choice, anti-impeachment, proreform candidate.

The Democrats' soft-money expenditures and money spent by their allies made a smaller difference because they bought much of their TV time late in the campaign, when TV stations were deluged with political ads. Some ads were not run, and sponsors of aired ads were forced to pay premiums, sometimes triple the regular rates. These late, inefficient TV buys were probably a function of two factors—a shortage of early money from the state and national Democrats and some "bad" strategic decision making.[35] In assessing the strategy of national Democratic signal callers, Baesler commented that "nobody thought the race was starting that early [in August]. They got fooled." Baesler asserted that the "Republicans probably had better media strategy from beginning to end. . . . They defined the race, and we didn't."[36] The attack ads also took their toll on Baesler, and the overall quality of Bunning's advertisements was superior.

Most importantly, thte Sixth District congressional race, between the liberal Democrat, Scorsone, and the conservative Republican, Fletcher, probably cost Baesler much of the vote margin he could expect in his own district. As the campaign progressed, questions about the Democrat's alleged alternative lifestyle and strong support for gay rights issues began to take on increasing importance. The religious right and other conservative groups in the Sixth District became energized by the congressional race, became heavily involved, and turned out in large numbers of voters. Polls indicate that Baesler received a third of the conservative Christian vote statewide, but there seems to be little doubt that the large anti-Scorsone turnout among conservative elements in the Sixth Congressional District had a significant negative impact on Baesler. He carried his home district against a northern Kentucky Republican by only about 21,300 votes. In past congressional elections, Baesler beat local Republicans by much larger vote margins.[37]

Given the ideological difference between the Sixth District congressional candidates, the contest was about who could convince the voters that they were closer to the center of the political spectrum. Throughout most of the campaign season both campaigns did a good job of maintaining their surface image as centrists but were unsuccessful in developing a widespread image of their opponent as an extremist. Eventually, however, supporters of Fletcher were able to better energize their own core constituency and raise concern about Scorsone. Scorsone, in contrast, was never able to make Fletcher seem dramatically and personally outside the mainstream. Fletcher attributed his victory to "good hard work. We both got the issues out . . . people knew where we stood. It was just a matter . . . of philosophical differences and who folks wanted to represent them."[38]

Fletcher had the clear resource advantage during the fall campaign. He had a lot more money, about $400,000; he received more support from his own party; and he had more significant help from groups outside the party and candidate-campaign organizations. Fletcher was able to neutralize much of the advantage that Scorsone was thought to have on the issue of Social Security and, with the help of the AMA, was able to refocus and make the health care issue his own. Fletcher's campaign, with the help of groups such as the NRA, continued to focus on the liberalism of Scorsone.

Given the large number of outside groups involved in trying to influence the outcomes of these elections, there was widespread recognition of their involvement by the statewide print media—the Louisville *Courier-Journal* and the *Lexington Herald-Leader*. The extent of the coverage, however, was heavily dependent on public records, the willingness of individuals to speak with reporters, and the strategy of key decision makers. When groups expended large sums of money for radio and TV advertisements, the print media provided timely coverage. When reporters were granted interviews with key interest-group and party individuals, the public received in-depth discussions of strategies. Al Cross and Bob Garrett of the *Courier-Journal*, in particular, exhibited an ongoing interest in the flow of party and interest-group monies. When a group perceived a strategic advantage in keeping its activities outside of the public limelight, coverage was limited and often after-the-fact.

Both Kentucky races reflected national developments in campaign finance and campaign strategies but exhibited a number of unique characteristics. Like congressional races nationwide, the Kentucky elections were more expensive, with significant soft-money expenditures, numerous issue-advocacy ads, large-scale party spending, widespread independent-expenditure campaigns, and candidates and groups utilizing multiple technologies, including user-friendly Internet websites. Interest-group activity was evident. As in other national races, the NRA, Right-to-Life, AFL-CIO, Christian Coalition, AMA, and other interests played prominent roles that were more extensive than in past Kentucky elections. The strategies of such interest groups in Kentucky races were also similar to what was occurring elsewhere: issue-advocacy TV and radio ads, phone banks, direct mailings, and personal contacts. Both parties had extensive GOTV efforts as in other states. All players used multifaceted strategies of sophisticated air and ground wars.

One of the unique characteristics of the Kentucky races involved the role of Kentucky Senator Mitch McConnell. As NRSC chair, McConnell was a major player in the Republican nationwide strategy to raise money and pick up additional Senate and House seats. After the election, McConnell received a great deal of criticism for a number of strategic miscalculations, especially the Senate races in Wisconsin, New York, California, and North Carolina.[39] In contrast, McConnell's help for both Bunning and Fletcher reflected his national role more intensely than elsewhere . . . and Kentucky bucked the nationwide pro-Democratic trend. While the Democratic ground war seemed superior in most of the states, it was the Republican ground war, that ruled the day in Kentucky.

Most importantly, Kentucky appeared to be part of nationwide trends that threaten electoral accountability. Large amounts of money were spent by sources that could not be traced; and independent organizations emphasized their own candidate themes. It has been increasingly difficult to follow the money, and the paradigm of this trends is to be found in Kentucky's Sixth District, where a predominantly anonymous lifestyle issue was a prime determinant in the election outcome, and played a critical role in the statewide Senate race as well.[40]

NOTES

We acknowledge the assistance of a talented group of research assistants at the University of Kentucky: Amanda Cooper, Jason Glass, Justin Hosie, Brooke Johnson, Adam Lawrence, Josh Mahan, Angela Van Berkel, and Kim Zargorski. Also, Professor Michael Morgolis and some students at the University of Cincinnati and Professor Gerald Watkins at Paducah Community College helped obtain media ad buy information for the Kentucky Senate race.

1. See Penny M. Miller, *Kentucky Politics and Government: Do We Stand United?* (Lincoln: University of Nebraska Press, 1994), for an in-depth look at the state's distinctive political culture, diverse regional influences, and unique political traditions.

2. Voter turnout rates in recent off-year congressional elections in Kentucky were: 40.5 percent in 1982; 39.1 percent in 1986; 52.5 percent in 1990 (this unusually high turnout was due to the clergy's successful efforts in support of a constitutional amendment making all church property tax exempt); and 38.8 percent in 1994. In addition, the 1998 turnout percentages can be seen as being biased downward because of the influence of Motor Voter Registration.

3. Valerie Honeycutt, "Fierce Contests Draw Record Numbers to Polls," *Lexington Herald-Leader*, 5 November 1998, A9.

4. The 45.1 percent turnout rate in the Sixth District in 1998 compares to turnout rates of 32 percent, 26 percent, and 35 percent in the off-year elections of 1986, 1990, and 1994, respectively. The total number of votes cast in 1998 in the Sixth District reflects a 63 percent increase over the total number of votes cast in 1994.

5. Information received from the advertising sales executive at the Lexington CBS television affiliate, WKYT.

6. Baesler joined the Blue Dogs, a small conservative group formed within the Demo-

cratic Party in 1995 after the GOP takeover of Congress. The Blue Dogs were in contrast to Democrats "so loyal it was said they would 'vote for a yellow dog' before lifting a finger for a Republican." James R. Carroll, "Independent Baesler Works Quietly, Steadily," Louisville *Courier-Journal,* 15 October 1998, B1.

7. Some effort had been made by Baesler supporters to get Henry and/or Owen out of the race.

8. David Beiler, "Where Experience Reigns," *Kentucky Gazette,* 11 August 1998, 8–9; Al Cross, "$1 Million Separates Bunning and Baesler," Louisville *Courier-Journal,* 15 October 1998, B1.

9. According to Mark Squier, Baesler's media consultant with Trippi, McMahon, and Squier, Baesler's theme was "Working for families, working for people." They wanted to emphasize that Baesler mirrored the moderate ideology of average Kentuckians. Mark Squier, interview by authors, telephone, 2 June 1999.

10. Bunning's media consultant, Doug McAuliffe, claimed that the "benign, father-hood-and-apple-pie visual introduction" of Bunning to potential voters in August and early September was "the most critical component of the race. . . . It gave people a sense that this guy was a genuine guy that they were going to take the time to listen to," in Robert T. Garrett, "Winning Campaign Strategy Possible Blueprint for GOP," Louisville *Courier-Journal,* 7 November 1998, A1 and A5.

11. "Center for Responsive Politics: Business / Labor / Ideological Split," *Center for Responsive Politics,* 1999, at <http://www.opensecrets.org/1998elect/dist_blio/98KYS8blio.htm>, 24 September 1999.

12. The geographic distributions of the Baesler television ads were light in heavily Democratic western Kentucky and nearly nonexistent in Bunning's Fourth District in northern Kentucky.

13. For most of the race, Bunning owned the radio airwaves around the state; Baesler's minimal radio spots were reserved for targeted areas only in the last few days of the campaign. To Baesler's detriment, radio is typically effective in rural counties, especially in western Kentucky.

14. Doc Switzer, Scorsone's media consultant, stated that the theme of the campaign was to focus on Scorsone's experience as a state legislator, identify the differences between Fletcher and Scorsone, increase Scorsone's name recognition, and protect Scorsone against attacks on his liberal voting record, which was not in line with the more conservative tendencies of the district. Doc Switzer, interview by authors, telephone, 2 June 1999.

15. Peter Baniak, "Fletcher's Win a Mix of Money, Message, Help," *Lexington Herald-Leader,* 4 November 1998, A19.

16. Since the nonallocable mail utilizes volunteers, the cost is approximately two-thirds of what similar mailings would cost a candidate.

17. Robert T. Garrett and Al Cross, "Soft Money Eclipsed Candidates' Spending: Issue Ads Avoid Limits on Giving in Senate Race," Louisville *Courier-Journal,* 28 December 1998, A6.

18. Al Cross, "Election 1998: Baesler Concedes Narrow Loss," Louisville *Courier-Journal,* 5 November 1998, A1.

19. Ibid.

20. Angie Muhs, "Baesler Misses Democrat Train Tour," *Lexington Herald-Leader,* 26 September 1998, A12.

21. Campaign for America said, "Statewide it placed orders for $467,000 worth of time for three rounds of commercials attacking Bunning in the campaign's final eighteen days. On election eve, the group spent $35,000 to buy four thirty-second commercials on Louisville's WLKY-TV—three on local newscasts and one on the prime-time show *L.A. Doctors*. For the same amount in September, the Bunning campaign had bought forty spots on the top-rated newscasts of WHAS-TV in Louisville, plus a handful of prime-time programs," in Garrett and Cross, Louisville *Courier-Journal*, 28 December 1998, A6.

22. Al Cross, "$325,000 Ad Blitz by National Group Supports Baesler," Louisville *Courier-Journal*, 21 October 1998, B1 and B6.

23. Garrett and Cross, "Soft Money," A6.

24. Cross, "$325,000 Ad Blitz by National Group Supports Baesler," B1 and B6.

25. Garrett and Cross, "Soft Money," A6.

26. Governor Patton's chief of staff, Skipper Martin, and former gubernatorial labor liaison, Danny Ross, were indicted by a federal grand jury for coordinating labor and candidate Patton's campaign activities in 1995. The Patton/Henry campaign was accused of coordinating "independent expenditures" of the International AFL-CIO to effectively violate the spending limits of Kentucky's new Public Financing Act (KRS 121.150[1]).

27. Cross, "Election 1998," A1 and A12.

28. Ibid.

29. Ibid.

30. Al Cross, "Race Goes Down to Last Precincts," Louisville *Courier-Journal*, 3 November 1998, A1.

31. Angie Muhs and Bill Estepp, "Bunning Had Plan, Kept to It," *Lexington Herald-Leader*, 5 November 1998, A16.

32. Jack Brammer, "Callers Disparage Scorsone," *Lexington Herald-Leader*, 1 November 1998, B1 and B6.

33. Geoff Mulvihill, "Push by Democrats to Get the Vote Out Helped Miller Win," *Lexington Herald-Leader*, 11 November 1998, B3.

34. See the *Lexington Herald-Leader* and Louisville *Courier-Journal* analyses of the U.S. Senate race on 4 and 5 November 1998.

35. "The Republicans aired about 17,000 TV commercials on the Senate race during the general-election campaign, while Baesler and his backers were able to broadcast only about 12,000." The average spent by both parties and candidates per Kentucky household by region includes: $3.93 in Lexington; $5.85 in Louisville; $4.15 in Cincinnati; $8.40 in Charleston and Huntington, W.Va.; $1.96 in Hazard; $3.05 in Bowling Green; $11.18 in Evansville; $9.32 in Paducah; and $1.69 in Hopkinsville (Louisville *Courier-Journal*, 28 December 1998).

36. Garrett and Cross, "Soft Money," A6.

37. In 1996, Baesler defeated Fletcher in the congressional race by almost 26,000 votes. More importantly, Baesler received 14,000 votes less in the Senate race than he did in the 1996 congressional race.

38. Fletcher won by more than 14,000 votes, with about 53.6 percent of the vote. Richard Wilson, "GOP's Fletcher Wins Seat Baesler Gave Up," Louisville *Courier-Journal*, 4 November 1998, 3, Special Section.

39. Gail Gibson, "Results Mixed for Strategist McConnell," *Lexington Herald-Leader*, 5 November 1998, A19.

40. Switzer and Squire, media consultants for Scorsone and Baesler, respectively, stated that hard-money expenditures are not the problem with campaign finance. The only problem with hard money, for them, is that the low contribution limits drive candidates to use soft money and allow independent expenditures to have too much power in an election. According to Switzer, independent expenditures "means that a nameless, faceless person can push a button and nuke you out of the water. Interest-group politics takes the campaign away from local people." Interviews by authors, telephone, 2 June 1999.

12

Conclusions and Implications

David B. Magleby

Most contests for the House and Senate in 1998 remained candidate centered, with incumbents exploiting their substantial advantages. The mean spending by House incumbents in 1998 was $631,726, compared with $252,322 for House challengers. In competitive races, House incumbents averaged $1.23 million while competitive challengers spent an average of $1.16 million. But the number of noncompetitive races in 1998 exceeded 80 percent of all House contests, a high for the 1990s. In these noncompetitive races, incumbents raised most of their money from PACs, sometimes giving as much as eight out of ten dollars. The smaller number of competitive races in 1998 helped the Democrats and their allied groups because they could narrow their focus and more effectively compete against the Republicans and their allied groups in fifty competitive races, rather than the one hundred or more that had been the norm in the 1990s. The Republican fund-raising advantage would have made a bigger difference in an election with more competitive contests.

Parties, more than individuals and PACs, are the campaign finance participants most willing to invest in challengers, but their spending rarely raises challengers out of obscurity. These same regularities continued in the 1998 election cycle in all but the relatively few competitive races.

The 1998 midterm election not only departed from the norm of past midterms, when the President's party picked up seats in the House of Representatives, but also in the expanded levels of electioneering by political parties and interest groups in competitive contests. Those competitive contests are pivotal in determining which party controls the House or Senate. In these strategic battlegrounds, there was an important shift from candidate-centered campaigns to campaigns with candidates competing with interest groups and parties for control of the election agenda and the attention of the voters.

How were the 1998 congressional elections in competitive contests less candidate centric? First, as we have demonstrated, much of the campaign was funded and run by entities other than candidates. In many instances, expenditures of outside groups exceeded candidate expenditures. Second, candidates in these contests often had to respond to the agenda of the opposing party or outside interest groups. Whether the issue was term limits in Utah, nuclear waste storage at Yucca Mountain in Nevada, or abortion in Oregon, interest groups and political parties were important to the content and tone of the campaigns. Sometimes outside money forced issues onto the agenda that would not have been discussed otherwise. In other contests, spending by noncandidate campaigns helped tilt the issue balance toward one candidate.

The dramatic growth of outside money in recent election cycles has come in part because of the close party balance in both houses of Congress, but especially in the House of Representatives. A shift of a few seats could alter party control of all the standing committee chairs and the speaker. With the stakes so high, every competitive seat has become a battleground. In these contests, party soft money and interest-group electioneering have also been concentrated, sometimes exceeding spending by the candidates. When is this noncandidate campaign activity likely to occur?

First, it occurs in competitive races. Those who allocate outside money are highly pragmatic and seek to determine the outcome of the overall election. They invest in races that the pundits call "toss-ups." Interest groups have a second motive that influences where they spend their money and that is agenda-setting for the next Congress. Groups like the League of Conservation Voters who target their Dirty Dozen not only want an overall Congress more favorable to their view, but they want to intimidate others in Congress to vote their way to avoid making future Dirty Dozen lists. Hence, victories against candidates like John Ensign in the Nevada Senate race serve a dual purpose.

Second, outside money is aimed at races where it can get the most bang for the buck; this, generally, to states or districts with less expensive media coverage or lower overall campaign costs. When faced with the decision about allocation of an additional $100,000 between the Nevada and New York Senate races, assuming all other things are equal, outside-money allocators will spend the money in Nevada because, for the same amount of money, they can buy far more advertising per voter. As a result it will not be surprising to see outside money flow into states like Nevada in future contests because parties and interest groups can get more bang for their buck there.

Many of those who spend outside money also contribute limited and dislosed money to candidates. For instance, labor PACs gave $45 million to congressional candidates in the 1997–98 election cycle, $41 million to the Democratic candidates, and $4 million to Republican candidates. Interest groups who favor Republicans behaved in a similar fashion. Business PAC contributions totaled $17 million, $13 million to Republicans and $4 million to Democrats.[1] For some groups, tracking their campaign activity is much more difficult. We don't know who contributed the $11.4 million spent by the term limitation movement in

1997–98, but it is likely that those individuals or groups also gave limited and disclosed contributions to one or both parties and to some candidates.[2]

The surge in outside money documented in this book would not have happened if contributors had not believed it important to invest in this strategy, often in large amounts. Although we know very little about the contributors to some interest groups who invest in election advocacy, their behavior in contributing so much money demonstrates that they see involvement as important.

HOW OUTSIDE MONEY IS SPENT

Before our study of the 1998 elections, scholars tracking outside money focused on broadcast advertising. The most visible interest-group campaigns, including those of labor unions in 1996, were largely done on television and radio.[3] But there were early indications of the importance of voter guides like those used by the Christian Coalition,[4] and party soft money used for voter registration and GOTV.[5] Our study is the first to monitor the full range of campaign activities by candidates and noncandidate entities.

Practicing politicians often say, "We fight the next election on the lessons we learned in the last contest." The first lesson learned in 1998 is the importance of the ground war in a low-turnout election like 1998. The second lesson is the importance of having a message that motivates voters to go to the polls. Both of these factors benefited the Democrats in 1998. Table 12.1 summarizes the relative importance of soft money, interest-group election advocacy, the air war and the ground war in primary, midterm general, and presidential general elections.

The theory summarized in table 12.1 is that in low-turnout settings like primaries and midterm general elections, the ground war is more important because activating marginal voters can make the difference, and such activation is better accomplished more directly. In a higher-turnout election context, the task is more one of persuasion than activation, and hence the air war becomes more important. Interest groups that can deliver their voters or that have issues that motivate people to vote are more important in low-turnout contests like primaries or midterm general elections and less important in the noisy environment of a presidential general election.

Table 12.1   Relative Importance of Campaign Activities in Different Election Settings

	Primary	*Midterm General*	*Presidential General*
Ground War	Very Important	Very Important	Important
Air War	Somewhat Important	Somewhat Important	Very Important
Soft Money	Less Important	Very Important	Very Important
Interest-Group Ads	Very Important	Important	Less Important

Party soft money has proven very important in both midterm and presidential general elections. Why might soft money play any role in primaries? The answer is in the small number of competitive contests, especially for the U.S. Senate, the parties have begun to spend soft money against the most likely opponent from the other party. One of the groups most active in pushing candidates to take pledges on public policy issues, Americans for Limited Terms, has promised to devote even more money to primaries in the future because "primaries look a lot better; in the primary, no one's confused about whether you're playing the party game."[6]

Midterm elections are different from presidential elections. Voter interest and turnout are lower. Turnout was low in 1998, only 36 percent. When voters are more engaged in the election and likely to turn out in the election as they are in presidential elections, then the air war becomes more important because it is reaching a larger segment of likely voters. Voter registration, identification, and activation will remain important and in a close election can make the difference. In races like those we studied in 1998, the ground war will remain essential.

Our research demonstrates that parties and interest groups invested heavily in the ground war in 1998. Organized labor mounted a large-scale voter identification and mobilization effort in targeted states. This person-to-person outreach also involved direct mail on key issues of concern to labor, such as Social Security and health care. Americans for Limited Terms ran phone banks in two of our contests. Direct mail was also integral to the strategy of groups, including the Republican and Democratic parties, the Sierra Club, and the National Right to Life.

As in the past, some groups chose to broadcast their message, often in combination with direct mail. The National Rifle Association used its famous president, Charlton Heston, in radio commercials. Some groups such as organized labor ran television and radio commercials in addition to ground-war tactics. Environmental groups ran ads early in the Nevada Senate race, in part to force environmental issues onto the agenda.

IMPACT OF OUTSIDE MONEY

Our intense study of outside money is limited to a single election, and while we have sixteen different observations, it is important not to overgeneralize from our data. Nevertheless, a summary and synthesis of what we learned about the impact of outside money provide a foundation for further research on what is a growing phenomenon.

Outside money is more effective when it reinforces candidate themes and messages. Issues relating to the environment were important to the Reid U.S. Senate campaign in Nevada and the Udall campaign for U.S. House in New Mexico.

Similarly, party soft-money spending by the Republicans often touted the accomplishments of the 105th Congress, rather than address the themes of concern to candidates in Iowa or Pennsylvania.

Outside money is more effective when it raises negatives about the opponent. We found a division of labor between the candidate and noncandidate campaigns, with the noncandidate campaigns generally taking a more negative approach. Putting a candidate on the Dirty Dozen is an example of such a tactic. And in the Iowa Third Congressional District, the Republican candidate believed that the GOP raised the wrong issues in the campaign, as he had to spend valued resources on attacking his opponent because the GOP did not.

Outside money is more effective when it is targeted to specific groups. The Udall campaign and its allied groups made a priority of voters who had voted for the Green Party in the previous election. Union voter identification efforts were often aimed at union households, and African American voter mobilization was aimed at black voters who were registered to vote in districts or states where their mobilization could make a difference. In a low-turnout election context, such segmentation of the electorate was part of the strategy of the more effective groups. Some critics of the Operation Breakout spending on the impeachment and Clinton character ads contend that the Republicans had the right message but the wrong strategy. Instead of broadcasting their anti-Clinton message, which had the potential of activating Clinton supporters and alienating fence sitters, they could have used telephones or direct mail to deliver the same message to those they most wanted to receive it and not angered and possibly mobilized others.

Outside money in midterm and primary elections is more effective when the ratio of ground-to-air campaigns is higher. Outside money spent on the ground war was very important to the outcome of several close races in 1998, most notably by organized labor. Yet as Steven Rosenthal has argued, "They [issue ads] were very hard hitting, and they drove home a message because the only way issue ads will work is if they're done in an electoral context . . . [it] is a very, very valuable tool in our legislative program."[7] But too much emphasis on an air war in 1998, as appears to have been the case with the NRCC, was a mistake. As Stephen Law, executive director of the National Republican Senatorial Committee, explained, "I do think the TV made a huge difference, and several races would not have been close before election day if we had not played a major role in issue advocacy on television. But I do think that you learn from the successes of your enemies."[8]

Outside money is more effective when the frequency of voter contact is high. Given the high volume of political communication in competitive congressional races, groups who only enter in a limited fashion are not as likely to succeed. Voters received as many as eleven pieces of mail from some parties or groups in 1998 and in the final days of the campaign may have received as many as five telephone calls urging them to vote. In such a contest the greater the frequency of voter contact and the more personal the communication, the more effective the campaign will be.

IMPLICATIONS OF OUTSIDE MONEY FOR ELECTORAL DEMOCRACY

We shift now to an assessment of the implications of outside money for electoral democracy in America. We begin by discussing the implications for candidates and then turn our focus to political parties, interest groups, and finally to the voters themselves.

Candidates

Elections in the United States have long been seen as under the control of the candidates. Our relatively weak political parties became weaker with the advent of the direct primary, which shifted the selection of party nominees from the parties to the voters.[9] Primaries encourage candidates to build a personal following and orient politicians to voters likely to vote in primaries rather than party leaders. Candidates also must raise money for two elections—the primary and the general election—and in the primary they generally do not receive money from the party.

The single-member district and winner-takes-all electoral rules of our democracy also reinforce the candidate-centered orientation of American politics. Congressmen and senators represent discrete groups of voters, and to hold office, they must win a plurality of votes. Candidates thus build relationships with these voters/constituents, motivated by their drive for election/reelection.[10] The result of our electoral rules and practices has been to make candidates and their campaigns the central cog in our electoral system. To an extent, the media report on the fairness and accuracy of the candidate campaigns, again assuming that the voters will hold the candidates accountable.[11] What does outside money do to the expectation of candidate control of elections and accountability for their content?

The surge in outside money in competitive 1998 congressional elections meant that candidates no longer controlled the tone of the campaign. Republican U.S. Senate candidate Bob Inglis of South Carolina dissociated himself from his party's soft-money ads because they were too negative.[12] A U.S. House candidate in Iowa disagreed with the advertising strategy of the NRCC in his contest. The heavy negative spending by Americans for Limited Terms (ALT) in the Utah Second Congressional District race made the candidate favored by this outside money appear more negative than she was, because voters assumed the ALT commercials were her own.

Outside money gave an overall more negative cast to the campaign. The Annenberg Center's "Issue Advocacy Advertising during the 1997–98 Election Cycle" found over half of the issue ads run after September 1 were pure attack ads, compared to less than one-quarter of candidate ads that were pure attack ads.[13] Ironically, even though candidates were no longer in control of the campaign agenda, voters blamed them if they did not like the campaign. One candidate described the implications of outside money as a double-edged sword. She benefited from the hundreds of thousands spent against her opponent but was hurt by the perception that she ran a negative campaign. In her defense, much of the negative communication came from the ads run by the interest group, but the distinction between candidate and noncandidate campaigns is lost on most voters.[14]

One tactic open to candidates is to disavow the tone of their party or the interest groups supporting them or opposing their opponent. This permits them to claim a neutral position on the attack but still potentially benefit from it. There appeared to be a division of labor between the Democratic candidates and Senate Republican candidates and their party committees, with the party ads generally more negative on their opponents while the candidate ads were more positive, sometimes on the same issue.

Here is how the process worked in several races. The opponent was attacked by the party ad for his/her position on Social Security, health care, or the environment, while the candidate favored by the party or interest group stressed his/her support for saving Social Security, securing better health care, and protecting the environment. The strategy thus aimed to elevate the favored candidate through the candidate campaign and to denigrate the opponent through the outside-money campaign.

How candidates respond to this multifaceted campaign environment is important. They not only need to run against their opponent but also the opponent's party and groups seeking to help the opponent. Waging a political battle on so many fronts is difficult. Moreover, the candidate cannot be sure his or her own party will really be of much help and has to worry that outside groups intending to hurt the opposition don't end up helping the opposition. In New Mexico, environmental groups ran an ad focusing on the reintroduction of the gray wolf that may have hurt the Democratic candidate, Tom Udall, among ranchers.[15] Clearly, the candidates and their races are pawns in a much larger interest-group battle. The problem with such thinking is that it distorts our electoral process from a choice between candidates to an election with multiple messengers and conflicting objectives.

All candidates in races with substantial noncandidate campaign activity should anticipate attacks from the opposing party and interest groups that may be more strident than those coming from the opposing candidate. Some advertising will be by groups that no one knows or that hide behind innocuous names. Our research shows that it is unlikely that the media will help voters much to untangle who is behind the noncandidate campaigning.

Parties

Both political parties made soft money a major part of their strategy in 1998. They were successful in raising record amounts of soft money, and they carefully allocated it to the most competitive races. Indeed, 70 percent of the noncandidate ads run after 1 September 1998 were political party ads.[16] Soft money was spent on all forms of communication with voters—TV, radio, print ads, telephones, and mail. Sometimes the content of a soft-money mailer was linked to the content of a candidate commercial.

Political parties have periodically tried to set the agenda of midterm elections, as with the Republican efforts in 1982 and 1994. In 1998, the Democrats identified three broad themes: education, health care, and Social Security. The party soft-money campaign attacked the local Republican and praised the local Democrat on one or more of these issues important to the district or state. In contrast, the House Republicans appeared to be without a theme or message of importance to voters, and unlike the Democrats, they put their candidates at a strategic disadvantage by not attacking the Democrats.

For decades political scientists have called for stronger parties that would more actively recruit, train, and fund candidates, that would provide more coherent party positions to voters, that would energize and activate public opinion, and that would hold officials collectively accountable.[17] What party functions has soft money enhanced? It has strengthened national and state parties as fund-raising institutions and has given greater power to national party committee leaders in allocation of these funds. National parties are also more heavily involved in deciding the strategy, theme, and message of their campaigns on behalf of candidates.

The new world of campaigns in competitive elections has clearly elevated the power of party committee leaders who allocate the millions of dollars of soft money. The most controversial decisions in 1998 took place in the Republican committees. On the House side, the decision to nationalize the President's scandal late in the game was widely seen as a mistake. Controversy also followed the allocation of NRSC money, which was seen as reflecting the views of NRSC Chair Mitch McConnell, an opponent of campaign finance reform. The charge was that McConnell spent money against campaign finance advocate Senator Feingold, Democrat of Wisconsin, while denying soft-money support to Republican Linda Smith in Washington, a supporter of campaign finance reform.[18] In McConnell's defense, polling numbers showed Feingold (D-WI) to be vulnerable and Smith (R-WA) to be trailing Patty Murray (D), but the allocation power of large pots of soft money clearly provides the dispenser with strategic advantage. Dave Hansen explained, "Contrary to what some people might think, we did not target Wisconsin simply because of Senator Feingold and his proposals on campaign finance reform. It was an opportunity state for us."[19]

While the more successful party soft-money spending in 1998 tailored its message to the local race, the control of the campaign was clearly national and professionalized in its reliance on polling, media advertising, and mail and telephone contacting by established national firms. As several participants told us, resource allocation was "by the numbers," meaning it was driven by polling numbers in competitive races. In the case of Senator McConnell, it is said he knew the content of virtually all the NRSC-funded commercials.[20] There is also evidence that parties were important in the ground war—voter registration, identification, and mobilization.

What is much less clear is whether the 1998 soft-money binge helps the state and local parties in future elections or if the spending was contest-specific and of no lasting party benefit. If the parties are largely fund-raisers and provide their own commercials, then there is little lasting benefit. But in contests where parties were more involved in grassroots mobilization—for example, in Kentucky—then there is likely to be a more lasting impact. The concentration of resources in the party campaign committees and the power of the chairs of those committees have the potential of increasing party discipline in roll-call voting and loyalty to the leaders of the party committees. What has long been thought of as the party-whip function now may shift to include the party campaign committee chairs who control the soft-money purse strings so essential in highly contested races. Under this scenario, we expect to see more party-line voting as a result of soft-money spoils. One factor that may mitigate this development is the close party balance in both chambers, which puts a premium on electing fellow partisans, regardless of their adherence to the party line in roll-call voting. In this context, a premium is put on winning a majority in the key organizing vote at the beginning of each Congress. With such a tight margin in both houses, maverick members can argue that they need to vote their district in order to be reelected and that to hold or gain the majority they need soft-money support. The extent to which the party committees follow party ideology or maximize their chances for a majority will be an important question for future studies.

Another possible development will be incumbents generally wresting control of soft money from the party committee chairs and allocating it among themselves more or less equally. Again, the narrow margin in both houses gives the party committee chairs and their supporters ample arguments for the kind of concentration of soft-money resources in a few races that we observed in 1998.

But it would be a mistake to overstate the impact of soft money on parties or elections more generally because, as we have repeatedly noted, it was very carefully targeted to the relatively few competitive races of 1998. For the vast majority of contests in 1998 there was a smaller party presence than in past years. Take for instance the dramatic decline in party-coordinated spending in 1998 U.S. Senate contests. As we documented in chapter 2, Senate committees in both parties provided little or no coordinated spending to U.S. Senate candidates; instead they transferred money to state parties.

One argument for parties having a larger role in campaign finance reform is that they may be a buffer between candidates and contributors and in so doing eliminate the quid-pro-quo nature of money going directly from contributors to candidates. The use of party fund-raising does help candidates who want to avoid accepting contributions from some organizations directly, like tobacco companies, labor unions, or even PACs. But the soft-money donors to political parties are well known to the candidates, and in at least one of the races we studied there was evidence that candidates urged donors who had maxed out in hard-dollar contributions to give soft money to the state party.

All participants in the new world of campaign finance in competitive elections have an incentive to claim credit for the help they provide winning candidates. Candidates likewise have a keen interest in who is spending money to influence the outcome of their election campaigns. Individuals who make large contributions to parties or interest groups, as well as the interest groups and parties themselves, all have a stake in the candidates' knowledge of their activity. This reality calls into question the idea that parties reduce the claim interested donors who invest heavily in a race have on the winner of that race. The new system does permit candidates to deny accepting money from some groups in direct and disclosed contributions to their campaign, while benefiting from party soft-money expenditures on their behalf that may be funded in part by those same groups. U.S. Senate candidates John Edwards of North Carolina and Russ Feingold of Wisconsin, both Democrats, took a "no PAC money" pledge for their campaigns, but the DSCC spent soft money that included PAC donations. Only after the protests of Senator Feingold did the DSCC halt the $200,000 independent expenditure ads and the $425,000 advertisement purchase made late in the campaign.[21]

How well did this more centralized and nationalized party activity impact legislative behavior? Will it make parties more disciplined on policy or will parties fund maverick legislators in hopes of retaining or gaining a legislative majority? To what extent will party caucuses assert a role in allocating soft-money resources or establishing party themes and messages in future elections? It is too soon to know how soft-money campaigning will change parties and Congress. But soft money has become increasingly important and has the potential to even more dramatically change parties, elections, and even the institution of Congress.

Voters

Voters casting ballots in competitive races have become the target of intense campaign activity, much of which does not come from the candidates. The noncandidate campaigns pose particular challenges for voters, as the groups paying for the ads often mask their identity. The place voters can turn to for neutral information on all of this campaign activity—the media—was generally not reporting on the activity by noncandidate campaigns in the 1998 races.

Voters find it hard to distinguish candidate ads from those run separately by their parties and also assume that many ads paid for by interest groups are candidate commercials. The frequent use of candidate photos and the emphasis on candidates' names, especially in the context of an election campaign, mean most voters assume the ads are candidate campaign ads. Adding a few words instructing voters to "call candidate X to express your views" does not change the overall impression of the ad nor its electoral context. For example, a direct mail piece sent out by Planned Parenthood in the New Mexico Third Congressional District contest encouraged voters to vote pro-choice on election day by showing a photo of Tom Udall, the Democratic candidate, with the photo caption "Pro-Choice."

Voters in competitive contests are inundated with communications by mail, phone, print ads, and radio and television ads about the candidates. In some of our congressional races, as many as eleven pieces of mail relating to that contest were received at one household.[22] The intensity of the campaign in these contested races and the saturation advertising made it hard for voters to sort through all the noise. In many of our races, the two candidates, both parties, and allied groups effectively canceled each other out in campaign communications. What made the difference was the greater resonance of the House Democrats' message and their success in turning people out to the polls on election day.

The length of the campaign has also been extended in part due to outside money. The Nevada Senate race started earlier, in part due to party soft money and early advertising by environmental groups.[23] One television station in Kentucky, anticipating a big year, had blocked out more advertising time for political advertisements in 1998 than it had sold in 1996, a presidential election year. All of the reserved advertising time had been sold by early September, forcing the station to turn away campaign ads from interest groups that arrived late in the campaign.[24]

The negative tone of many of the noncandidate ads has the potential to reinforce alienation and cynicism among voters.[25] Several of our case studies found a tendency for the party ads and interest-group ads to be more negative, while the candidate ads were not quite as negative. One possible explanation for this is that parties and interest groups conduct the candidates' dirty work of beating up the opposition while permitting the candidates to disavow any connection to it. North Carolina Democratic Party coordinator Mike Davis explained, "I think [the party spots] made a difference. It allowed John [Edwards] and his campaign to stay on the high road by and large. And it allowed the party to be the one to take out the long knives."[26]

What is the impact of outside money on turnout? Is there evidence to support the claim by Kentucky Senator Mitch McConnell that more spending in campaigns increases voter turnout? The answer to that question is that heavy spending did not boost turnout in Nevada or North Carolina, where turnut in 1998 was lower than in the most recent midterm election with a U.S. Senate contest on the ballot. Turnout, however, was up in Kentucky and South Carolina.[27] But as we have argued previously, it is hard to separate out the effects of a competitive race, a well-funded race, and other stimuli on the ballot, like the South Carolina video poker referendum. Even with all the money spent in North Carolina and Nevada, the turnout in these two states was below the national average of 36 percent, the lowest turnout in the past thirty years.[28]

Interest Groups

In 1998, we found evidence of continued growth of interest-group electioneering under the guise of issue advocacy. We have also documented the extensive direct voter contacting conducted by interest groups through mail, telephone contacts, and in person. In competitive races, interest groups behave very much like old-fashioned political parties, working on behalf of candidates and mobilizing voters.

This mobilization was most successful with interest groups that made a better case for linking their campaign messages to a legislative agenda. The term Dirty Dozen for legislators on environmental issues is not only an effective negative label, it gives the group a possible tool against legislators in the future. Not surprisingly, groups like the League of Conservation Voters tout their success rate in defeating legislators placed on their target list. When groups expend $300,000 or more in House races, they can force their issue onto the agenda. Term limits would not have been an issue in the Utah Second Congressional District if Americans for Limited Terms had not made it an issue; the environment would have been an issue in the Nevada Senate election and New Mexico Third Congressional District Race, but the investment by interest groups in environmentally related issues elevated the issue and helped some candidates while hurting others.

Ultimately, when groups appear to help elect or defeat a candidate, they can and do use this as leverage against incumbents over the next few years after the election. Senator Reid will be reminded of the importance of organized labor and the League of Conservation voters to his victory, while Senator Bunning will be reminded of the importance of conservative right-to-life groups to his victory. When a group singles out a candidate for attack and then is not successful, it reduces the credibility of that group in future elections. Our most conspicuous example of this was Merrill Cook's withstanding the $380,000 attack by Americans for Limited Terms in 1998.

Interest groups can also be important in the ground war by activating their members or stressing issues to targeted groups. When they make a difference, the influence of the group rises with those they helped elect. Whether interest-group activity actually made the difference in any of the close elections we studied is hard to say. In several races, one interest group canceled out another. But in contests like the Nevada Senate, New Mexico Third Congressional District, and Illinois Seventeenth Congressional District, most observers in both parties saw interest groups as having been important to the outcome. As Mark Emerson, chief of staff for John Ensign, put it, "With a decision by only 401 votes, everything works." As congressional races become more competitive, most activity will have an impact.

Interest groups expanded the use of "pledges" in 1998 on policy questions ranging from taxes to saving the flag. The group that has used this technique the most is the term limitation movement, spending $11.4 million in 1998 and promising to spend $20 million in 2000. If other groups decide to use the pledge technique, candidates could face many opposing groups if they refuse to sign all pledges. We doubt that voters understand the nuances of pledges; they simply see this as advertising for or against a candidate. Some candidates will be tempted to sign all pledges in hopes of arraying the maximum range of groups campaigning against an opponent. Congressman Maloney in the Connecticut Fifth District essentially made this choice in signing three pledges in 1998. Future elections will test the ability of the term-limits groups to punish those who violate their pledge by voting against legislation consistent with the pledge or by seeking a term of office in excess of their term-limit pledge.

As we have shown, political parties and interest groups have a range of ways they can influence the outcome of congressional elections. Some of their activities are fully disclosed and available to public scrutiny through the Federal Election Commission. But for both parties and interest groups, there is a growing tendency in competitive contests to seek to influence elections by spending money in ways that are not disclosed. The distinction between interest groups and parties is being further blurred by the decision of some party committees to encourage the creation of issue-advocacy organizations that will invest in selected races. There is also the reality that with relatively few competitive contests, there will unavoidably be coordination between interest groups and parties. This only reinforces one of our findings that outside money from parties or interest groups is shifting our electoral system from a candidate-centered system to one with more power vested in interest groups and political parties.

Outside money enlarges the power of interest groups because they have more ways to influence legislators. In addition to the limited and disclosed contributions to candidates, they are a major provider of disclosed but not limited soft money. The intensity of candidate and party fund-raising is escalating.[29] Groups must now contribute to incumbents to remain on friendly terms with those candidates, even though they are not in jeopardy of losing their seats, and contribute to party committees often to curry the favor of legislative leaders. With the party balance so close, many groups elect to give to both parties and their prospective leadership PACs. Finally, we have now added the unlimited election advocacy that groups pursue in races like those studied in this book. In these races, groups often engage in a bidding war against competing groups and parties.

Media

The ground-war dimension of the 1998 story was almost always missed by the media. The academics who participated in our study carefully monitored news coverage of their races, and only occasionally did reporters talk about the role of party money or interest-group electioneering. This is not surprising, given the tight deadlines reporters operate under and the desire on the part of the parties and interest groups to keep their activities low key.

Following outside money is difficult because of the absence of disclosure, the efforts of some groups to mask their identity, and the reality that much of the outside-money spending comes late in the campaign. To report on outside money effectively requires stations and newspapers to commit more resources to reporting on elections and politics. Because the dynamic we document in this study occurs only in a small fraction of contests and because news media outlets may not be aware of the spending binge coming their way, they often are caught unprepared and are unable to provide their viewers and readers with answers to important questions relevant to a voting decision.

But the absence of news coverage of these extraodinary expenditures by parties and groups to influence voters left those same voters in the dark about the agendas of those seeking to persuade them. For reporters to be able to correct this news void will take a lot of work and considerable investment on the part of news organizations. This reality, when combined with the Annenberg Center's finding that local television news devoted less time to congressional campaigns in 1998, means voters were allowed to pick and choose from among the many messages, without much help.

One deterrent to expanded media coverage of outside money is the reality that broadcasters and cable station operators reap a huge financial windfall from soft-money and interest-group election advertising. Unlike candidate campaigns, which can claim the broadcast time at the lowest unit rate for that time slot,[30] advertising funded by outside money must pay whatever the station demands. There was evidence of some inflation of rates in 1998. There are some headaches associated with outside money for broadcasters. They face hard decisions about which commercials to run; what priority to give candidates, as compared to party or interest-group ads; and whether to refuse to run some noncandidate ads because of accuracy issues. When advertising was run by candidates, stations did not worry so much about the content of commercials that might be misleading or false, but with outside money, stations must evaluate the content more carefully.

CONCLUSION

In the landmark *Buckley v. Valeo* decision, the U.S. Supreme Court distinguished campaign communications that urged voters to elect one candidate or defeat another from speech that lacked the explicit "vote for" or "vote against" language. Left dormant in a footnote, this distinction between what the Court calls express and issue advocacy has permitted individual donors and interest groups to circumvent the Federal Election Campaign Act's contribution and disclosure provisions. Independent expenditures, which the court insisted by unlimited, were required to be disclosed under the *Buckley* ruling. Political parties are experimenting in the 2000 cycle with forming groups that can exploit the same distinction between express and issue advocacy and thereby avoid disclosure of their activity. Party soft-money expenditures already permit contributions without limitation but require disclosure of the contribution.

The 1998 election demonstrated that in competitive elections, outside money is unconstrained, and American electoral democracy now has two distinct types of elections: those without serious competition, by far the larger type, in which incumbents milk the PAC cow for money and exploit their other advantages; and competitive elections, which have the potential to decide which party controls the House, Senate, or both chambers. In this context, the *Buckley v. Valeo* express-versus-issue advocacy distinction has been used to circumvent contribution limits in what is clearly election advertising. This development, when combined with the soft-money loophole for parties, means that in competive House and Senate races, noncandidate campaign spending does, can, and will exceed candidate spending.

The heavy outside-money investment by interest groups in recent election cycles has added to the money chase by parties and candidates and by other interest groups. The spending by organized labor in 1996 motivated not only the business community to launch its own outside-money operations, but the Republican Party used the labor activities as a prod to raise more money for the party. As we enter the 2000 election cycle the Republicans have formed a separate issue-advocacy effort aimed at raising and spending $20 million in 2000 in an effort to counter the issues of advocacy of organized labor. The surge in soft money and interest-group election advocacy spending motivates candidates to raise more money, which in turn reinforces the parties' and groups' desire to raise and spend even more.

Barring a change in election law to limit issue-advocacy or soft-money spending, we anticipate additional growth in the use of these devices in the 2000 presidential and congressional elections and the 2002 midterm elections. The tendency for interest groups to push their message in primary and special elections will continue because the media attention generated advances the agenda of the group. Candidates fearing this prospect will not only want to raise money early, but also have allied groups or PACs that can push issues favorable to them in the primary and general election campaigns.

One of the most important implications of the surge in party and interest-group spending independent of candidates is that large contributors are back in the system in a big way. A large part of the motivation behind the Federal Election Campaign Act was to reduce the power, influence, and access of large contributors. The act included contribution limitations for individuals and political action committees. While groups and individuals could spend independently, such spending was disclosed and rarely of much significance.

But soft-money and interest-group spending in recent cycles has changed that. Parties place a premium on large soft-money donors, and some interest groups do not even disclose who their donors are or the average contribution. Hence we can have a small number of individuals or corporations set up issue advocacy operations and not know anything about them. No one knows how much is being spent to influence the election and where that money comes from. When asked to reveal the source of funds for Americans for Limited Terms, Eric O'Keefe, the group's president, responded, "My donors are not famous, they're not Congress, they don't run big companies, and they're not the issue. . . . I have a policy that our board adopted of not disclosing who gives to us. We believe it's in our best interest as an organization to do that."[31]

We expect many groups and the party committees to apply the lessons of 1998 in their planning for 2002. Parties will likely target more of their resources to ground-war tactics, and all committees will assume that they need to have even more soft money in 2002 than they had in 1998. Candidates in 2002 will also assume that if they are in a competitive race, they will have a harder time controlling the message of the campaign, and if they hope to control the message, they will need a lot of money. Unless news organizations commit the resources and develop the expertise to track this outside money, voters will continue to be uninformed about this influential dynamic.

Beyond dramatically increasing the amount of money spent communicating with voters, the outside-money campaigns raise fundamental questions for our electoral democracy. Who is in charge of the content of campaigns—the candidates, parties, interest groups, or wealthy individuals acting on their own? When voters do not like the content of outside-money campaigns, how do they hold someone accountable? Given the conflict of interest for broadcast media who reap substantial windfalls from outside-money campaigns, who will help inform voters about those seeking to persuade them? Given the limited disclosure requirements for interest groups or individuals hiding behind the issue-advocacy language, how effectively can those reporters who want to cover this story access relevant data for their reports? These questions suggest the need for a fundamental reexamination by legislatures and courts of the campaign communication dynamic and if a more sensible standard that protects electoral democracy.

NOTES

1. "Total Misc. Business PAC Contributions to Federal Candidates, 1997–1998," Center for Responsive Politics, at <www.opensecrets.org/pacs/sectors.htm>, 3 August 1999.

2. U.S. Term-Limits Press Release, "Term Limits Movement Announces Plan to Spend $20 Million in 2000 Election Cycle," 25 January 1999.

3. Darrel M. West, *Air Wars* (Washington, D.C.: Congressional Quarterly, 1997); Lynda Lee Kai and Dianne G. Bystrom, eds., *The Electronic Election: Perspectives on the 1996 Campaign Communication* (Mahwah, N.J.: Lawrence Earlbaum Associates, 1999).

4. Mark J. Rozell and Clyde Wilcox, eds., *God at the Grass Roots* (Lanham, Md.: Rowman & Littlefield, 1995).

5. Herbert E. Alexander and Anthony Corrado, *Financing the 1992 Election* (New York: M. E. Sharpe, 1995), 162–63.

6. Eric O'Keefe, lunchtime discussion panel at the Pew Press Conference, "Outside Money: Soft Money & Issue Ads in Competitive 1998 Congressional Elections," National Press Club, Washington, D.C., 1 February 1999.

7. Steve Rosenthal, lunchtime discussion panel at the Pew Press Conference, "Outside Money" National Press Club, Washington, D.C., 1 February 1999.

8. Ruth Marcus, "Outside Money Wasn't Everything," *Washington Post,* 5 November 1998, A39.

9. V. O. Key Jr., *Politics, Parties, and Pressure Groups,* 5th ed. (New York: Thomas Y. Crowell Company, 1964), 342; Austin Ranney and Willmoore Kendall, *Democracy and the American Party System* (Westport: Greenwood Press, 1956), chapter 12.

10. David R. Mayhew, *Congress: The Electoral Connection* (New Haven: Yale University Press, 1974); Morris P. Fiorina, *Congress: Keystone of the Washington Establishment* (New Haven: Yale University Press, 1978).

11. Darrell M. West, *Air Wars,* chapter 5.

12. See chapter 6, 100.

13. Jeffrey D. Stanger and Douglas G. Rivlin, "Issue Advocacy during the 1997–98 Election Cycle," a report by the Annenberg Public Policy Center. Pure attack ads are defined as "a case made only against the opposing position."

14. Jack W. Germond and Jules Witcover, "Turning Issue Ads into a Big Issue," *National Journal,* 20 September 1997.

15. See chapter 8, 144–45.

16. Stanger and Rivlin, "Issue Advocacy."

17. Austin Ranney, *The Doctrine of Responsible Party Government* (Urbana: University of Illinois Press, 1962), chapter 2.

18. David Postman, "Murray's Schedule Not Too Tight," *Seattle Times,* 15 October 1998, B5.

19. David Hansen, lunchtime discussion panel at the Pew Press Conference, "Outside Money" National Press Club, Washington, D.C., 1 February 1999.

20. Dave Hansen, interview by author, telephone, 9 August 1999.

21. "Democrats Pull Ads at Feingold's Insistence," *Milwaukee Journal Sentinel,* 25 October 1998, 5.

22. See chapter 9.

23. Michael Bowers, Tim Fackler, Nathalie Frensley, Eric Herzik, Ted Jelen, and Todd Kunioka, "A Profile of the Nevada Senate Race," in *Outside Money: Soft Money & Issue Ads in Competitive 1998 Congressional Elections,* ed. David Magleby and Marianne Holt (report of a grant funded by the Pew Charitable Trusts, 1999), 42–52.

24. Chris Baker, WKYT-TV general sales manager, interview by Penny Miller and David B. Magleby, Lexington, Ky., 22 October 1998.

25. Overall, our findings about content and strategy of broadcast ads by interest groups

and political parties mirror those of the Annenberg Center, which found issue ads to be just as likely to attack as in 1996—40.9 percent were pure attack in 1998.

26. Thad Beyle and Ferrel Guillory, "Profile of North Carolina Senate," in *Outside Money*, 53–62.

27. Turnout for the four sample U.S. Senate races in 1998, 1994, 1990, and 1986. Turnout is calculated by dividing total votes cast for the Senate race by total voting age population (VAP). See table 12.2 below.

Table 12.2   Turnout for Four U.S. Senate Races

	1986	1990	1994	1998
Kentucky	24.09	33.43	—	38.31
Nevada	32.58	—	34.97	33.10
North Carolina	33.64	40.89	—	35.39
South Carolina	30.02	29.02	—	37.02

Source: Data from *America Votes*, 1986, 1990, 1994, 1998.

28. Stephen Ansolabehere, Shanto Iyengar, Adam Simon, and Nicholas Valentino, "Does Attack Advertising Demobilize the Electorate?" *American Political Science Review* 88, no. 4 (December 1994): 829–38.

29. B. Drummond Ayres Jr., "In Fund-Raising Race, Democrats Set Pace," *New York Times*, 25 April 1999.

30. Most candidates in competitive races in 1998 purchased non-preemptable time, which is not charged at the lowest unit rate, and therefore paid closer to prevailing rates in the general-election campaign.

31. Eric O'Keefe, lunchtime discussion panel at the Pew Press Conference, "Outside Money: Soft Money & Issue Ads in Competitive 1998 Congressional Elections," National Press Club, Washington, D.C., 1 February 1999.

Index

abortion groups, Kentucky U.S. Senate and Sixth Congressional District races and, 201–2

Abramson, Jerry, 200

absentee voting, 67–68; New Mexico Third Congressional District race and, 148; South Carolina U.S. Senate race and, 101; Utah Second Congressional District race and, 176–77

ad campaigns, 214, 215; attack ads, 25, 49, 221; Clinton and, 30–31; Connecticut Fifth Congressional District race and, 153, 156, 158–59, 161, 163–66, 167n17, 168n18; fund-raising for, 35; importance of, 213; Kansas Third Congressional District race and, 77, 80, 81, 85–86, 88, 89; Kentucky U.S. Senate and Sixth Congressional District races and, 28, 55, 190, 192–94, 197–201, 205, 206, 208n14, 209n36; Lewinsky scandal and, 6; medium for, 30–31; monitoring of, 11; National Republican Congressional Committee and, 30–31, 35, 39n44; Nevada U.S. Senate race and, 36–37, 114, 115, 117, 118–20; New Mexico Third Congressional District race and, 136, 140–46; political parties and, 5, 28, 29; soft money and, 35, 220–21; South Carolina U.S. Senate race and, 99–101, 103, 106, 107–8; state parties and, 23; Utah Second Congressional District race and, 173, 175–81, 184; voters and, 220–21. *See also* candidate ads; interest group election ads; issue advocacy; radio ads; television ads

Adelson, Sheldon, 123–24, 126–28, 131n33

AFL-CIO, 41; Connecticut Fifth Congressional District race and, 162, 164–66; disguised identity and, 54; election advocacy by, 46; Kansas Third Congressional District race and, 79, 81, 86–88, 91n22; Kentucky U.S. Senate and Sixth Congressional District races and, 200, 201, 206; Nevada U.S. Senate race and, 118; New Mexico Third Congressional

District race and, 49, 139, 140–41; television advertising and, 63; Utah Second Congressional District race and, 183

African Americans: cable and radio ads and, 55; Democrats and, 4; mobilization and registration of, 28, 30, 72–73, 101–4, 215; voter turnout in, 4

AFT-Kentucky, 200

agency agreements, 18

air war. *See* ad campaigns; radio ads; television ads

American Association of Retired Persons, Connecticut Fifth Congressional District race and, 168n28

American Federation of State, County, and Municipal Employees, Kentucky U.S. Senate and Sixth Congressional District races and, 204

American Medical Association (AMA), 42; HMOs *versus*, 53; Kentucky U.S. Senate and Sixth Congressional District races and, 200, 202–3, 206; Pennsylvania Thirteenth Congressional District race and, 57

American Postal Workers Union, Kansas Third Congressional District race and, 91n22

Americans for Job Security, South Carolina U.S. Senate race and, 105, 107

Americans for Limited Terms, 47, 214, 226; collusion and, 52; ground war of, 51, 69, 73; pledges and, 51; South Carolina U.S. Senate race and, 107; Utah Second Congressional District race and, 171, 176, 178–81, 184, 186n23, 216, 222

Americans for Tax Reform (ATR), 46; Nevada U.S. Senate race and, 131n29

Anderson, Ross, 172

Angle, Matt, 28, 30, 72

Annenberg Public Policy Center, 25, 43

Armey, Richard K., 158

Ashcroft, John, 23, 117

229

About the Contributors

Sandra Anglund, former visiting assistant professor of political science at Trinity College and lecturer at the University of Connecticut and the University of Hartford, is the author of *Small Business Policy and the American Creed* (forthcoming). She is a former corporate public affairs executive and consultant.

Lonna Rae Atkeson, assistant professor of political science at the University of New Mexico, researches political behavior, public opinion, political psychology, and the media. Her articles have appeared in the *American Political Science Review,* the *American Journal of Political Science,* and the *American Politics Quarterly.*

Michael Bowers, professor of political science and public law at the University of Nevada, Las Vegas, is the author of *The Sagebrush State: Nevada's History, Government, and Politics, The Nevada Constitution: A Reference Guide,* and more than two dozen other publications.

Allan J. Cigler, Chancellor's Club Teaching Professor of political science at the University of Kansas, received his doctorate from Indiana University. His research and teaching interests include interest-group politics, political parties, and participation.

Anthony C. Coveny, Ph.D. student at the University of New Mexico, received his master of arts degree in Latin American Studies at UNM. He currently researches electoral behavior and congressional politics.

Tim Fackler, assistant professor of political science at the University of Nevada, Las Vegas, researches and teaches in the fields of political behavior, institutions and processes, political economy, and political communication. His current research examines the effects of different types of news coverage on citizens' political judgments and decisions.

Nathalie Frensley, assistant research professor of political science at the University of Nevada, Las Vegas, researches and teaches in the fields of political behavior, conflict processes, international relations, and political communication. Her current research examines the effects of media and party framing on conflict terminations and in U.S. foreign policy.

Jay Goodliffe, assistant professor of political science at Brigham Young University, received his Ph.D. from the University of Rochester. His research and teaching interests include positive political theory, political methodology, and American politics, with an emphasis on campaign finance in the U.S. Congress.

Donald A. Gross, associate professor of political science at the University of Kentucky, has written numerous articles on congressional elections and campaign finance. His book, *Money Matters,* coauthored with Robert K. Goidel and Todd G. Shields, was published in spring 1999 by Rowman & Littlefield.

Eric Herzik, chair of the department of political science and director of the Great Basin Policy Research Institute at the University of Nevada, Reno, has edited four books and authored over seventy journal articles, research monographs, and book chapters, mostly focused on state politics and policy making. His most recent book is *Towards 2000: Public Policy in Nevada.*

Marianne Holt was the head researcher on the *Outside Money* project. She received her degree in political science from Brigham Young University and currently works at the Center for Public Integrity in Washington, D.C.

Ted G. Jelen, professor and chair of political science at the University of Nevada, Las Vegas, has published extensively on religion and politics, public attitudes toward social issues, and church-state relations.

Todd Kunioka, assistant professor of political science at University of Nevada, Las Vegas, teaches and researches in the field of public policy, with an emphasis on environmental policy and bureaucratic behavior. His work has been published in *Journal of Policy Analysis and Management, Public Administration Review,* and *Journal of Socio-economics.*

David B. Magleby, distinguished professor of political science at Brigham Young University, was the principal investigator on the *Outside Money* project. He has also published several books, including *The Money Chase: Congressional Campaign Finance Reform* and *The Myth of the Independent Voter.*

Clyde McKee, professor of political science at Trinity College, is past president of the New England Political Science Association, founder and president of the

Connecticut chapter of the American Society for Public Administration, and visiting lecturer at Queens University. He studies and writes about Connecticut state and local politics.

Penny M. Miller, associate professor, is director of undergraduate studies in political science at the University of Kentucky. Author of *Kentucky Politics and Government: Do We Stand United?* she researches and teaches in the areas of legislative processes, political parties and elections, local and state government, and Kentucky politics.

Bill Moore, distinguished professor of political science at the College of Charleston, is author of *Political Extremism in the United States* and coauthor of *South Carolina Politics and Government.*

Danielle Vinson, assistant professor of political science at Furman University, received her Ph.D. from Duke University. She researches and writes on media in the American political system and on international political communication.